Praise for
"Out of the Loft"

I just finished *Out of the Loft* and am so excited to tell others about this book. From the time I started reading until the very last page, I found it very difficult to put down! This story of Don's ministry within his church choirs is not just a story about typical choir tours. In fact, if I were to look for the book in a local bookstore, I could find it under scripture devotion, ministry encouragement, and ministry "how to and how not to," as well as travel adventure and tour guide...to mention a few. I was touched, in so many instances, as Don shares from his heart how God used him and many others to accomplish purposes far beyond their imagination. The use of scripture throughout the book, in addition to powerful lyrics from music the choirs performed, helps keep the book's focus on the most important aspect of their ministry. Don's ability to relate detail in a fascinating way kept me reading almost non-stop to the end. I found myself feeling as if I had been a participant in the many adventures that were told! But mostly, I found myself encouraged by the way God uses music ministry and willing people to accomplish His purposes around the world. After reading Don's story, it will be hard for me to do ministry "the same" ever again!

Ed Cobb, Choral Director, Fresno, CA

Reading *Out of the Loft* made us feel we were right there with the choirs on their ministry trips to Central and Eastern Europe. . . . We appreciated the comments by Don King and other tour participants on how their experiences brought them closer to the Lord.

Cal and Kae Eiland, Escondido, CA

This is a very special story of a call to ministry and the many people who committed their time, talents, and dedication to the "Out of the Loft" mission. This is also a story of the many people and nations who were touched by the choirs' message of love and hope. I was privileged to be part of two of the choir tours to Europe and my life was changed forever because of it. In addition, this is a story of God's love and faithfulness to every person who either participated in this ministry or was touched by it. In every situation that could occur, from language barriers to border guards to illness and finances, God was faithful. *Out of the Loft* is a reminder that all we have to do is let the love and joy that Jesus Christ has brought to our lives reflect from our faces to the world around us. Then "Righteousness will shine and Salvation will blaze!" Isaiah 62:1-2

Penny Hecker, Sanctuary Choir and Bells of Praise,
Lake Avenue Church, 1984 & 1989
Current choir member, Redding First Church
of the Nazarene, Redding, CA

Don King has been involved in and committed to the implementation of the "Out of the Loft" ministry from its inception. He shared Dan Bird's vision of a ministry that would take church musicians outside of the traditional loft setting to reach people who had not heard the gospel in church but would attend a concert where that message was given. This is Don's story of the ups and downs of that journey. Beyond Don's personal story is the greater truth of how God used him, Dan, and two church choirs to go to spiritually and materially needy people beginning in West Germany, Austria, and Switzerland and branching out to Eastern Bloc countries during and after the tumultuous fall of the Iron Curtain. Don tells of the lasting friendships choir members made with many of the people who learned about and experienced God's love through this "Out of the Loft" ministry. That outreach continues to this day in many forms. This book is a must-read for those with a heart for church music ministry.

Joan McCuen, Newtown Square, PA

I have been blessed with Don and June King's friendship most of our adult lives, so the choir trips to Central and Eastern Europe are familiar to me. However, it wasn't until I read Don's book, *Out of the Loft,* that I realized the scope of this ministry. The book gave me a better understanding of how much work went into planning the choir tours, the depth of the friendships choir members made with people in Europe, the challenges the choirs faced before and during their mission trips, and the wonderful way God overcame the difficulties they encountered. What is most inspiring to me is the level of dedication to God shown by those who participated. It is clear that the "Out of the Loft" ministry has been blessed by the Lord in a special way. I am very touched and humbled by the dedication and work of everyone involved, and I feel fortunate to have been along on these trips through the pages of this book.

Barbara Lewis, Novi, MI

Don King's *Out of the Loft: A Memoir of Music and Ministry* is a highly personal and readable account of Don's thirty-year effort to spread the Christian message by organizing and leading repeated choir tours to Europe. The reader will discover within these pages the joys and difficulties of world travel, vivid images of Europe before and after the fall of the Soviet Union, descriptions and historical information about the places the choirs visited, and the blessings received by those doing the work of the Lord. And the best part is that the work goes on! Out of the Loft is the inspirational story of what can be accomplished by people totally dedicated to the service of God.

Paul Sparre, Waterford, MI.

OUT OF THE LOFT

*To Felician
Merry Christmas!

Jon Kr*

OUT OF THE LOFT

A Memoir of Music and Ministry

DON KING

"Out of the Loft: A Memoir of Music and Ministry"

Copyright C 2014 Don King. All rights reserved.

ISBN: 1494733013
ISBN 13: 9781494733018

This book is non-fiction. All dates and events, persons, dialogue, and description of locales and places are as accurate as possible, based on the recollections and impressions of the author.

No part of this book may be reproduced in any form or by any electronic or mechanical means including information storage and retrieval systems, without permission in writing from the author. The only exception is by a reviewer, who may quote short excerpts in a review.

Published in the United States by Chorister Press and CreateSpace, an Amazon.com company. First Edition.

Book cover design by Robert Henslin

Printed in the United States of America.

"Out of the Loft: A Memoir of Music and Ministry" is available at:

https://www.createspace.com/4578604

http://www.amazon.com

Scripture marked (NIV) taken from the HOLY BIBLE, NEW INTERNATIONAL VERSION®. NIV®. Copyright © 1973, 1978, 1984 by International Bible Society. Used by permission of Zondervan. All rights reserved worldwide.

Scripture quotation marked ((NASB) taken from the NEW AMERICAN STANDARD BIBLE®, Copyright © 1960,1962,1963,1968,1971,1972,1973,1975,1977,1995 by The Lockman Foundation. Used by permission.

Scripture quotations marked (RSV) are from Revised Standard Version of the Bible, copyright © 1946, 1952, and 1971 Division of Christian Education of the National Council of the Churches of Christ in the USA. Used by permission. All rights reserved.

Scripture quotation marked (NRSV) is from the New Revised Standard Version of the Bible, copyright © 1989 Division of Christian Education of the National Council of the Churches of Christ in the USA. Used by permission. All rights reserved.

Scripture quotation marked (NLT) is taken from the *Holy Bible*, New Living Translation, copyright ©1996, 2004, 2007 by Tyndale House Foundation. Used by permission of Tyndale House Publishers, Inc., Carol Stream, Illinois 60188. All rights reserved.

Scriptures quotation marked (GNB) are from the Good News Bible © 1994 published by the Bible Societies/HarperCollins Publishers Ltd UK, Good News Bible© American Bible Society 1966, 1971, 1976, 1992. Used with permission.

Scripture quotations taken from The Message by Eugene H. Peterson Copyright © 1993,1994,1995 by Eugene H. Peterson Used by permission of Tyndale House Publishers, Inc. All rights reserved.

Scripture quotations marked (NCV) are from the New Century Version®. Copyright © 2005 by Thomas Nelson. Used by permission. All rights reserved.

DEDICATION

*To June, my beloved wife,
who always sees and brings out the very best in me.*

In Memorium

Donald William Fee
1922-2013

"[You] have fought the good fight, [you] have finished the race, [you] have kept the faith." (2 Timothy 4:7 – NIV)

"Well done, good and faithful servant!" (Matthew 25:23 – NIV)

Bill Fee exemplified a true "servant heart" in the Solana Beach Presbyterian Church Chancel Choir. In addition to his singing in the bass section of the choir, Bill used his gifts of photography and graphics as the choir's pictorial historian at SBPC and on our two Eastern European Ministry trips. He never allowed his physical difficulties to keep him from serving the choir and the Lord.

ACKNOWLEDGMENTS

First of all, I want to thank Marguerite Walker, who challenged me to write the story of the Out of the Loft ministry four years ago. To all the many people who have been involved in the ministry and have shared some of their "stories," I extend my heartfelt thanks; there are just too many to name each and every one of you.

However, I must make special mention of a few people. Tony Bohlin and Mike Maduras have been with me in this ministry from its inception in 1982. They both have shared their stories from the ministry and have read my manuscript to make sure the book is accurate.

Also, this book could not have come to fruition without the unbelievable editing assistance I received from Dawn Bell. Dawn participated in our very first European Ministry Tour in 1984 and played a significant role in extending our ministry to Eastern Europe. In that regard, I must also express my appreciation to Ildikó Barbarics Dobos—our dear friend from Hungary who has been such a significant partner in our ministry. Special kudos also go to Rob Henslin, who has shared his first-hand knowledge on how to self-publish one's book and who designed the book's cover.

Finally, I want to extend my deep gratitude to the one person without whom there would never have been an Out of the Loft ministry. That is my friend, my spiritual mentor, and my inspiration for these past thirty-plus years: Dan Bird—who has served as minister of music and worship at Lake Avenue Church and currently holds the same position at Solana Beach Presbyterian Church. His example of faithfully following God's calling in his life has helped me in attempting to do the same in mine. Dan, I thank you with all my heart!

Early the next morning the army of Judah went out into the wilderness of Tekoa.
On the way Jehoshaphat stopped and said, "Listen to me, all you people of Judah and Jerusalem! Believe in the Lord your God, and you will be able to stand firm.
Believe in his prophets, and you will succeed."
After consulting the people, the king appointed singers to walk ahead of the army,
Singing to the Lord and praising him for his holy splendor. This is what they sang:
"Give thanks to the Lord; his faithful love endures forever!"
2 Chronicles 20:20-21 (New Living Translation)

CONTENTS

Acknowledgments   xv

Forward   xxi

Chapter One	Dawn of a Ministry (1982-1984)	1
Chapter Two	God Is Our Song (August 10-28, 1984)	15
Chapter Three	The Macedonian Call (1984-1989)	47
Chapter Four	Out of Despair, HOPE! (July 27-August 19, 1989)	81
Chapter Five	Ministry Aborted (1989-1996)	121
Chapter Six	Ministry Restored (1996-2003)	141
Chapter Seven	Dawn of a New Day (June 26 – July 14, 2003)	169
Chapter Eight	Music With a Mission (2003-2010)	207
Chapter Nine	Seeing God at Work (June 25 – July 10, 2010)	251

Chapter Ten	The Song Goes On (August 2010 – Present)	299

Epilogue	307
Appendix	315
Update on Choir Proposal – February 20, 2007	315
MUSIC WITH A MISSION 2009	
Executive Summary October 30, 2007	319
2009 CHOIR MISSION TRIP	
Mission Trip Task Force	325
Tour Information Packet	327
Word of Life Hungary Global Mission Proposal	331
Tour Documentation	335
Audio Equipment Used for Ministry	
Travels To Europe	339
Continuing the Ministry	343
Final Thoughts	345

FORWARD

Out of the Loft takes the reader on a fascinating journey as Don King leads two groups of church musicians beyond the choir loft into a unique international missionary calling. Don shares how he used his skills—some of which he didn't know he had—to help director Dan Bird and two Southern California church choirs make a global impact for Jesus Christ. It is a fascinating story of incredible, sometimes-difficult planning and challenging, but exciting travel to Central and Eastern Europe. Every music director needs an ally like Don who helps bring to reality the uniquely wonderful vision of changing the world through music.

    This is also a story of imperfect people and the disappointments that can come when people don't agree or see situations in different ways. I had the unique challenge and privilege of leading the choir at Lake Avenue following Dan Bird's departure from the church. The story of how God brought redemption and restoration between our two choirs and congregations continues today in all of our lives. The gifts that Dan brought to Lake Avenue Church still impact the musical ministry of the Sanctuary Choir. God was at work then and He is still doing His work in both Lake Avenue Church and Solana Beach Presbyterian. It has been a miracle to experience.

Don is one of a kind. I honestly can't think of anyone who has given himself to international choral ministry like he has. Thousands of people will never be the same because of Don's sacrifice of time and energy over the past thirty years.
Duane Funderburk
Co-Director, Worship and the Arts
Lake Avenue Church, Pasadena, CA

CHAPTER ONE

Dawn of a Ministry

> "I will praise you, O Lord, among the nations;
> I will sing of you among the peoples." Psalm 57:9 (NIV)

Our three buses were rolling into the city of Wroclaw, Poland, on that hot Sunday afternoon in the summer of 1989. The choir had been scheduled to sing at St. Elizabeth's Catholic Church at 4:00 p.m., but it was now 5:45. What were we going to do? This was before cell phones, and the government did not allow buses to use their radio communication.

We had left our hotel in West Berlin in plenty of time to make our estimated 2:00 p.m. arrival at the church and to prepare for the next concert on our European ministry tour. Unfortunately, the Communist bureaucrats in East Germany and Poland decided we should meet our "official" Polish guides at the Frankfurt-an-der-Oder border crossing instead of the one closest to Wroclaw, increasing our travel time. On top of that, we were delayed three hours at the border waiting for our passports and visas to be cleared before we could proceed. Thus, we had not only missed our estimated arrival time, but the concert time as well.

When we finally arrived at the church in Wroclaw, I jumped off the bus, along with Mike Maduras and Dan Bird, our choir director, and dashed to find the priest at St. Elizabeth's. At almost the same time we found the priest, a young woman came running up and introduced herself as Niusia. She had been asked by Halina, our 1988 Polish interpreter, if she would interpret for us that summer. Niusia had been at the church from 2:30 that afternoon until almost 5:30, waiting for us to arrive. She had finally given up and was headed for a bus to take her home when her cousin saw our three buses and guessed that the choir was arriving. He contacted Niusia and brought her back to the church just in time.

The priest, while gracious enough, was obviously unhappy that this "Protestant choir" from America had totally missed the concert. It had been rather embarrassing for him, even though he understood the problems with border crossings. He told us, "If you still want to sing, it will have to be at 8:30 p.m. after the last Mass." We were unsure about what we should do, since the people who had planned to attend the concert had long since departed, and the priest could not guess how many people, if any, would stay to hear the concert that evening. We had just a few moments to decide whether or not we would sing, but we immediately agreed that we had not come all the way to Wroclaw just to spend the night in a hotel. We would make the effort and leave the matter of the people up to the Lord.

All we had to do in the next couple of hours was get ourselves to the hotel, check in, eat dinner, get back to the church, and be ready to set up. It was quite a sight as 139 people jammed into the hotel lobby, carrying all of their bags and trying to get onto two small elevators. Any person with an ounce of common sense would have said that it was impossible for all of us to "get to the church on time." However, the set-up crew was able to get to the church by 7:40 p.m. and began to unload the van. The bulk of the choir arrived around 8:20 p.m. and quickly grabbed their robes. At 8:30 sharp, the set-up crew started carrying risers and bell equipment into the church while the rest of the choir hurriedly assembled in the two side aisles. By 8:42 p.m., the set-up was complete and the choir began to sing our opening anthem, "Heilig, Heilig" ("Holy, Holy").

As the monk in the Xerox commercial used to say, "It's a miracle!" Every seat in the church was filled; people were standing in the back and outside on the steps. After the choir had moved onto the risers, even the side aisles became filled with people. The reserved decorum one would expect in a Catholic church was forgotten as the audience cheered, clapped, and blew kisses at the choir. The audience clambered for more until the priest finally indicated we should bring the concert to a close.

After the program, nearly everyone was hugging and sharing—choir members and parishioners alike. As we were all standing outside the church, the priest pointedly told his congregation, "This choir has brought us a desperately-needed message of joy and hope, and we are one in Jesus Christ." He then said to us, "If you are ever in this area again, you <u>must</u> sing at St. Elizabeth's." The priest stayed out on the sidewalk, waving and saying goodbye, until the last bus had been loaded and had pulled away from the curb.

As I look back on this experience, I cannot help but see the Lord's hand constantly guiding this entire ministry. What were we, a Protestant choir from Pasadena, California, doing behind the Iron Curtain in 1989 singing at a Catholic church in Poland? How did this "Out of the Loft" ministry get started? To answer this question, we have to go back some seven years to the fall of 1982.

2

That fateful Choir Cabinet meeting took place on a Friday night in October, 1982, at the home of Chuck and Judy Gilbert. Those present that evening included Dan Bird, the minister of music and worship at Lake Avenue Church, and his wife Linda; Ed Fischer, director of the church handbell choir, and his wife Leta; and the new choir officers—the Gilberts, Larry and Bev Johnson, Mike and Jane Maduras, and my wife June and I.

Dan was relatively new in his position at Lake Avenue, having arrived at the church in June of 1981, just a little over a year before. Ed Fischer, on the other hand, had been involved in the music ministry at Lake Avenue since 1948! Ed now served as the assistant choir director and director of the church handbell choir; he and Leta were like Mom and Pop to everyone involved in the music ministry. Dan and Ed made a great team. Both had a revolutionary way of looking at the choir's ministry. They believed that singing in the choir was not a "voluntary" activity, but a "called" one. The church's previous choir director, Dr. Bruce Leafblad, had first introduced the choir to this idea and had helped us gain a deeper understanding of the biblical foundation of music and worship.

Singing in the Sanctuary Choir under Dr. Leafblad had been very demanding. One of the first major pieces we presented was "The Conversion of St. Paul" by Felix Mendelssohn. The music not only had to be memorized, but also staged and acted in costume. It was a phenomenal experience, but one that proved to be too much for my wife, June. She decided that maybe she was not "called." When June told Bruce Leafblad she was leaving the choir, he asked her why. June told him she felt her voice was not up to the demands of the choir. Bruce then asked her, "Have you prayed about it?" When she responded that she had, Bruce told her to go and pray about it some more. June later told me, "It would be easier to get out of San Quentin Prison than to get out of the Sanctuary Choir!" Dan took the idea of being "called" just as seriously.

Dan's approach to the Choir Cabinet was different from that of most choir directors. Instead of using the choir officers primarily to implement his own plans for the choir and its ministry, Dan viewed the officers as colleagues—people who would come alongside him in planning and carrying out the ministry of the choir, bringing skills and talents which would complement his own. Since I was the new choir president, I especially appreciated Dan's collegial approach.

We began our Choir Cabinet meeting with a delicious potluck dinner. As usual, Chuck Gilbert and Mike Maduras managed to eat several helpings of everything! After dinner and a great time of getting better acquainted with each other, the twelve of us started the meeting with a time of prayer and praise, followed by a discussion of general agenda items. So far the meeting had moved along a familiar track. Then it was Dan's turn to share his "update and wisdom." None of us realized at that point what a profound impact Dan's words would have on us and on the choir's ministry!

Dan began by telling us about a visit by a group of 49 German pastors which our church had hosted during the summer. They had come to America to visit a number of churches and discover what was making these churches so alive and effective. One reason Lake Avenue Church was on their itinerary was that one of the group's leaders was Roger Bosch, an American missionary supported by Lake Avenue Church, who was working with Campus Crusade in Germany. He lived in the town of Pohlheim, where he was very involved with the local village church, the Christus Kirche. Pastor Ernst Maschmann of the Christus Kirche was one of the pastors in this group.

As a part of their visit, the German pastors had met individually with each of the Lake Avenue pastors to find out more about the church's different areas of ministry. During their session with Dan Bird, the pastors talked about what an important role music plays in worship. These Germans had been impressed by the beautiful church service, but also by the fact that the Sanctuary Choir sang every Sunday. Their choir sang only on holidays and for special Sundays in the liturgical calendar, so they usually presented just a few concerts a year. At this point in their meeting, Dan asked the German pastors if they might like a visit by an American church choir. They immediately said that a choir like Lake Avenue's Sanctuary Choir would be most welcome.

After concluding his summary of the German pastors' visit, Dan looked each of us straight in the eye and said, "I've been thinking about my time with the German pastors and I'd like to share an idea with you." He then asked a startling question: "What do you think about the possibility of taking our choir to Europe?" You should have seen the expressions on our faces! We had never contemplated such a thing, and yet there was something inside us that yelled, "Yes!" Dan said that if we were to take such a trip, it would not be a typical "choir tour" during which we would sing a few concerts in great cathedrals as part of a European vacation trip. If we were really going to do this, he said, it would be done as an extension of our call to ministry. By the end of the meeting, we had agreed that we needed to pursue this idea and share it with the whole choir.

I don't think any of us had the slightest idea of what would be involved in taking a large choir to Europe or what an impact the tour would have on our individual lives and on the choir as a whole. Everyone is familiar with the saying, "Ignorance is bliss." I don't know if this saying is true, but I can definitely state that if we had known all of the "zigs and zags" through which this ministry would take us, we might not have been so eager to endorse the idea at our October meeting. Little did we realize that the Lord was taking us on a challenging, yet exciting "journey of faith."

3

The first task we faced was deciding where God was calling us and figuring out how we would get there. We shared the tour idea with the whole choir, who were enthusiastic and supportive. Then we talked with our senior pastor, Dr. Paul Cedar, and introduced the idea of a European ministry tour to the Board of Nurture, the church body that oversaw the church's music and worship. We also sent letters to various Lake Avenue Church-supported missionaries in Europe—Roger Bosch in West Germany; Hal Leaman in Salzburg, Austria; Ed Moehl in Vienna; and Rod Johnston near Geneva, Switzerland—asking them about possible ministry opportunities for the choir. We told these missionaries, "We believe our choir will be an encouragement to the people in your country, as well as a blessing to your ministry."

Lake Avenue Church had always had a strong missions program, and this was one way we could make our own contribution. Our ministry is summarized in Acts 1:8 (NIV), *"And you shall be my witnesses in Jerusalem, and in all Judea and Samaria, and to the ends of the earth."* Our primary ministry was at Lake Avenue Church in Pasadena, our Jerusalem; then throughout Southern California, our Judea and Samaria; and, finally, to our "ends of the earth" in Europe.

Replies from our missionaries were encouraging. We set the summer of 1984 as our target date and began to develop an itinerary. This, of course, raised an important question: Just how long should the trip be? Some argued for a trip of 10-12 days, the usual length of "group tours," while others pushed for a longer time. We eventually decided on a tour of nineteen days, which would give us three full weekends to minister in Germany, Austria, and Switzerland.

Now that we had a basic itinerary, we needed to find a tour provider for the ministry. Many church choirs use tour providers who specialize in organizing "choir tours" and arranging places for them to sing. That was not what we were looking for. We were not going on a trip just to sing, but also to minister—along with our missionaries—in these three European countries. We therefore needed to find a tour provider who could help us plan a very different kind of tour than most choirs experience.

I don't know if anyone had ever chosen a tour provider this way before, but Mike Maduras and I got together and wrote out an eighteen-page bidding document. Mike had extensive experience in working up bidding documents for his business, but we had never seen one used to find a tour provider. We sent out the bidding document to several tour agencies which had been recommended to us or which had expressed an interest in submitting a bid. The bid proposals were to be submitted to us no later than May 1, 1983. After analyzing each of the proposals, the Choir Cabinet selected the bid submitted by a local travel agency which would use DER Tours of West Germany for the European arrangements. Their proposal seemed to meet all of our requirements and was the lowest bid: $2,400 per person.

When we told the choir how much the trip would cost, many of them felt overwhelmed. How would they ever come up with that kind of money? It is not surprising that the greatest test of faith was raising the funds for the trip. As each choir member committed to the ministry tour, he was asked to make a "faith commitment" of the amount he believed the Lord would enable him to pay for the tour. All choir members were encouraged, of course, to commit the full amount, but we understood that not everyone would be able to do so. Most people committed to paying the entire $2,400; others decided to pay even more. In addition, some of those who were not able to participate in the tour committed to help others financially.

Tom, a tenor in our choir, shared with me how the Lord provided a way for him and his wife to go on the tour: *"When the tour was* announced, I just knew it was something I had to do. I had been in the Sanctuary Choir at Lake Avenue since leaving high school and had been singing in choirs since the third grade. I knew that the tour would become part of the fabric of the choir and would influence the choir for years to come. Don't ask me how I knew this at the ripe old age of 30, but I did! The largest problem facing me was how to do it financially as a newly self-employed father of two, with another on the way.

Early in the process, we were asked to give a deposit of $300.00. This was a tough nut to crack, and it was just a small portion of what would eventually be needed. However, a few weeks later I received a check in the mail from Volkswagen of America. Many months earlier we had purchased a VW minivan to accommodate our growing family. Unbeknownst to me and apparently unbeknownst to the dealer, there was a rebate on this particular model. That rebate was in the amount of $300.00!

That week during choir rehearsal, Dan asked me to share with the choir how my deposit money had come in. I told the choir my little miracle story. I added that I still had no idea where the rest of the money would come from, but I was trusting God for it. That night after rehearsal, a choir member came up to me and told me that I had nothing to be worried about: she had talked to Dan and wanted to cover the rest of my tour costs. I wasn't even acquainted with this lady, so what a surprise that conversation was!

I also needed money to pay my brother-in-law to do deliveries for me while I was away. Another choir member stepped up to cover that expense! Then I told Dan that it would be really nice if my wife could go, even though she would be seven months pregnant by the time the tour concluded. Done and done. Every obstacle was knocked down. As a result, my wife and I were able to experience not just a magnificent choir ministry trip, but we were also able to be a part of God's miracles and be blessed by the overwhelming generosity of others as God moved them to act on our behalf.

I had recently purchased my business from my dad. It was, and still is, a one-man operation, so leaving the business for two weeks was a difficult thing to do. When I told my dad that I was going on the tour, he was upset. He felt that my taking the trip was a risky thing which could endanger the health of the business. Perhaps he was concerned about the financial impact on him, as I was giving him monthly payments. I told my dad, 'Everything we own is God's and He can do with it what He pleases. Certainly, God can cause the business to survive for two weeks in my absence.' However, that reply didn't make an immediate change in my dad's attitude.

A few weeks later the choir was singing in the first service, which at the time was at 7:30 a.m. I don't remember what the choir sang that morning, but my dad and mom were there. After the service, as I was visiting with friends at the beginning of my adult Bible study class, my dad sought me out. He then confessed to me that he had been wrong in his attitude towards the tour and my participation in it. He acknowledged that God was the true owner of all we have and he essentially gave me his blessing to go on the trip! This removed the final hurdle and freed me to go forward with the choir tour. The peace that God gave to my father was truly remarkable!"

The first step in the choir's journey was finding a way to pay our initial deposits to the airlines and the tour provider, which were due during the summer of 1983. Summer was a tough time to do fundraising, especially since the choir was off from the end of July until after Labor Day. However, over the summer we were able to persuade the airlines and the tour provider to delay our initial deposit deadlines until October.

When the chairman of the Board of Nurture met with us in September, he could not believe that the European ministry tour was still alive. "The tour providers' willingness to delay your initial payments until later in the fall," he told us, "is evidence that the Lord is truly in this ministry." He promised to recommend to the Board of Nurture and the Board of Trustees that they give their support to the tour. Hallelujah! Just when everything looked hopeless, we saw God change hearts and make the impossible a reality. As we moved through the fall of 1983 and into the winter of 1984, we were able to make each payment to our tour providers as it came due.

4

By January of 1984 we had just seven months left to prepare for the ministry tour. Here we were, still novices, trying to figure out what else had to be done. Our missionaries were a great help in finalizing our ministry opportunities; with their assistance, we arranged for the choir to give eight full concerts and to lead worship in three Sunday morning worship services. It would be a demanding schedule! Meanwhile, the choir members had their own daunting task: to learn and memorize an entire program of music, including four pieces sung in German.

Another project which needed to be done was designing our printed program. We decided the program should be in the language of the people to whom we would minister. This meant we needed to have the program translated into German (for Germany and Austria) and into French (for the French-speaking part of Switzerland around Geneva). We would also print an English version of the program, since our audiences might well include English-speaking visitors. The final version of our program included the words to every piece of music we would sing—in all three languages.

Tony Bohlin, the husband of one of our choir members, saw the need for two special teams—a medical team and an audiovisual team.

At the time, we did not realize how essential these people would be. Tony was a paramedic as well as an RN. He understood that taking a group of 120 people on a nineteen-day ministry tour could have medical implications for individuals and for the whole group, so he asked three other RNs in the choir to become part of a medical team. Then Tony contacted Dr. Marshall Welles, a retired medical missionary to China and Thailand who was then practicing in Pasadena. Under Dr. Welles's auspices, Tony acquired various medicines, including antibiotics, to bring on the trip. Tony also developed a medical history form which he asked everyone to complete and return to him.

In addition to the medical planning, Tony decided we needed to document the trip for our congregation, as well as for the trip participants. He had begun the video ministry at Lake Avenue Church in the fall of 1983, so he arranged to bring a video camera and audio recording equipment on the tour. Tony's foresight proved invaluable during and after the trip. In fact, both of his ideas—for a medical team and for making an audiovisual documentary of the tour—proved so necessary and successful that they became a basic part of all our future trip planning.

The Board of Trustees had told us we would need to have the full amount for the tour, approximately $265,000, by the end of July, less than two weeks before the start of our trip. As we approached this date, we realized we would come up short by $25,000 to $30,000. Our senior pastor, Paul Cedar, asked Dan for some time at the end of our rehearsal the first Thursday in July to talk to the choir about the ministry tour, so Dan stopped the rehearsal around 9:00.

Pastor Paul reiterated his support for the European ministry tour and presented the challenge to the choir—the need to raise the additional funds. All of the choir members had not completed their payments for the tour and we needed to find out if those payments would close the financial gap. We went into a time of prayer for God's provision. Following the prayer, Pastor Paul challenged each of us to respond to four questions: "Am I still committed to going on the ministry tour?" "Will I be able to complete my 'faith promise' by the deadline?" "If not, how much will I be able to pay?" "If I can complete, or have already completed, my faith promise, can I give more—and if so, how much?"

People were given pieces of paper on which to record their answers to these questions. Mike and I then took their responses back into Dan's office to figure out how much money we had. About twenty minutes later, we reported back to the choir that we had reduced our deficit to under $10, 000. Pastor Paul asked us again to go to the Lord in prayer. When we finished praying Pastor Paul said, speaking through tears, "The Lord has laid on my heart that if I am asking the choir to sacrifice, I also need to sacrifice." He then wrote out a check for $1,000 to the tour. We were awestruck! It was now getting close to midnight, so Pastor Paul asked us, for the second and last time, to respond to the four questions. The results from the choir's second response showed that we had not only made up the deficit, but also had a small surplus! There was not a dry eye in the place! All we could do at that moment was exalt the Lord, so we closed the night by singing the Doxology.

> *"Praise God from whom all blessings flow; Praise*
> *Him, all creatures here below;*
> *Praise Him above, ye heavenly host; Praise Father,*
> *Son, and Holy Ghost. Amen."*

We had come a long way from the Friday night in October of 1982 when Dan had first shared with us his meeting with the German pastors and his vision for the choir. During those two years, we had often talked about what we should call this ministry. Finally, we came up with the phrase that would forever identify our mission. We were being called to go "Out of the Loft and Into the World" to share the love of Jesus Christ through vital spiritual singing.

CHAPTER TWO

God Is Our Song

> *"God is our song. We sing with jubilation!*
> *Great is His name and great is His creation;*
> *The boundless heav'ns to Him belong."*
> From *"God Is Our Song"* by Ludwig van Beethoven

D-Day, or "Departure Day" for our European Ministry Tour finally arrived on Friday morning, August 10, 1984. The buses taking us to Los Angeles International Airport were parked across the street in the church parking lot. An air of excitement surrounded the 120 people who stowed their bags on the buses and headed back to the church sanctuary for a short time of worship and prayer. As the buses pulled out of the parking lot, choir members tearfully waved good-bye to family being left behind.

We had planned to leave for the airport by 10:00 a.m. because we did not know if we would encounter major traffic problems near the Los Angeles Coliseum. This was a possibility, since we had to drive through downtown L.A. in the middle of the 1984 Olympics! As it turned out, we sailed right by the Coliseum without any problem. We thus arrived at the airport before noon. Despite a difficulty with our tour provider related to baggage handling costs, we lifted off from LAX as planned. We were finally on our way to Europe!

On board our 747 flight, we felt more and more excited. Everyone seemed in a jovial mood; choir members were constantly running around the plane talking with each other. A number of people were either reviewing their music or were trying to memorize some piece they had not yet mastered. The transfer of planes in London went smoothly and we arrived at the Frankfurt Airport in Germany at 11:15 a.m., where it was already the next day. Needless to say, after flying through the night we were feeling the effects of jet lag.

Everyone who travels abroad knows that the first thing a person does upon arriving at a foreign airport is to go through passport control. Since most people in our group were U.S. citizens, they did not need visas to enter the German Federal Republic, or "West Germany." As we moved from passport control to the baggage claim area, a burly, tall German with a bushy mustache came up to me and introduced himself as Joe Leonards. Joe was to be one of our tour escorts representing DER Tours and was the person in charge. I did not have the slightest idea when I met Joe that our friendship would continue for over thirty years.

Shortly after we arrived, Joe told me that one of our choir members, Hwai-tang, had a problem. She was originally from Taiwan and carried a Taiwanese passport, but she had not checked with her consulate to find out if she would need any visas for the trip. When she tried to go through passport control they stopped her, saying that since she did not possess a visa to enter the country, she would have to return to the United States. Joe took me to the passport control office to see if we could work things out. I told the German authorities that Hwai-tang was a vital member of our choir and asked if she might be given a temporary visa. After 45 minutes of deliberation they agreed to do so, provided that she went to the consulate in Düsseldorf within five days to obtain a regular visa. Hwai-tang was able to do this and had no further problems.

By the time Joe and I were ready to leave the airport, the rest of the group already had their bags and were waiting for us on the three buses. Choir members commented on how impressed they were that every vehicle in the long line of taxis at the airport was a Mercedes-Benz!

Our check-in at the Hotel Hilton in the city of Mainz went smoothly. When June and I arrived at our room, I walked over to the window and found myself looking out on the mighty Rhine River. It now sank in that we were really in Germany and that I was seeing one of the most famous rivers in Europe. That evening we all enjoyed an elegant welcome banquet, listened to Joe's entertaining description of what we should expect during our travels, and ended with a brief rehearsal. Our heads were swirling by the time we flopped onto our beds that night.

The familiar phrase, "hit the ground running," certainly described our group as we began the first full day of our European Ministry Tour on Sunday. The "complete American buffet breakfast" we enjoyed was a far cry from the dry Continental breakfast so many tour groups are served. We could choose from several kinds of dry cereals, cold cuts, breads, and rolls, along with scrambled or boiled eggs, sausages, bacon, broiled tomatoes, fresh fruit, and juices. What a way to begin the day!

Actually, the events of the day had begun before most people entered the dining room to have breakfast. In the hall outside our hotel room, I heard excited voices. Entering the hall, I found Tony Bohlin leaning over the prostrate form of a woman from our group. Tony was checking her pulse and other vital signs. Early evidence seemed to indicate that she might have suffered a heart attack. Joe Leonards joined Tony and called for paramedics, who then took her to a hospital.

We eventually found out that this lady had not been entirely truthful on her medical history form. She had not indicated that she had high blood pressure and heart problems because she was afraid that if we knew about her medical condition we would not let her go on the trip. Unfortunately, she never was able to rejoin our group; she spent several days in the hospital and was eventually flown back home. This incident reminded us how important it is for everyone on a trip to be thorough and honest regarding his or her medical history. This incident had been a close call, and we were lucky it had not been more serious.

We were scheduled to leave the hotel by 9:00 a.m. and arrive in Pohlheim in time for the 10:00 worship service at the Christus Kirche. A choir spouse remarked that her first impression of Pohlheim was the sound of church bells ringing, calling the villagers to worship. I can still picture our arrival in front of the Volkshalle, the town hall. Since we were going directly into the church when we arrived, we had all dressed in our "tour outfits"—navy blue blazers, gray slacks, white shirts, and rose-colored ties for the men, and rose-colored floor-length dresses for the ladies. The group looked sharp. However, the ladies began to refer to their outfits as "pink elephant" dresses. I assume the reference was to the dresses and not to the ladies themselves.

We lined up in front of the Volkshalle and then entered the church for the service. We did not even have time to warm up or practice any of our music before the service began. The church was packed, perhaps due in part to curiosity about who these Americans were. It was an inspiring time of worship. Pastor Maschmann conducted the service and preached, while Dennis Griggs translated everything into English. The love and bonding we felt with the German congregation made us better understand the truth of the great hymn,

> *"In Christ there is no East or West, In Him no South or North;*
> *But one great fellowship of love Through-out the whole wide earth."*
> Words by John Oxenham (1908)

When the church service was over, everyone moved to the Volkshalle across the street for a reception. As coffee and snacks were served, Roger Bosch and Dennis Griggs welcomed our choir. When Dennis Griggs saw me, he informed me that he had placed June and me with a wonderful family who spoke good English. This was a relief, since the only German I knew was "Ja," "Nein," and "Wo ist die Toilleten, bitte?" or "Where is the toilet, please?" All of us were wondering just how well we would communicate with our German hosts. Dennis then introduced me to Günter Wehrenfennig, in whose home June and I would be staying. Since Günter said very little to us, I thought, "If this family speaks good English, heaven help those choir members who are staying with families who speak limited English or none at all!"

After all the other choir members had been connected with their host families, Günter drove June and me to their home. We noticed that most of the houses in town were located right on the street, with a tall wooden gate shutting off the driveway and yard. The Wehrenfennig home had a well-kept back yard with a flower and vegetable garden which extended all the way back to a pedestrian alley at the rear of their property. We were met at the front door by Günter's wife, Adelheid; their four children; and the friendly family dog. We soon discovered that Adelheid spoke good English. Keeping her German-English dictionary with her at all times, she made sure we understood everything that was said.

As I think back on that afternoon, I realize that we were almost immediately enfolded into the Wehrenfennig family. In fact, the Wehrenfennigs' youngest son, Bernhardt (age 7), who spoke no English, said to his parents before we left, "They [June and I] are not just friends; they are family." We enjoyed a flavorful Sunday dinner; then Günter took me on a drive to see some of the historic sites in Pohlheim and the surrounding area while June took a nap. One of the children had given up his bedroom so we could have a room to ourselves, which we greatly appreciated.

OUT OF THE LOFT

At the end of a post-concert reception, I returned home to the Wehrenfennigs and found June and Adelheid chatting like old friends. June had been too tired to attend the concert, so Adelheid had stayed home with her. During the hours the two of them had spent getting better acquainted, they discovered they had much in common. Adelheid and June have been close friends ever since. I noticed that the dining room table was again set with food for the *abendessen*, or evening meal. Evidently, we were to be fed at every opportunity. June barely made it through the meal before she fell asleep, but I was still so emotional from the concert that I could not have gone right to sleep if my life had depended on it.

Dawn, one of our choir members, had a very different experience. She later related her story to me. *"I spoke a little German, so I was placed with hosts who didn't speak much English. Since I was the only choir member assigned to this home, I found it difficult to carry on a conversation all by myself. My German hosts had prepared an absolute feast for the noon meal. The table was loaded with several kinds of meat, two different potato dishes, a variety of vegetables, breads, desserts, you name it. I tried to eat as much as I could, but they insisted that I take more, so I kept stuffing myself because I didn't want to offend them.*

When they asked me what I wanted to drink, I said I'd like some water. They looked confused. I found out later that people don't drink water with their meals in Germany; the beverage of choice is beer. (We also found out that there were no water fountains in Germany. We even had to pay extra to be served water along with our meals in restaurants.) Since my host family didn't feel comfortable serving me water, I asked for milk. This request seemed even crazier to them—several family members tried to stifle a laugh. Why would anyone want to drink milk from a cow?! Finally, they brought me carbonated fruit juice, which was actually quite good. All this time, I was struggling with jet lag and literally had trouble keeping my eyes open. I finally was able to get away to my room for a little shut-eye. When I rejoined the choir at the Volkshalle, I almost cried. I was so relieved to be back with people who spoke English!"

Around 5:00 p.m. the choir assembled for our evening concert. We needed time to put up the risers, handbell tables, and audiovisual equipment, as well as to warm up our voices. Since it had been six days since we had sung together, we worried that we might not remember the music. We also wondered how many people would show up. Before we left Pasadena, we were told that because we were going to Europe in the summer, we would find many people away on vacation or "on holiday," as Europeans call it, so we were advised not to be disappointed if we had small audiences at the concerts.

However, we intended to sing our hearts out, no matter how large the audience was. Every concert began with our surrounding the audience and singing Mendelssohn's "Heilig, Heilig" or "Holy, Holy." As we walked in from the rear of the Volkshalle, we were amazed to see the hall completely filled with people, with some even standing in the back. The atmosphere during the entire concert was electrifying; if any of us forgot any words or notes, I am sure the audience never knew it.

It was interesting how the choir connected with the audience. After the first few choir numbers there was only polite applause, but when the Son-Light Bells began to play a little later in the program, the people went "bonkers." They literally came out of their seats with loud and long clapping, a new style of clapping we had not experienced in the United States. The applause began with the normal random clapping and then changed into loud, unison clapping which became faster and faster as it went on. We learned that in Europe this kind of clapping denotes the audience's desire for more. From then on, the people in the Volkshalle responded with great enthusiasm to every song the choir sang. In fact, at every concert thereafter, the Son-Light Bells proved to be the catalyst which bonded the choir to the audience.

Another first for us was when the audience began shouting "Bravo!" over and over at the end of the concert, an exhilarating response we would hear throughout our tour. But the biggest surprise came after Hermann Georg, the town's *Burgermeister* (mayor), greeted us warmly at the conclusion of the concert. As he walked off the stage, he went over to Joyce, a soprano in the first row, and gave her a big kiss on the cheek. That moment was recorded on video and became one of the video clips we will always remember with a smile.

After breakfast the next morning, we were returned to the Christus Kirche, where we had a time of sharing and praying together. The short weekend we had spent with the people of Pohlheim did more to prepare us for the rest of our ministry tour than anything else we could have imagined. We had begun this tour praying that God would be glorified and that He would use us in amazing ways. As our buses pulled away from the church, the Apostle Paul's words found in Ephesians 3:20-21 (NIV) were also written on our hearts: *"Now to Him who is able to do immeasurably more than all we ask or imagine, according to His power that is at work within us, to Him be glory in the church and in Christ Jesus throughout all generations, for ever and ever! Amen."*

Roger Bosch, the Lake Avenue missionary who arranged for us to sing in Pohlheim, told me recently that as the choir prepared to leave in 1984, Pohlheim's mayor said to Roger, "I am so sorry to see the choir leave this area, as they not only brought an excellent musical program to the community, but they also touched the personal lives of everyone with whom they had contact." The mayor was standing next to Roger as the people of Pohlheim waved good-bye to us. Roger noticed that the mayor had tears in his eyes and that he kept waving his white kerchief until they could no longer see the buses. Roger summed it up well when he said, "There were many, many friendships forged during the brief stay of the choir in Pohlheim which carry on to this day, almost 30 years later."

One example is the friendship June and I have enjoyed with Günter and Adelheid Wehrenfennig and their family ever since the 1984 tour. Not long ago, I asked Adelheid to write about how the choir's visits and our friendship with her and her family have affected them over these years. She then wrote this lovely letter to June and me: "*We often and fondly remember the choir visits in our church. Your music helped motivate our choir. Many people were impressed by the trouble you took and the money you invested in order to visit people, to encourage them, and to preach the good news to them through song. We believe that especially the trips to the Eastern Bloc have been full of blessings. However, surely you too have been richly rewarded by the joy, love, and gratitude of the people you have met. Some people in the village still cultivate friendships with their guests from the choir tours. People from the Catholic church also continue to speak of your concert at their church; everyone back then was especially impressed by the bell choir.*

We remember with great joy your first visit to us. You had been but a few hours with us when June told me, 'I can hardly believe that we have never seen each other and that half the world lies between us.' It was really something like 'love at first sight.' Our children have always been crazy about you. Both of you are a steadfast and beloved part of the childhood memories of our now grown-up children. I asked them what they can remember about your time here and got spontaneous answers from all of them. They remember the anticipation and suspense of wondering what it would be like to have you stay with us. They enthusiastically cleaned up their rooms and 'moved in together' so that you would have a bedroom. They were totally thrilled by the way you marveled at our garden, our trees, and our vegetables, and how you noticed that everything was so green here in the summer.

For us and our children, your visit was our first impression of, and contact with, people from the other side of the globe, which was exciting and positive for us. All of us have experienced how faith in God connects people and turns them into real, true friends. You have often said and written that we are your German family, as you are our American family to this day. During one of our visits with you and Dan Bird, Dan gave Anke the "All Day Song" after he spontaneously wrote it down on a sheet of paper with notes and words. This made such an incredible impression on her that she has kept that sheet of paper like a treasure. Annette and Martin still cultivate the friendship of Scott and Lisa that arose from the choir trip, and Annette always tells me when she has met Don 'on the web.'

In the 30 years of our friendship much has changed. You gave us record albums of the choir in the beginning. Then they became tapes, and now they are CDs. We have always enjoyed them and hear the outstanding quality of the choir in all of the recordings. We want to take this opportunity to thank you again with all our hearts for these gifts of music. Of all our experiences with you, the most wonderful one was visiting you in California in 1998. To this day, that trip is a highlight of our lives. Together with you, we saw the unbelievable beauties of your country. It was a very special time thanks to your enormous hospitality and all your caring love. We have experienced wonderful times together. Our many shared memories and our joyous faith bind us together. We are sure that God brought us together and that is why our friendship has persisted for nearly 30 years." (Translated from German by Wolfgang Bluhm)

One of our most significant stops after Pohlheim was the great German city of Cologne with its magnificent cathedral. We were aware that the Romans originally founded Cologne; we even saw some of the old Roman ruins while we were there. It was the Cologne Cathedral, however, which most caught our attention. During World War II, Cologne was heavily bombed, but the Allies made every effort to avoid hitting the cathedral. Although the cathedral sustained considerable damage, it remained standing tall in an otherwise flattened city. It is amazing that Allied pilots were able to spare such a tall building even before the invention of the smart bombs we hear about today.

The Cologne Cathedral is the most famous Gothic cathedral in the world, and I found it to be the most impressive and awe-inspiring edifice I had ever seen. The cathedral took more than six centuries to build and was the world's tallest building until 1884, when it lost this title to the Washington Monument. However, the Cologne Cathedral still boasts the largest church facade in the world: the total area of the cathedral measures over 86,000 square feet and has room for more than 20,000 people. With its interior vaults soaring up 150 feet and its 515-foot-high twin towers dominating the landscape outside, everything in the cathedral points upward. Standing in the central aisle and looking up toward the ceiling far above, I glimpsed the glory of our great God.

Joe Leonards had made arrangements for our choir to sing three songs in the cathedral that morning. We took our places near the front of the church and began to sing "Ubi Caritas." The first line of that piece, which we sang in Latin, says, "Where charity and love are, there is God." We felt the love and presence of God as we sang and heard our voices echoing over and over in the huge cathedral. The reverberation in the cathedral was so great that I believe our choir could have sung a piece, sat down, and heard it resound back to us in its entirety. Singing in the Cologne Cathedral made me think of the passage in which Paul writes: *"I pray that out of His glorious riches He may strengthen you with power through His Spirit in your inner being, so that Christ may dwell in your hearts through faith. And I pray that you, being rooted and established in love, may have power, together with all the saints, to grasp how wide and long and high and deep is the love of Christ, and to know this love that surpasses knowledge—that you may be filled to the measure of all the fullness of God."* Ephesians 3: 16-19 (NIV).

Our last song was a spiritual called "Give Me Jesus." Bill, a choir spouse, was sitting out in the church with people who had come in to see the cathedral. When they heard our choir begin to sing, many of them sat down to listen. After we finished "Give Me Jesus," Bill noticed a man sitting next to him with tears running down his face. The man told Bill that he had left his faith many years before, but that while we sang "Give Me Jesus" God had touched his heart and he had decided to recommit his life to Christ. When Bill later shared his experience with the choir, we realized that no matter where we were or what we were singing, the Lord was using us in the lives of others who needed Christ.

Before we could leave the following morning, we had to take care of a medical problem. Fritz, one of the choir basses, fell in the hotel, breaking his collarbone. Tony Bohlin went with him to the hospital to have the bone set. Tony's wife, Judy, was concerned that Tony and Fritz might not catch up with us before we arrived in Koblenz and boarded our boat for a cruise on the Rhine River. She had a right to be worried; Tony and Fritz, his arm in a sling, made it to the boat just before it pulled out into the river. Fritz's fall was probably due to his instability from multiple sclerosis. Fritz was an amazing example to the choir, as he never complained about his disease, even though he could not walk without the aid of a cane, and he never allowed his physical challenges to deter his ministry. He did not sing in the concert that night in Limburger Hof, but he sang in every concert thereafter. Fritz was not going to let a little thing like a fractured collarbone stop him from singing!

The cruise on the Rhine River was spectacular, taking us through the Rhine River Gorge, a 40-mile section of the river. This gorge was carved out of rock over many centuries, leaving the river with steep walls over 600 feet high in some places. We cruised the river from Koblenz to the town of St. Goar, the stretch of the Rhine which passes the ruins of a myriad of medieval castles that dot the hills on both sides of the river. It is one of the most beautiful parts of Germany.

Perhaps the most famous feature along the Gorge is the Lorelei, a rock on the eastern bank of the Rhine which soars some 400 feet above the waterline. It marks the narrowest part of the river between Switzerland and the North Sea. A very strong current and the rocks below the waterline have caused many boat accidents there. Lorelei is also the name of a feminine water spirit similar to a mermaid or "Rhine maiden" and is associated with this rock in popular folklore. I tried to hear the maiden's voice, but the choir was making too much noise.

As we began our four-hour cruise, Dan was in high spirits as he quipped, "Maybe we should sing 'Shall We Gather at the River.'" As our boat moved along at a relaxed pace, many people standing on the banks of the river or sitting in front of their houses waved to us and smiled as we went by. That day was Lois and Dick's 25th wedding anniversary. Lois fondly recalls, *"Dick bought me a bouquet of flowers as we cruised down the Rhine River. We received many anniversary cards and felt the love of the choir. It was a great day for us as a couple and for the choir."* It is clear that the Rhine cruise was one of the special blessings we experienced during the tour.

We disembarked at St. Goar and were met by our three buses, which took us to the town of Limburger Hof to present our last concert in West Germany. This concert had been arranged by Lake Avenue missionary, Ed Moehl. When Ed had brought up the idea of a concert in Limburger Hof, the local church leaders told him he should try to find a relatively small church for the concert because many people would be away on holiday. However, Ed insisted that the concert should be held in the Ortszentrum, Limburger Hof's large concert hall. He admitted it was a huge step of faith, but he encouraged the church leaders to trust the Lord for the results. Ed also mobilized small Bible study groups from several area churches to plan for the concert. They even decided to provide a large potluck dinner for the choir before our program. And what a dinner it was! Stuffed with all kinds of tasty German dishes, we were somehow expected to sing afterwards!

The Ortszentrum can seat around 1,000 people. As we gathered outside for a time of prayer, we gave the evening over to the Lord. Then, as we walked into the concert hall, we found ourselves singing for the largest and most enthusiastic audience of our time in Germany. It was an uplifting experience to sing for these people and share God's love. It was also heartening to see how the Lord had honored Ed Moehl's step of faith. Not only was the place packed, but our time there also brought together people from a number of churches in service to the Lord.

4

Our destination the next day was Salzburg, Austria, with a stop in the city of Munich along the way. This was our first day off from singing since we had arrived in West Germany. We had never had a chance to get over jet lag before we began our ministry, and we had traveled to a new city every day. Thus, having a day free to see the beautiful and historic city of Munich and to enjoy a special dinner in the evening at a charming Austrian sport chalet, the Gut Brandlhof, was something we were all looking forward to. We also were thrilled to be spending two nights in the same place!

The Gut Brandlhof is located in the foothill village of Saalfelden, about a forty-five minute drive from Salzburg. When we arrived, Joe Leonards was informed that the hotel did not have enough rooms for our whole group and that twenty of our people would have to be housed elsewhere. To say that this was a disappointment, especially for those who would have to make the move, would be an understatement. Everyone was exhausted and just wanted to fall into bed. The hotel had prepared a delectable buffet dinner for us that night, but the meal did not make the group of twenty feel any better. What should have been a time of great food and fellowship turned into an evening of grumbling and disunity. I wondered if we could ever recover from this experience and continue to minister with a good spirit. Satan had used his two most effective tools, discouragement and division, in an attempt to disrupt the tour.

After a night of much prayer, we felt God's loving grace and healing touch. The group which had been sent into exile came back to the Gut Brandlhof full of enthusiasm about the hotel in which they had stayed. They had loved the smaller, more intimate setting of their hotel and were no longer bitter about the change. It also helped that everyone was anxious to spend the day in Salzburg, one of the most fascinating cities in Austria. Lake Avenue missionaries Hal and Liz Leaman ministered in Salzburg and would be there to greet us.

Salzburg, the birthplace of Mozart and the setting for the movie "The Sound of Music," lay before us in all of its splendor. Towering over the Altstadt, or "Old Town City," was the Festungsberg with its Hohensalzburg Castle. This 900-year-old citadel is the place in which archbishops took refuge during the battles between the Ottoman Empire and the medieval Kingdom of Hungary. Fortress Hohensalzburg is an unmistakable landmark, creating the city's world-famous silhouette. The narrow cobbled streets below the fortress were filled with the cacophonous sounds of street vendors, blaring music, and hundreds of tourists. Dan Bird could not wait to begin our bus tour of Salzburg so he could see Mozart's birthplace museum, the Mozart Gerburtshaus.

Of course, we also visited some of the famous sites from the movie, "The Sound of Music." Mirabell Gardens contains the famous steps where the song "Do-Re-Mi" was filmed. Leopoldskron Palace, where visitors can see the Captain's back yard and private gardens, stands next to the lake known for the movie's boating scene. The gazebo where the two young lovers sang "16 Going on 17" and where Maria and Baron von Trapp kissed, is located in the gardens of Hellbrunn Palace, once the summer palace of the Archbishops of Salzburg. Nonnberg Abbey, where the "real" Maria was a novice and where she and Baron von Trapp were married in real life, is still an active convent today. Just outside Salzburg the buses drove past Lake Fuschl and Lake Wolfgang, where panoramic shots and scenes of the picnic were filmed. And in the little town of Mondsee, we had the chance to see the church where the wedding of Maria and Baron von Trapp took place in the movie.

After the bus tour, we were free to have lunch and explore the quaint, narrow streets of Salzburg on our own. Around 2:00 p.m. the choir met in front of St. Peter's Monastery and Church to change into our tour outfits and move into the church to warm up. The actual concert was scheduled to take place at 4:00 that afternoon outside in the Alter Markt, a busy shopping area. We had chosen the Alter Markt as the location for the concert (provided, of course, that it didn't rain) because it was usually full of tourists and townspeople and was surrounded by tall buildings, which would allow the sound of our singing to reverberate off the buildings and would keep our music from floating out into space.

A good number of people were in the square when we began our concert, but as the sound of our singing began to blanket the square, more and more people were drawn in. By the end of the concert, there must have been a thousand people jammed into the Alter Markt. Even after we finished, the crowd hung around, hoping we would sing some more. Some corralled various choir members into conversations. One young boy even asked Dan to autograph his program.

Dick, who sang bass in the choir, recalled his experience at the Alter Markt: *"After we finished the concert in the Alter Markt, we tried to share with the people in the audience and talk about our love of Jesus Christ, as we did after every concert. It was always an exciting time, but it made me a little nervous since I didn't speak their language and was apprehensive about what I would say. As we circulated around the square, I met a lady from Lichtenstein who spoke very good English. I had the opportunity to share with her about the Lord and why the choir was there—to glorify God. She seemed to understand, and I enjoyed our conversation.*

At this point, my wife joined me. We encountered another lady who came by passing out tracts. This lady happened to be a member of the church that had arranged for our singing in Salzburg. She told me how fantastic it was to have us there. 'It is like heaven, like angels singing,' she said. 'You just do not know what it means to have you here.' Then her voice cracked and she began to cry. Even though we were standing in the Alter Markt with hundreds of people around, I said to her, 'We need to pray for you right now.' All of us grabbed hands, formed a circle, and prayed that God would take care of this lady. We then assured her that we would be praying for her and her ministry in Salzburg. That was an experience I will never forget."

That evening the choir was treated to an entertaining dinner and folklore show. Costumed dancers sang, swung, kicked, and slapped to delightful Austrian folk music. During the show, some of the dancers "invited" (actually, coerced) some of our people to join them in the dances. Those who were asked to dance were good sports and at least put on a "good face" when asked to participate. One set of dancers was called "The Fauffinger Girls." Some young ladies in the choir remembered these dancers on the last evening of the tour, when we had a farewell dinner and fun night. They put on an hilarious skit, calling themselves "The Four Finger Girls." We laughed so hard that tears rolled down our faces.

Denise, who was part of "The Four Finger Girls," recently shared her memories of the impromptu dance group she and her friends organized. *"During the 1984 ministry tour to Germany, Austria, and Switzerland, we enjoyed so many wonderful times with our choir group. One evening we were treated to a special dance troupe, the Fauffinger Girls, who were terrific! The troupe performed synchronized dancing and played cowbells with gusto. They were very impressive! The women wore the traditional 'dirndl' with aprons, and the men wore 'lederhosen' with feather hats.*

The last night of the tour, three of us—Kathy, Robin, and I—decided we would pay tribute to the dance troupe we had seen. We couldn't convince any men to join us, so we put our heads together and named ourselves 'The Four Finger Girls.' We had purchased the dirndl skirts and aprons, so we were set with costumes. To keep in sync with one another, we linked our arms together, held up our four fingers, and folded our thumbs down, creating the image of four fingers. We picked out a spirited folk tune and proceeded to dance together on stage. At the apex of the dance, we picked up some cowbells and attempted to play them in time with the music. During our grand finale, Kathy led us in a high-stepping gig which included giving each other the 'boot.' It was truly memorable!"

The drive to Vienna the following day made us want to join Maria von Trapp in singing, "The hills are alive with the sound of music." The mountains stood tall against the deep blue sky and the valleys were a verdant green. Every so often we would come upon small villages with picturesque houses clinging to the hillsides and small churches pointing their onion domes high into the sky. Everyone was anticipating our stay in Vienna, not only because it is one of the great capitals of Europe, but also because we would stay in the same hotel for three nights. I was also looking forward to celebrating my 50th birthday on August 18th, the day we arrived in Vienna. A special choir dinner had been arranged for that evening in Baden, a town less than an hour from Vienna, at a famous 400-year-old inn called the Streiterhof. What better place could a guy celebrate his big "5-0"?

Tables had been set up for us in a garden patio, the evening was clear and balmy, and an elderly gentleman entertained us by singing and playing his accordion. We were all in a festive mood as we talked, drinking in the Austrian atmosphere and the pungent aroma of two whole pigs being roasted over an open hearth. I have never tasted such tender and succulent roast pork! As the dinner came to a close, Joe Leonards stood up and, on behalf of the choir, presented me with a special birthday gift. When I opened it, I found a beautiful medieval illuminated manuscript depicting scenes from the Book of Genesis. I was absolutely blown away! When we got home from the tour I had the manuscript framed, and it has had an honored place on the wall of our home ever since.

The next morning the choir sang in the Sunday morning service at the Vienna International Chapel. The chapel ministers to the English-speaking community living in Vienna—diplomats, business people, and expatriates. The church is located right next to the Israeli Embassy. As we got off the bus, we were met by armed guards toting sub-machine guns, which shook up a few of our people. We immediately understood that Israel takes security very seriously!

Following lunch, we went on a tour of Vienna, including the Ringstrasse and the Schönbrunn Palace. The Ringstrasse surrounds the inner, historic city where the old city walls used to stand. The tour included many of the sites the choir had hoped to see, such as the Vienna Opera House and the Hofburg Palace, the main residence of Austrian emperors during the Hapsburg dynasty. Naturally, the choir wanted to visit the Opera House. If only we could have attended one of their outstanding productions! Our final stop was at Schönbrunn Palace, completely rebuilt by the Empress Maria Theresia, which became the preferred summer residence of the imperial family. Its gardens form a magnificent backdrop to the palace itself.

Our evening concert was held in the Lutherische Stadtkirche. This Lutheran church is the oldest Protestant church in Vienna, having been founded by Imperial Edict in 1783. Inside it looked much like any other Protestant church . . . except it had two very high balconies. The organ and choir loft were located up in the second balcony, which seemed to hover near the ceiling, a breathtaking distance above the main floor. Our choir would be singing from the two sides of the second balcony, with Dan perched out on a small platform in the center balcony. The handbell tables were set up downstairs in front of the chancel, which meant that the bell ringers had to walk up and down two steep flights of narrow stairs each time they played. Some choir members, especially those with a fear of heights, felt somewhat unsteady as they looked down from the "rafters," so they clung to one another to keep from feeling like they were falling over the railing. Also, because the lighting in the balcony was dim, Dan said later, "I felt like I was directing an invisible choir!"

Our final day in Vienna was more relaxed. Some of us went sightseeing, while others took naps at the hotel. That evening we went to the Prater, a large public park in Vienna's Second District, to ride the Giant Ferris Wheel, one of Vienna's most famous symbols. Anyone who has seen the movie "The Third Man" will remember that part of Vienna. The last stop of the evening was a point high up in the Vienna Woods which overlooked the city. As our buses huffed and puffed up the steep incline, Hans, one of our bus tour escorts, described the magnificent view of the brightly-lit city which we would see when we reached the top. He explained that we would see "the city of Vienna eliminated at night." Since Hans had a few problems with his English, he wondered why we were all laughing so hard. Throughout the rest of the trip, people talked about seeing Vienna "eliminated" at night.

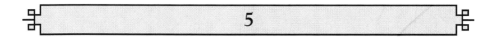

The choir then entered a kind of "interlude" in our ministry schedule, which we used for physical and spiritual renewal. We would spend two days in the Bavarian village of Oberammergau and two days in the Swiss city of Lucerne—with no concerts scheduled. Our drive through the Alps to Oberammergau was stunning. Located 62 miles south of Munich, the village of Oberammergau is set in the lush meadows and foothills of the Bavarian Alps. The village has grown up alongside the River Ammer and today is home to some 5,300 inhabitants. It is a pretty town with leafy parks and typical Bavarian houses, their carved wooden balconies and gardens bright with summer flowers. Many of the buildings have ornately painted exteriors, some of them dating back to the 18th century. These *Lüftlmalerei*, or frescoes, usually depict religious themes or scenes from fairy tales. Oberammergau is famous for its woodcarvers as well as its Passion Play.

Being able to attend the Oberammergau Passion Play was one of the highlights of the tour. The history of the Passion Play is captivating. Gripped by war, poverty, and plague, the villagers of Oberammergau vowed to put on a "passion play" every ten years if God would allow them to survive. That was back in 1633. God did indeed preserve them, and the villagers performed the first Oberammergau Passion Play in 1634. Ever since, their descendants have continued to fulfill that vow. For the past four centuries the tradition has continued, once every ten years.

Only villagers are allowed to take part. They devote a year of their lives to re-enacting the life, death, and resurrection of Christ. All performers are laypeople who, along with preparing for the Passion Play, pursue their usual careers as woodcarvers, housewives, and businesspeople. In 1984, for instance, Jesus was played by a psychologist and Mary Magdalene worked as a flight attendant. By taking on their roles in the Passion Play, the villagers were not only fulfilling the promise their ancestors had made to God, but they were also expressing their own faith and sharing it with the world. In 1984 Oberammergau was celebrating the 350th anniversary of the first Passion Play.

Except on Sundays, people attending the play in Oberammergau arrive in the afternoon and stay in village homes and inns. Because 5,000 people attend each performance, the visitors are housed not only in Oberammergau, but also in surrounding villages. The next day is filled with the play itself—beginning at 9:00 in the morning, breaking for lunch, and then continuing until 5:00 in the afternoon. Included in the deal were housing for two nights, two dinners, two breakfasts, and one lunch, plus admission to the play. Approximately 100 performances take place between mid-May and the first of October in the years the play is performed. It is easy to see why it is done only once every ten years!

Our experience in Oberammergau was all we had hoped it would be. The weather was exceptional and the choir seemed to enjoy the various homes and inns in which they were staying. When we met in front of the Passion Play theater on the morning of the play, Dan and his wife Linda experienced the surprise of their lives. Our group was waiting to go into the theater when a man and woman came over to speak to Dan. He stared at them in disbelief. Standing before him were his mom and dad! They were in another group attending the play on the same day we were. Dan's parents had not said anything about this ahead of time because they wanted to surprise Dan and Linda. They certainly did! That moment was a real serendipity.

The play itself was a moving experience. Even though it was all in German, each of us had a program containing the entire script in English so we could follow along with the action. A fascinating aspect of the production was that the play was a combination of theatrical action, a musical chorus, and beautiful dramatic tableau portraying different scenes from the Bible. It was also exceedingly long. Thank goodness, we had rented cushions to sit on or our bottoms might never have recovered!

The next morning, we set off for Switzerland and the city of Lucerne. On the way, we took a tour of Schloss Neuschwanstein ("New Swan Stone Castle"), the most famous castle in Germany, which stands on the top of a mountain overlooking the picturesque Hohenschwangau Valley. Built by King Ludwig II, who is sometimes called "Mad King Ludwig," this fairy tale castle is the epitome of the neo-Romantic style. In fact, Walt Disney used Neuschwanstein as the model for his Sleeping Beauty Castle at Disneyland. We were overwhelmed by the many ornate, gold-covered walls and furnishings, including the Throne Room, in which ethereal paintings of angels surround the site for a throne. (Ironically, there is no throne in the Throne Room, as Ludwig died before it was finished.) King Ludwig was a great admirer of the world-renowned composer, Richard Wagner; thus, Wagner's characters inspired many rooms in the castle's interior. In fact, the Singers Hall, which occupies the entire fourth floor of the castle, contains characters from Wagner's operas.

After the tour we had lunch in the small village at the base of the castle. While we were there, Dan stepped off a curb the wrong way and sprained his ankle. His foot would bother him for the rest of the trip.

That afternoon we arrived in Lucerne, a small city in the heart of Switzerland. It is across the lake from the town of Altdorf where, according to legend, William Tell shot an apple off his son's head. Founded in the 12th century, Lucerne is a major tourist destination. Since it is situated at the foot of Mt. Pilatus, which is nearly 7,000 feet high, the scenes are spectacular, with wonderful views of Lake Lucerne and the Swiss Alps. Perhaps the most famous site in Lucerne was the more than 500-year-old Chapel Bridge spanning the River Reuss, said to be the oldest wood bridge in Europe. As we crossed the bridge, we could view nearly a hundred pictures of 12th century city life and Swiss history. Tragically, the bridge burned down in 1993, after we were there. It has since been rebuilt.

We had the next day to ourselves, so a group of us took an excursion up Mt. Pilatus. Rumor has it that the mountain is named after Pontius Pilate who, also according to tradition, was thrown—or flung himself—into a nearby lake and still haunts the mountain. More likely, the name comes from the Latin word "pileatus," which means "cloud-covered." At the village of Kriens, we boarded aerial panorama gondolas and then transferred to the aerial cable car, which took us to the peak of Mt. Pilatus. The trip back down the mountain via the 100-year-old Pilatus Railway, the world's steepest cogwheel rail, was also a memorable experience. Riders have to lean backward to keep from falling forward and perhaps falling off!

Someone has compared the view from the top of Mt. Pilatus to the view from Mt. Olympus. As we gazed from the mountain's peak at the surrounding mountains, valleys, towns, and lakes below and saw the majesty of God's creation, we could not help but burst out in praise of the Lord. One of the choir's favorite pieces was "The Majesty and Glory of Your Name" by Tom Fettke, with words by Linda Lee Johnson, which is based on Psalm 8.

> *"When I gaze into the night sky*
> *and see the work of Your fingers:*
> *The moon and stars suspended in space.*
> *Oh what is man that You are mindful of him?*

You have given man a crown of glory and honor
And have made him a little lower than the angels.
You have put him in charge of all creation:
The beasts of the field, the birds of the air, the fish of the sea.
But what is man, oh what is man that You are mindful of him?
O Lord, our God, the majesty and glory of Your name
Transcends the earth and fills the heavens.
O Lord, our God, little children praise You perfectly
And so would we, and so would we.
Alleluia, alleluia, the majesty and glory of Your name.
Alleluia, alleluia!"

Back in town, Joe Leonards asked Mike Maduras and me to go for a walk with him after dinner, so the three of us took a leisurely stroll along the lake shore that evening. Joe said he had been talking with the other guides and bus drivers about the usual "gratuity" which is traditionally given at the end of the tour. Mike and I were taken aback, since we believed these gratuities were included in the agreement with our tour provider. It turned out that our tour representative did not have the money, which left us in a difficult situation. Since we were near the end of the tour, we figured that few of our people had saved that kind of money. Our three guides and drivers had been doing a fine job, especially Joe, and we believed that not only our credibility, but also the testimony of our church and of Christians in general, was on the line.

We got back to Joe the next morning and explained the misunderstanding with the travel agency. We emphasized that even though we did not have the money now, we would send the proper amount to each of the guides and drivers after we got home. Joe looked at us with an expression that said, "Once these people fly home, we will never hear from them again." Even after we repeatedly assured Joe he could count on us, we suspected he still had doubts they would ever see the checks.

He did, however, give us the addresses for each of them, on the chance that we might actually be faithful to our word. And we were!

6

When our buses pulled out of Lucerne on Saturday morning, August 25, we were entering the area of Switzerland in which French, not German, is the language spoken. Pam, one of our choir members, commented later that while she had loved our time in Oberammergau and Lucerne, she was anxious to start singing again. It had been several days since we had sung and we missed it! Our ministry during that last weekend was full, but most memorable.

That night we presented a concert for the opening evening of a family Christian convention in the town of Morges. A number of large tents were set up in an open field on the edge of town. We ate dinner in one of the tents and performed in the largest tent, a rather unique experience! Because of his sprained ankle, Dan had to hobble up to the platform with a crutch under his arm. Even with his crutch, he conducted with his usual vigor, dancing up and down on his good foot. At one point between numbers, Dan turned and asked the audience, "Do you know how I hurt my foot?" He paused. "My wife stepped on it!" The people responded with peals of laughter.

It was an exceptional concert and the audience was wonderfully enthusiastic. After our drive back to Geneva, many people in our group were so exhilarated that they went for a walk along the shores of Lake Geneva in spite of the late hour.

Sunday was a full day of ministry. It began with the morning worship service at the 800-year-old Lausanne Cathedral, located on a hillside overlooking Lake Geneva. While it was originally a Catholic cathedral, it became a part of the Reformed tradition in the later 16th century. The construction of the cathedral began in the 12th century, was dedicated a century later, and has been a "work in progress" ever since. Like many cathedrals we visited in Europe, Lausanne Cathedral has a long nave, with a ceiling towering over the congregants far below. Appropriately, the theme for the service that morning was "mission." Although we sang several songs, the one which most stands out in my memory is "When I Survey the Wondrous Cross." We were overcome with gratitude as our voices echoed, *"Were the whole realm of nature mine, That were a present far too small; Love so amazing, so divine, Demands my soul, my life, my all! Amen!"* The music soared up to the heavens and the hand of God touched us all.

That evening we presented the final concert of our European Ministry Tour in the town of Chenebourg, located near the Swiss-French border. The concert was to take place in Chenebourg's town hall rather than in its local church because our missionaries, Rod and Fran Johnston, believed we would need the larger seating capacity of the town hall. They were right! By the time the concert began at 8:00 p.m., the auditorium was packed. People were standing along the sides, and every inch of the lobby was jammed with people. Since we began every concert by surrounding the audience, this presented the choir with a problem: "How on earth will we ever get through the mob of people and move down the side aisles in order to surround the audience?" The answer, of course, was "Super Joe"—our very own tour escort, Joe Leonards. We set our "Prussian Warlord" loose and he cleared the aisles. Don't ask me how he did it. It was just done.

From the moment we began singing, the atmosphere in the hall was charged with emotion. The choir was so energized by the packed-out audience and by the fact that this was the last concert of our European Ministry Tour that we literally sang their hearts out! It was undoubtedly our finest performance of the tour. On our drive back to our hotel in Geneva, the choir was flying high. There is nothing like concluding a two-year project on a high note. Truly, "the Spirit of God had filled that place!"

Our final full day in Europe took us from Geneva to Zurich; we would fly home from there the next day. The farewell dinner that evening was a time for everyone to sit back, relax, and let their hair down. In addition to eating good food, watching entertaining skits, and helping Ed and Leta Fischer celebrate their 49th wedding anniversary, choir members shared how they had seen God at work during the ministry tour.

Our Pan Am flight was scheduled to fly from Zurich to New York's JFK Airport. There we would go through passport control and customs and then take another flight to Los Angeles. The change of planes in New York should not have been a problem, but, predictably, we had to deal with one final difficulty. We were told that our flight was delayed because a food truck had struck one of the plane's wings. (No, I'm not making this up!) It took Pan Am three hours to find another plane and get it ready before we could board. Those three hours seemed to last forever! Our people were stretched out all over the lounge—on chairs and on the floor. We were all exhausted and could not wait to get home.

One of the first things Mike Maduras and I did after we arrived back in Pasadena was to reconcile our tour financial records with those of the church business office. Since our bidding document had stipulated that ten percent of the total land costs would not be paid to the travel company until after we returned home, we needed to see how much money was left in our account. Also, we were committed to sending the guides and bus drivers their gratuity checks. Mike discovered that the church records showed a substantially smaller account balance than did our records. Evidently, the church had not entered some of the deposits Mike had made. Despite the disparity, John Raymond, the church business administrator, generously agreed to accept our records and wrote the checks to fulfill all of our financial obligations. Hallelujah!

After two years of planning and nineteen days of traveling, the European Ministry Tour was completed. In spite of the variety of problems we had encountered on the tour, the ministry had exceeded our wildest dreams. Dan Bird summarized the impact of the ministry tour best when he said, *"The goals for going were instilled in us very early in the game. They were basically to do this: to share the glory of God and of Jesus Christ through vital spiritual singing to the people of Germany, Austria, and Switzerland; to encourage our missionaries and other Christian leaders in those countries; to enlarge our view of what God can do in and through our lives; and last, but most important, to greatly enlarge our vision of God Himself.*

Praise God! All of these goals were accomplished as we saw how the Lord had prepared the hearts and lives of our audiences even before we arrived. It was God who had allowed us to sing to 'standing room only' audiences—a total of over 12,000 people. We realized that we now needed to let God show us even bigger visions. Though our first priority was to ministry locally at Lake Avenue Congregational Church in Pasadena, we knew that sometime in the future the choir would again leave the loft and go into the world."

I recently came across Debbie, a choir member from the 1984 trip, on Facebook She offered the following reflections—some 30 years later—on what this European ministry tour meant to her. I believe that her story and the impact of the ministry tour on her life help to validate the "Out of the Loft" ministry. *"The European choir tour was one of the greatest events of my life. Being a part of this ministry at the young age of 24 was a pivotal and significant experience. My memories involve singing in quaint village churches, in the Cologne Cathedral, along the Rhine River, in Salzburg, and in village squares. The privilege of seeing the Passion Play in Oberammergau was probably the climax of the trip. It was absolutely incredible! Dinner with my grandfather's 80 year-old sister and her son in Munich was also a once-in-a-lifetime event for me, a memory I have always cherished.*

I feel almost weepy recalling how significant that time was for me. Singing such glorious music to our Lord and Savior, in the midst of people who may never have heard His message through such beautiful song, and knowing that God was using our choir for His glory was a great honor! The blessing and privilege of singing with so many gifted voices, so many dear friends, and such a gifted and lovingly charismatic director, Dan Bird, was truly all joy for me. Grateful for the gift of music and the opportunity to take His song to the world, even if only this once, I feel blessed beyond measure."

In September, Tony Bohlin and crew produced a half-hour video of the trip. It was to be shown to the church, but he wanted the choir to see it first. So on a Thursday night in the fall of 1984, we all gathered in the video overflow room below the church sanctuary to preview the video. Tony's production had no narration except for a short introduction, so it was almost entirely a musical presentation. As the video clips and photos from the trip appeared on the screen, music we had recorded on the tour played in the background.

From the moment we heard the Son-light Bells begin to play "Glorious Things of Thee Are Spoken," not a sound could be heard. We were spellbound! We remained mesmerized throughout the video as we listened to the majestic works we had sung: "God is Our Song," "I'm Gonna Sing," "Ubi Caritas," "Now Thank We All Our God," "Kum Ba Yah," and "The Majesty and Glory of Your Name." Then as we watched and listened to the final anthem, "When I Survey the Wondrous Cross," we dissolved into tears. There was no applause when the video ended. No one could speak a word without choking up. The impact of the tour and what God had accomplished during those nineteen days in West

Germany, Austria, and Switzerland simply overwhelmed us. All we could do was give glory to the Lord!

> *"Praise the Lord!*
> *Praise God in His sanctuary,*
> *Praise Him in His mighty heavens.*
> *Praise Him for His acts of power;*
> *Praise Him for His surpassing greatness.*
> *Praise Him with the sounding of the trumpet,*
> *Praise Him with the harp and lyre,*
> *Praise Him with timbrel and dancing,*
> *Praise Him with the strings and pipe,*
> *Praise Him with the clash of cymbals,*
> *Praise Him with resounding cymbals.*
> *Let everything that has breath praise the Lord!*
> *Praise the Lord!"*
> Psalm 150 (NIV)

CHAPTER THREE

The Macedonian Call

> *"During the night Paul had a vision of a man of Macedonia standing and begging him, 'Come over to Macedonia and help us.' After Paul had seen the vision, we got ready at once to leave for Macedonia, concluding that God had called us to preach the gospel to them."*
> Acts 16: 9-10 (NIV)

The choir which returned from the European Ministry Tour in August of 1984 was a different choir than the one that had left; there was a greater vitality and spirit evident in our singing every Sunday morning. We had seen how God had used us to strengthen people in West Germany, Austria, and Switzerland, and we sang with that same power and energy at Lake Avenue Church. The concept of "Out of the Loft" did not die with the end of the 1984 tour. Instead, our focus was simply transferred from "the ends of the earth" to our own Jerusalem, Judea, and Samaria.

Over the next two years, the Sanctuary Choir and Son-Light Bells shared the love of Christ through vital spiritual singing and ringing in a number of churches throughout Southern California. Then several events occurred which made us think about another European ministry tour. In 1986, the Sanctuary Choir was invited to sing for the Western Regional Convention of the American Choral Directors Association (ACDA). This was a singular honor for the choir, as choral groups are chosen to participate through a "blind audition." The selection committee listens to the tapes of various college, community, and church choirs which have been submitted for consideration. The committee members do not know what choir they are listening to or the name of the choir director; thus, it is a "blind audition." The Sanctuary Choir was one of only three church choirs invited to sing at the convention.

That year the convention was to be held in the city of San Jose, California, from February 12-15, with the choir scheduled to sing on Saturday afternoon, February 15th. Since the Lincoln's Birthday and the Presidents Day holidays were being celebrated on Friday and Monday, the choir leadership decided to plan a 5-day mini-tour to Northern California. We scheduled concerts at Grace Church in San Luis Obispo on Thursday night and at First Baptist Church of San Jose on Friday night, followed by our 30-minute program for the ACDA convention on Saturday afternoon. Our mini-tour would conclude with the Sunday morning worship services and an evening concert at Menlo Park Presbyterian Church before we returned home on Monday.

In addition to the Sanctuary Choir and Son-Light Bells, this mini-tour included a brass ensemble. Dan Bird had written a festival anthem, "Canticle of Faithfulness," for choir, brass, and organ in honor of the 100th anniversary of Glendale Presbyterian Church, and we decided to end our ACDA program with Dan's piece. On Thursday morning, February 13th, we boarded three buses, accompanied by a rental truck carrying all of the handbell equipment, choir risers, and choir robes, and set off for San Jose.

As we began our journey, we didn't realize that a "monkey wrench" the previous evening had almost derailed the tour. Dan Bird had received a phone call from Joe, the church accompanist, saying he was not able to make the trip. Dan's stomach dropped to the floor. What could he do? He called Nancy Lewis who, in addition to singing in the choir, was also an excellent pianist. He asked her if she could fill in and accompany the choir on the tour. Fortunately, Nancy was a great sight-reader and responded affirmatively to Dan's desperate request. God was faithful to provide for our needs, even at the "last minute."

One of my most vivid memories of the mini-tour was how much and how hard it rained. 1986 was definitely not one of California's drought years. In fact, it rained so hard every day that some in the choir started talking about looking for Noah's ark! Loading and unloading the truck in a downpour at each of our concert venues was not the most pleasant thing to do. Another very different memory I have of the trip are the dinners which were provided for us. Every church seemed determined to prepare its best lasagna for our group, evidently thinking that lasagna was one thing everyone would like. We loved lasagna, but by the end of the tour we felt as if we'd been stuffed to the gills with the Italian dish.

While our first two concerts went well, it was mainly the opportunity to sing for the ACDA on Saturday afternoon which had brought us to Northern California. Even though we would not be officially "graded" by the ACDA, we all wanted to do our best. We began the program, as we did all of our concerts, by singing "Heilig, Heilig" in the round and then processing up to the risers as we sang "Thank the Lord." We then performed several pieces we had sung in Europe, including the spiritual "I Can Tell the World," which was the "theme song" of the 1984 tour, and the moving piece, "Give Me Jesus." Our final number was Dan's festival anthem, "Canticle of Faithfulness," with brass and organ. When the choral directors joined the choir in singing "Great is

Thy Faithfulness" near the end of the anthem, the church was filled with resounding praise! The choir's energy during the 30-minute program was so Spirit-filled that the room seemed to come alive with God's presence. Many of the choral directors told Dan they had been deeply moved by the performance.

It would have been easy for our singing at the Menlo Park Church the next day to be anti-climatic. However, Dan had served as minister of music at Menlo Park for seven years in the 1970s, so for him it was a kind of "homecoming." The choir caught his enthusiasm and again sang with great vitality. When Monday morning dawned bright and clear for the first time on the trip, we felt God was saying to us, "Well done, good and faithful servants."

Another event which led us to explore a new European ministry tour took place during the summer of 1986, when the Sanctuary Choir had the privilege of hosting forty-five members of the Christus Kirche from Pohlheim, West Germany. The Germans stayed in the homes of Sanctuary Choir and other Lake Avenue Church families for approximately ten days before they traveled north to the Monterey Peninsula and San Francisco. Our choir was enthusiastic about the opportunity to return the hospitality the people of Pohlheim had so graciously shown us in 1984. Some of our choir members even planned their vacations around the Pohlheim visit. We hoped that as our German friends lived in our homes, participated in special activities with the choir, and attended two Sunday worship services at Lake Avenue Church, they would see how American Christians live out their faith and would sense the sweet aroma of Jesus around us.

When the Pohlheim bus pulled into our church parking lot on a Friday afternoon in July, the group was welcomed by a huge contingent of families from the choir and the Lake Avenue congregation. There was great rejoicing as we greeted and hugged each other. Despite the fact that our choir had spent only about 24 hours with the people in

Pohlheim in 1984, their arrival two years later was like a family reunion. God had knitted our hearts together in the "bond of love."

An activity we wanted our German friends to attend was a "small group Bible study" with their host families. Small groups were a big part of life at Lake Avenue, but the Christus Kirche in Pohlheim did not have small groups. To make it easier for everyone, we combined some of the groups so English and non-English-speaking people would be together. Our German guests were particularly impressed that, in addition to having a time of fellowship and Bible study, we shared personal needs, followed by prayer for those needs. Most of the Germans had never experienced this type of sharing before. We learned several months later that the small groups had had such an impact on our guests that a number of them formed small group Bible studies when they returned to Germany.

Our first major group activity was enjoying a concert at the Hollywood Bowl. This famous venue, a 1920s amphitheater in Los Angeles, is used primarily for music performances. It is known for its band shell, a distinctive set of concentric arches set against the backdrop of the Hollywood Hills and the famous "Hollywood sign." The "Bowl" refers to the shape of the concave hillside from which the amphitheater was carved. It is the home of the Hollywood Bowl Orchestra, the summer home of the Los Angeles Philharmonic, and the site of hundreds of musical events each year.

The program we attended was called "An Evening in Vienna," an ideal program for our guests. One unique aspect of the Bowl experience is that many people bring a picnic dinner to the concert, eating in their seats or in one of the Bowl's picnic areas. Since we were a large group, I had reserved one of the group picnic areas, in which we enjoyed the dinner we had brought with us. Being able to listen to music out under the stars while feeling the cool breezes from the nearby Pacific Ocean made this a special evening.

The second group activity, the annual choir picnic, took place on the last Saturday the Germans were with us. One family in our church had a lovely home where we could swim, play volleyball, or just fellowship with others on the large lawn during the afternoon. In the evening we set up several grills to cook our meat. The rest of the meal was potluck; choir and host families brought appetizers, salads, vegetable dishes, and desserts. It was quite a feast! After dinner, we had a "fun night" featuring different skits and one of Dan Bird's famous stand-up comedy routines, which are always hilarious. The evening was lots of fun, and the Pohlheimers entered into the fun with the rest of us.

On the first Sunday of the Pohlheimers' visit, our guests attended one of Lake Avenue's three morning worship services. For the evening service, the Germans who sang in the Pohlheim church choir joined our Sanctuary Choir in singing an anthem. Pastor Maschmann preached, with Dennis Griggs translating. On the last Sunday of the group's visit, the morning worship service was unusual. One service for the entire congregation was held in the parking lot because this Sunday was the "groundbreaking" for the new sanctuary and ministry center the church was starting to build. All attendees were given a plastic "hard hat" to wear at the service. We found out later that the Pohlheimers kept their "hard hats" as a souvenir of their visit.

Inevitably, the time came for us to walk our German friends out to the front sidewalk on Lake Avenue, so they could board their bus and depart for Northern California. After we had spent ten days together, it was hard to say good-bye. We exchanged long hugs and shed tears as we tried to sing a benediction, but all we could produce were a few choked-up sounds. The only thing we could do was wave as the bus drove off. The bond between our choir and our friends in Pohlheim had continued to grow stronger in spite of the fact that we lived thousands of miles apart and did not speak the same language. This bond reminded us that the Church, the Body of Christ, is forever united by "one Lord, one faith, and one baptism."

2

Taking a mini-tour to Northern California and hosting the Pohlheim group led us to seriously explore the possibility of another European ministry tour. The choir agreed we should return to Pohlheim, but our other destinations were unclear. One intriguing possibility was to minister in Scandinavia. June and I were members of the King's Couriers adult Sunday School class at Lake Avenue, which, along with the church, had a heart for missions. The class helped support a number of missionaries financially, and pastors and missionaries who visited the Pasadena area would often attend our class.

One such visitor was Frank Matre, a pastor from the town of Sandefjord, located southwest of Oslo, Norway. He and his family had been attending Lake Avenue Church for a year while Frank worked on his doctorate at Fuller Theological Seminary. He loved our church, our worship, and our choir. I decided to ask him the same question Dan had asked the German pastors back in 1982: "Do you believe our choir could have an effective ministry in Norway and other Scandinavian countries?" Frank excitedly replied, "Yes!" As a result, the Choir Cabinet began to explore how we could put together a ministry tour to Scandinavia and West Germany.

We laid out several possible itineraries, all of which began in Norway and ended in Pohlheim. Through the assistance of Frank Matre and others in the congregation, we were introduced to several churches in Norway and Sweden. The responses from these churches indicated their great interest in having our choir come and sing. However, as we began to seek approval for such a ministry tour, our church leadership was reluctant to give it. Lake Avenue Church had embarked on a major fundraising program for the new building, and our plan for a ministry tour in 1988 looked like a financial conflict. We were told to put the ministry tour "on hold" and look at the possibility again the next year.

Therefore, in the fall of 1987 we renewed our attempt to obtain approval from the church boards for a ministry tour in 1989. After we gave a presentation to the Board of Trustees about the planned trip, we were told to reexamine how we planned to finance the ministry tour and then return to the Board of Trustees with a new proposal. Mike and I went "back to the drawing board!" We put together a new bidding document which outlined plans for a 1989 tour to Scandinavia and West Germany. More importantly, we revised our budget plans; the new document specified that the choir would be responsible for raising all of the funds for the trip.

We received bids from several tour providers and arranged personal interviews with the most promising ones. By the end of January, 1988, we had settled on the bid from Wilma Webb of Koopman's Travel. It seemed that our plans were back on track and that we were moving ahead with our next European Ministry Tour in the summer of 1989. We felt sure we were now following God's plans for our ministry. How wrong we were!

The Choir Cabinet had planned another "mini-tour" in February of 1988, again over the Presidents Day holiday weekend. We would begin the trip with a concert in San Diego on Friday evening, continue on to Phoenix, Arizona on Saturday and Sunday, and return home on Monday. Our "Out of the Loft" ministry was back in operation. One reason we had chosen Phoenix was that former choir members, Dawn and Bruce Bell, were then living in Arizona. Dawn had gone on our 1984 European tour, and as a result, the Bells had spent four months in 1987 on a short-term mission assignment working with Hal Leaman, a Lake Avenue missionary who now lived in Munich, Germany. While they were in Germany, the Bells had visited another Lake Avenue friend, Julia Winterberg, who had established a Christian music ministry in Hungary. The group, called "Jubilate," was patterned after the Continental Singers, a Christian ministry group popular in the United States at that time. Now Dawn and Bruce wanted our Sanctuary Choir to sing at their church in Phoenix. We would present a full concert there on Saturday evening and then sing for two worship services on Sunday morning. The church would also host a dinner for us following the morning services.

After the Saturday night concert, Dawn introduced us to her friend, Ildikó Barbarics, a member of the "Jubilate" group whom Dawn and Bruce had met while visiting Hungary in 1987. Ildikó already had her law degree, but she wanted to improve her English. As a result, the Bells felt led to invite Ildikó to the United States to live in their home while she studied English at Arizona State University during the spring of 1988 on a student visa.

Once the Sunday services were over, we moved to the fellowship hall to eat the grand buffet dinner the church had prepared. During lunch, Ildikó and Dawn came over to the table where Dan, Mike, and I were sitting. Ildikó began by telling us a little about herself, but then she launched into the main reason she wanted to talk to us. She had been so impressed by our choir that she was convinced we needed to share our music with the people of Hungary, who desperately needed to hear our message of joy, hope, and salvation. Ildikó had heard that we were planning another ministry tour in 1989 and thought we should make Hungary a part of our itinerary. Ildikó recalls that fateful lunch: "I said to Dawn, 'I wish this choir could sing in Hungary one day.' It was actually more like a wishful sigh than a statement. I was kind-of surprised when Dawn said, 'You should talk to Dan, Don, and Mike about this.' A few minutes later I did."

We told Ildikó that our plans for the 1989 tour were set, but that we would consider Hungary for a possible future tour. Ildikó would not take "no" for an answer. She insisted that Hungary needed us now. The rest of our conversation ranged over a number of topics, but Dan, Mike, and I had already dismissed the possibility of adding Hungary to our 1989 itinerary. After all, we were finalizing our contract with Koopman's Travel for a trip to Scandinavia and West Germany. Going to Hungary was an interesting idea, but not one we thought we could consider for 1989.

Have you ever thought your plans were God's plans, only to find out that the Lord was leading you to do something else? It was Solomon who said, *"Many are the plans in a person's heart, but it is the Lord's purpose that prevails"* (Proverbs 19:21 - NIV). The choirs returned home from the mini-tour excited about the following year's trip to Scandinavia, but there was a problem: our plans were not God's plans. He was in the process of revealing to us His heart for the hurting people of Eastern Europe.

A couple of weeks after our return from Arizona, I received a phone call from Ildikó. She told me that two leaders from her home church in Hungary—Géza Kovács Jr., and Gyorgy Kovács (no relation)—would be in the Los Angeles area the next week to attend a workshop. Ildikó asked, "Would it be possible for the three of you to meet with these men while they are in Southern California?" She added, "If so, I'll fly in from Phoenix and join you." As Ildikó told me months later, during our phone call she had been thinking, "It cannot be an accident that they [Géza and Gyorgy] are coming over right at this time. I will ask them to extend an 'official invitation' to the Lake Avenue choir to sing in Hungary."

We found out later that while Géza, Gyorgy, and Ildikó were waiting to meet us for breakfast, Géza asked Ildikó, "Who is this choir, what is so special about them, and why do you want us to meet these people and invite them to Hungary?" Ildikó replied, "I think they can communicate the Lord's love in a way that I have never heard anywhere else before." She was disappointed when Géza did not show a great deal of interest, saying only, "O.K., we'll see." Ildikó remembers that Géza's nonchalant response "was like a cold shower on my excitement about the choir."

When Dan, Mike, and I met Ildikó, Géza, and Gyorgy at the church, both men had cameras strung around their necks and looked every bit like casual tourists. However, as we walked several blocks to the restaurant, the men did not sound at all like tourists. Géza became the interviewer and we became the interviewees. In those ten minutes of walking, he asked probing questions about our beliefs. Géza wanted to know our view of what constitutes a true saving relationship with Jesus Christ and how that relationship should be lived out in the world. This left us with the clear impression that, had we shown ourselves to be merely nominal Christians, the breakfast chat would have been brief. No lighthearted banter here! Dan, Mike, and I quickly became aware of the seriousness of this meeting, which we had thought would be a casual gathering to get acquainted. Fortunately, we answered Géza's questions to his satisfaction, and the bond among us as Christians became firmly and permanently established.

This breakfast meeting, which we had thought might last about an hour, continued for four hours. At the restaurant Ildikó explained that Géza and Gyory were elders in the Budafok Baptist Church, which

Géza's father pastored. Géza then painstakingly detailed for us the condition of the church in Hungary and the brokenness of Hungary's society after long years of Russian occupation. He also shared his passion for giving his fellow Hungarians the hope of an eternal relationship with Jesus Christ. Ildikó, Géza, and Gyory ended the meeting with an impassioned plea that we bring our musical message to Hungary to inspire the Hungarian people.

We ended our time together by promising to pray for Hungary and to thoughtfully consider their desire for us to minister in their country. Ildikó well remembers that crucial breakfast meeting. "We spent several hours just getting to know each other, learning about the mission of the choir, and even exchanging doctrinal views on the Bible. At the end, all of our hearts were knit together in Christian love." As I think back on this 30-year ministry, I have come to believe that what took place in February of 1988 was the pivotal event in the life of the "Out of the Loft" ministry. Our encounter with these three Hungarian Christian leaders had transformed the choir's ministry tours from being just another series of "choir trips" into a missionary outreach to Central and Eastern Europe.

When Dan, Mike, and I met for Sunday worship the next morning, we exchanged remarks about the previous day's meeting, but we were careful not to plunge into a discussion about a radical change in our tour itinerary based on one breakfast conversation. Instead, we agreed to individually place the Hungarians' plea before the Lord's throne and ask for His leading, but we had no idea of what would result from our prayers.

The following Thursday night, choir rehearsal brought the three of us together again. Each of us had something on our hearts to share with the others, but we were reluctant to do so. At the end of the rehearsal, one of us broke the ice. Out tumbled three identical reports of how God had taken hold of our thinking. There had been absolutely no communication between any of us for four days. Each of us had individually communicated with the Lord and had sought His will even as we went about our daily tasks. Words are not adequate to describe our feelings as we realized God had said the same thing to each of us: that we should change our tour plans and include Hungary in our 1989 tour itinerary. We intuitively knew we were not in control of what was unfolding. We were just participants in a greater plan, following a script which God had given us to follow.

At this point, we felt like the Apostle Paul when his plans to visit Asia were interrupted by his vision of a man from Macedonia imploring him to "come over to Macedonia and help us." Our plans were literally being turned upside down. We did not know how we could make the change, but we believed the Lord was calling us to go in a totally different direction. This would require a couple of things right up front. First, we would need to approach the Choir Cabinet and then the entire choir with what we believed God was calling us to do. If we got the "green light" from them, we would then need to contact Wilma Webb at Koopman's Travel about changing the tour itinerary. The bid we had accepted called for a 19-day tour to Scandinavia and West Germany. Now we needed to add Hungary to our tour plans.

4

A serious discussion took place at our next Choir Cabinet meeting. The possibility of taking the choir behind the Iron Curtain to minister was a scary thought. How safe would the choir be? How free would we be to share our faith? We certainly did not have all the answers, but we were convinced God was calling us to something new. We could either say "no" to God, or we could say "yes" and then, by faith, put our complete trust in Him. After much discussion, followed by earnest prayer, the cabinet took the bold step of saying to God, "Yes, we will follow wherever You lead."

With the cabinet's support, we took the matter to a special meeting of the choir and shared with them what we believed was a new call and direction for our ministry. The result was strong support from the choir. In fact, several members told us afterwards that they had not felt a call to go on our original tour, but they were enthusiastic about the new plans. Now that we had the choir's support, the question became, "Would the church leadership approve our new proposal for the ministry tour?"

Before we could go to the church for approval, we needed to develop a new itinerary. I phoned Wilma Webb and told her we were scrapping our plans for Scandinavia and were adding some places behind the Iron Curtain. She was deeply concerned about our proposed changes since she did not feel competent to handle land arrangements in Communist countries. She told us we needed a tour provider with experience in that part of the world. One of the bids we had received for our initial itinerary was from Icontas Service in Munich, West Germany. I told Wilma I would ask Joe Leonards, who had been our lead tour escort in 1984 and who had recommended Icontas Service, whether he believed Icontas would be open to bid again on a new itinerary behind the Iron Curtain.

Looking back on the limited means of communication we had in 1988, it seems miraculous that we were able to get anything done. We did not have e-mail, phone calls were expensive, and first-class mail to Europe usually took a week in each direction. When we heard back from Joe Leonards, he told us he had talked with Peter Wisst, the president of Icontas Service, about bidding on our new itinerary. Peter said they would be glad to give us a bid. Now that we needed a different kind of expertise, Icontas was obviously the best choice.

Once Icontas was on board, we began to put together a new tour itinerary. At just the right time, God directed us to several contacts. The first was a music teacher and organist from West Berlin, Dieter Wunderlich, who was vacationing in Southern California with his wife, Brigitte. I am not sure how they found their way to Lake Avenue Church, but they introduced themselves to Dan after one of our worship services. They told Dan how much they had loved the music that morning and then shared a little about their lives in West Berlin. When they heard we were planning a ministry tour for the choir in 1989, they said that we should consider singing in Berlin.

The second contact was a young couple who had just returned from a mission in Poland. They gave us the names of several people in Krakow and Wroclaw who might be able to help us. I wrote to these contacts in Poland, who told me there were several possible places for the choir to sing. We thus set out to develop an itinerary which included these new ministry opportunities. What had originally been a 19-day trip to Scandinavia and West Germany became a 24-day European Ministry Tour to West Germany, East and West Berlin, Poland, Hungary, and Austria! We went to the Board of Nurture to tell them about what we believed to be our new calling. They were skeptical about whether such a ministry was feasible, but they gave us permission to explore what the tour would involve.

In May I received a letter from Géza Kovács in Budapest asking me to call him. He said we needed to talk about several issues which could not be conveyed easily in a letter. After giving me the day and time of the call, Géza mentioned in the letter that we should use only first names, not last names, when talking to him on the phone. He doubted that the "authorities" would be listening in on the conversation, but that was always a possibility. This statement brought home to me that we would be ministering to people whose individual freedom was still restricted by the government.

During our phone conversation, Géza told me it was imperative for us to send someone from the choir to Hungary during the summer to work out the specifics of the tour. He said we would have to obtain permission from various authorities for each place the choir wanted to perform in Hungary, and that the authorities would want to meet us personally. We brought his request to the Choir Council, who agreed a planning trip was essential and insisted that both Dan and I go. But we believed one other person was essential—Mike Maduras. Mike had been deeply involved in the planning of the 1984 and 1989 tours, and we highly valued his insight and counsel. Going behind the Iron Curtain would require the gifts of all three of us.

The Choir Council agreed to send Dan, Mike, and me on the planning trip. Therefore, working with Koopman's Travel and Icontas Service, we developed an itinerary for the planning trip, which was to take place during the first three weeks of August, 1988. In a way the three of us felt like Caleb, Joshua, and the others who were sent by Moses to spy out the "Promised Land." In our case, there would be only "three spies"—or maybe a better name for us was "The Three Stooges"!

According to Ildikó, *"Our meeting led to the first planning trip of Dan, Don, and Mike to Hungary that same year—even before I returned from the States. It is still exciting for me to see how the Lord put all the pieces together, even during the weekend in Arizona when I first heard the choir. In 1989 I organized the Hungarian part of the tour with great excitement. What had seemed only a dream had become a reality within only eighteen months! The choir's singing was a great blessing to all the people who heard them in Hungary. 'To God be the glory, great things He has done!'"*

5

While we were not traveling to the Promised Land, we were making our own "journey to Macedonia." We trusted the Lord to guide us as we sought to discern the places where He was calling the choir to minister. We flew out of LAX on the afternoon of Sunday, July 31, 1988. After we arrived at the Frankfurt airport the next morning, we took the shuttle to pick up our rental car. The vehicle waiting for us was a Mercedes 190 compact sports car. Mike was thrilled to see it and was anxious to take it on the road. (Mike, even in his "dotage" today, is a sucker for a German-engineered stick-shift rocket like that 190!)

When we met with Joe Leonards later in the afternoon, he asked what kind of car we were driving and whether it ran on gas or diesel. When we replied that the Mercedes required unleaded gas, Joe told us we had a problem. He explained that unleaded gasoline was not available everywhere in Eastern Europe. While we could easily obtain the right fuel in Hungary, we would have trouble getting unleaded gas in Czechoslovakia and Poland. The only place that had unleaded fuel in the parts of Czechoslovakia where we would be traveling was the city of Ostrava, near the Polish border, and no unleaded fuel was available in Poland. Only when we reached East Germany would we be able to obtain more unleaded gas.

Joe urged us to return to the rental agency and ask them to substitute a car with a diesel engine, since diesel fuel was readily available throughout the East. However, when we returned to the agency to see what they could work out, the answer was simple: "No." We would have to stay with our gasoline-powered Mercedes. However, the rental agency gave us a map which supposedly indicated all of the places in which we could obtain unleaded gasoline. It is unbelievable how much of a pest a little thing like "petrol" can be!

Our immediate objective was to drive to Pohlheim, the village in which we had begun our 1984 ministry tour. Returning to the village after an absence of four years was an emotional event for each of us. When we drove into the village and parked in front of the Volkshalle, with the Christus Kirche across the street, we got out of the car and just wandered around for several minutes. None of us said a word. Memories came flooding over us of the 1984 tour and our time spent in this town.

We were jolted out of our reveries when we heard someone calling out to us. It turned out to be Reiner Schaefer, whom we had met in 1984 and who had been part of the German group that came to Pasadena in 1986. He came bounding over, giving each of us a big hug. At that moment, we realized how much Pohlheim was an integral part of our ministry and that we were being welcomed back into "family." Later that morning we had a meeting with Dennis Griggs to talk about the kind of ministry we could have in Pohlheim in 1989. Dennis told us the church leadership wanted the choir to stay for a whole weekend, rather than for just one night. They believed Pohlheim families would be eager to host the Lake Avenue group in 1989 because many people from Pohlheim had gotten to know us in 1984 and had visited us in 1986.

We, along with Dennis, were invited to have dinner that evening with the Wehrenfennigs. I had not seen them since we were there in 1984, so I was looking forward to our visit with them. Dennis had a couple of extra bicycles at his house and suggested we bike over to the Wehrenfennigs' home. I had not ridden a bike for years, but I managed to get the hang of it. We had a great evening catching up with their family and talking about our projected trip the next summer.

After a few days in Germany, we drove on to Hungary. As we approached the Hungarian border, we noticed that the fields were devoid of any buildings or homes; the only thing we saw was an occasional guard tower, which we assumed was used to spot anyone trying to enter or leave the country illegally. We had our passports and official visas to enter Hungary, but we were still uncertain of what we would encounter upon reaching the border. When our turn came, the border official took our passports and asked us to open the trunk of the car so he could inspect it. When he told us we could move on, we gave a sigh of relief and headed for Budapest. The sense of heaviness we felt as we moved into Hungary reminded us that Americans often take freedom for granted, while many people in the world struggle under totalitarian rule. It was also a clear reminder of the seriousness of our choir's call to minister to these people.

The highlight of our time in Budapest, the capital of Hungary, was meeting Géza's dad, Pastor Géza Kovács Sr., and attending his church's Thursday evening service. Before the service, Pastor Kovács met with us in his apartment and talked about the choir's proposed visit the next summer. "Young" Géza, the pastor's son, had told us earlier about his dad's ministry under the Communists. Pastor Kovács had been pastoring the largest and most active Baptist church in Budapest, which did not ingratiate him with the Communist Party. Therefore, he was dismissed from the church and was not offered a new pastorate.

Being the bold Christian he was, Pastor Kovács began preaching on the streets of Budapest. Though threatened with imprisonment, he continued his preaching. Rather than put him in prison and make a martyr of him, the Baptist Union assigned Pastor Kovács to a tiny church in Budafok, one of the city's suburbs, as a way to get rid of him. Not surprisingly, the Budafok Baptist Church became an active and vibrant church. God's hand was obviously on this fearless preacher of the Word.

Géza took us to meet two leaders of the Baptist Union, whose approval we would need to sing in any Baptist church in Hungary: one was the president of the Baptist Union, the other its secretary. After the meeting, Géza told us that one of these men had once been a close friend of his. Later, however, in order to curry favor with the Communist government, this man had turned against Géza's father and was responsible for the troubles Pastor Géza Kovács had experienced. Despite this history, we received permission to minister in the Budafok church or any other Baptist church in Hungary. God had given us favor in the eyes of these church officials.

Before we left Hungary, we had to take care of one final item. Naturally, it was related to our nemesis—unleaded gasoline! We needed to find gas cans that could be properly sealed to carry the extra unleaded gas we would need to get through Poland and into East Germany. Praise the Lord, we found a store which carried this item and bought ten 5-liter cans with the proper seals.

From Budapest we crossed the Czech border and proceeded north toward Poland. Whenever I rode in the front "navigator's seat" of our Mercedes, I used the opportunity to take pictures with my video camera. I was shooting out the front window as we began to gain on a slow truck when Mike calmly but forcefully warned me, "Put the camera down!" He had seen that the truck in front of us was full of Russian soldiers! I quickly lowered my camera, hoping no one in the truck had seen me taking pictures.

When we arrived in the Czech town of Banská Bystrica, we inquired at the hotel desk about how to purchase gasoline coupons, which all visitors were required to use while in the country. The hotel clerk told us the bank was the only place to purchase official gasoline coupons and that the bank would be closing in ten minutes! We rushed over there and Mike got in line in front of a teller window. Dan and I sat on a bench and waited for him, hoping the window would not close before Mike got there.

While we were waiting, Dan whispered in my ear, "Have you noticed the young man standing over there?" I shook my head. "I think this man has been following us ever since we left the hotel!" Our minds raced to thoughts of the KGB or its Czech equivalent. We wondered if they had noticed our Mercedes with a West German license plate, a rare sight in Czechoslovakia. When Mike returned, he told us the teller had not understood his initial request for unleaded gas coupons, so Mike had bought coupons for the most expensive type of gasoline, figuring that this kind of coupon would cover us no matter what. This assumption proved to be incorrect, but God still opened the way for us to get the gasoline we needed.

As we walked back to the hotel, Dan told Mike about the man he had seen following us. Then, as we looked back, we saw the same man emerge from the bank and head in our direction. In fact, he was picking up speed, as if intending to overtake us. When the man came up and began speaking to Mike, Dan and I held back a bit. Suddenly the man broke off his conversation with Mike and walked away. When we asked Mike what was going on, he explained that the man had asked us to exchange some of our U.S. dollars or West German marks for Czech money. Of course, Mike told him "no." We never found out if the man was simply trying to get some hard currency or if he was a KGB plant trying to get us to do something illegal so they could arrest us. It was spooky!

We arrived at the outskirts of Ostrava late in the afternoon. Since our map was no help in locating the one "natural gasoline" pump in the city, we just drove around looking for the elusive "needle in a haystack." We stopped at one busy gas station. The attendant told us in Czech that they did not have unleaded fuel, but that one other gas station might have it. Even though we did not completely understand what he had said, we drove off and promptly got lost. It was closing time as we neared a large factory, so "Mike the Wise" got the great idea of stopping across from the factory and asking one of the workers if he could direct us to the gas station.

What followed was a comic pantomime. Mike approached a young man, led him to the gas fill of the Mercedes, and pointed—all the while exclaiming, "Natural gas – *bleifrei*," over and over. Remarkably, the young man got the idea when he saw the smaller fill pipe of the Mercedes which was made specifically for unleaded gas. When we asked for directions, he nodded, gestured into the distance, and told us in halting English how to get to our destination. After energetically shaking his hand, we drove off to find unleaded gasoline.

We drove and drove and got lost again. As darkness started to fall, we began to lose hope that we would ever find the station. Then, as we turned a corner and stopped at an intersection, a car pulled up next to us and someone waved for us to follow him. The driver turned out to be the same young man who had given us directions at the factory parking lot! He led us directly to the one gas station in Ostrava which had unleaded gas. With his mission accomplished, the man drove off into the night. It was clear that God had been directing us!

Mike pulled up to the gasoline pumps and looked to see which one dispensed "natural gasoline." He told us he was planning to fill the tank first, and then go up to the attendant and pay for it. He figured he'd better get the gas right away; then if our coupons turned out to be the wrong ones, at least he would have already filled the tank. As Dan and I waited in the car, Mike and the station attendant talked for a long time. We could see that the man was getting more and more angry as he and Mike engaged in an increasingly-intense conversation. Trying to think of a language the man would understand, Mike decided to speak a few words to him in Ukrainian. Bad move! The attendant, who thought Mike was speaking Russian and concluded that we were from Russia, became even more infuriated. Apparently, he had no use for Russians. He threw up his hands and screamed, "*Durak*!" The kindest possible translation of this word is "stupid moron." Having been called worse names in his life, Mike tried to suppress a laugh. After all, this "stupid moron" had managed to get a tank full of unleaded gas without possessing the proper coupons!

Meanwhile, we noticed a police car drive into the gas station and wondered if the gas station attendant had called for the police to arrest us. As Mike and the attendant continued to communicate with hand and arm gesticulations, the police drove up to the pump to get some gas. Mike boldly suggested that we ask them for accurate directions. The officers turned out to be young, so they felt completely overwhelmed about having Americans approach them. As a result, they fell all over themselves trying to help us.

Language was again a barrier, so we thought of the word, *Zoll*, which means "border crossing," and pointed to the place on the map where we intended to cross into Poland. The policemen indicated we should follow them, and we did—right to the Czech-Polish border crossing station! God's hand had surely been on us all day as we tried to buy gasoline coupons in Banská Bystrica, searched for the only station in Ostrava that sold "natural gas," and finally arrived at the border crossing in český Těšín. All of this had been accomplished without our being able to speak one word of Czech to people who spoke no English. It was obvious our family and friends at home had been praying for us. God does indeed answer prayer!

Our day, however, was not yet over. We still had to cross the border into Poland, drive through the night to the city of Krakow, and then try to find our hotel. Because we were driving a new Mercedes-Benz, we experienced an unusually long delay at the border. The Polish border officials thought we might be attempting to drive the new Benz into Poland so we could sell it on the black market. In the end, they let us pass and keep our ten cans of unleaded gasoline. Now on the Polish side of the border, we looked for the highway leading to Krakow. It was pitch black outside and we had no idea where we were going, so for the second time that evening we engaged the border control officers and asked where we could pick up the highway to Krakow. They probably figured that this threesome did not have the brains to sell a Mercedes-Benz on the Polish black market, so they graciously told us how to get to the highway.

6

Finally, we were on our way to Krakow. It was after midnight when we arrived on the outskirts of the city and checked into our hotel. The next morning we met our Polish interpreters. Halina, an English professor at the University of Wroclaw, was to be our primary interpreter, and her friend, Anna, would assist her. Both were strong Roman Catholics who were committed to helping us in any way they could.

That afternoon we met with the parish priest of St. Elizabeth's Catholic Church. Poland is nearly 95% Catholic, so if we wanted to sing in a church it would likely be Catholic. Lake Avenue Church missionaries had previously told us that the priest at St. Elizabeth's was looked upon as a maverick by Catholic Church hierarchy. He proved to have a gracious spirit and responded warmly to the idea of arranging a choir concert at his church the following summer. However—and this was a big "however"—he said we would need to obtain the approval of Cardinal Henryk Gulbinowicz, the prelate in charge of the Wroclaw diocese.

We looked at our interpreters. Their faces told us this could be a huge problem, especially since we were scheduled to leave the next morning for Berlin. Halina said they would contact the diocese offices early the next morning to see if Cardinal Gulbinowicz was available to meet with us. About 9:00 a.m. we received a phone call from Halina informing us that a meeting with Cardinal Gulbinowicz was scheduled for 10:00 and that they were on their way to join us. As we drove to the cardinal's office, the ladies told us they had gotten the meeting scheduled only by refusing to take "no" for an answer, continually rephrasing their request until the cardinal's secretary finally gave in and scheduled the meeting.

When we were ushered into the cardinal's office, Dan and I were in a daze; we could not believe we were really going to meet with a Polish cardinal. Our interpreters were beside themselves with excitement. After all, this was their top prelate! Cardinal Gulbinowicz welcomed us warmly. Then he asked about our church, what we believed, and how he could help us. Cardinal Gulbinowicz listened carefully to what Dan had to say and followed up various points with probing questions. We never felt he was trying to put us on the spot, but he certainly took the measure of this Protestant trio sitting in his office.

He asked if we had any churches in mind for our concerts, so we mentioned that St. Elizabeth's had excellent acoustics and would be an ideal venue for our program. To our great surprise, Cardinal Gulbinowicz told us about several other churches which he believed would serve our purposes, and he promised he would ask the priest at each of the churches to show us his church's facilities. God had opened the way for us again!

By now, we were seasoned travelers behind the Iron Curtain. We had traveled over two thousand kilometers and had made it across several borders. Crossing from Poland into East Germany was not particularly intimidating, and we were soon tooling along at the posted speed of 30 miles per hour on a concrete highway pointing straight as an arrow to West Berlin. As we approached the city, we saw tall guard towers at major highway intersections checking all travelers.

Suddenly, an East German policeman appeared in the center of our lane and motioned for us to pull over and stop. He indicated that Dan, who had been driving, should get out of the car. Mike and I remained inside, wondering what the problem could be. Dan had certainly been watching his speed, since we knew the East Germans were notorious for stopping and fining people who exceeded the 50 kilometers per hour speed limit. When Dan finally returned to the car, he told us he had been charged with making an unsafe lane change as he approached the highway intersection. Although Dan had done no such thing, he had to pay a fine right there on the spot.

After this little adventure, we continued on to the border of West Berlin. We noticed that the authorities were checking and processing documents through a succession of five windows. Our progress through Windows #1, #2, #3, and #4 was going well until the official at Window #5 noticed that we had entered East Berlin via Poland. We were directed to a concrete bunker about half a mile away; there we were processed by Brunhilde, a brawny female border control guard whom we nicknamed "Brunnie." She ordered us to exit the car, completely unload the trunk, and remove the rear seats. She then checked through our luggage and carefully examined every cavity in the car, engine compartment, and trunk, ending with a thorough examination of the car's under-carriage using a roller-mounted mirror. Brunnie had taken more than an hour to make certain we were not smuggling anyone from Poland into West Berlin!

To this day, Mike is certain "Brunnie" understood some of the comments we made in English as she examined the car, which evidently had only added to her determination to give our car the "ultimate" inspection. Upon the completion of her work, Brunnie returned our documents and left us on the concrete with a disassembled car interior and luggage spread everywhere. If anyone would like to know how to quickly take apart a 1988 M-B 190, please call us.

The prosperity of West Berlin was on display in the beautiful shops, stores, restaurants, and luxury hotels located along the tree-lined Kurfürstendamm Strasse, West Berlin's main thoroughfare. What a contrast it was to the cities we had visited in Poland and Czechoslovakia! Life on the Strasse continued late into the night. Even though West Berlin was an island surrounded by Communist East Germany, it felt as if we were visiting a prosperous country in Western Europe.

Dieter Wunderlich, whom we had met at Lake Avenue Church when he was vacationing in California, met us the next day and drove us to see several churches where we might be able to sing. Once we had finished our survey of churches, Dieter showed us around West Berlin, pointing out many places of interest. Of course, we wanted to walk to the Berlin Wall in front of the Brandenburg Gate. It was here that President Reagan declared, "Mr. Gorbachev, tear down this wall!" We also drove past "Checkpoint Charlie," the major crossing point between West and East Berlin. We loved our time in Berlin and could not wait to bring the choir there the following summer.

After visiting the German cities of Hamburg and Göttingen, we drove back to Pohlheim, the place our "journey to Macedonia" had begun three weeks earlier. We met one more time with Dennis Griggs, Erhard Jung, and Pastor Maschmann to finalize our plans for the tour. Then we drove to the Frankfurt airport for our return flight to Los Angeles. After we got through customs and immigration at LAX and walked into the terminal, we were met by a cheering crowd of choir members welcoming us home. Their support meant the world to us! Many things still needed to be done to prepare for the 1989 European Ministry Tour, which would begin in less than a year. If we had known some of the problems we would have to deal with before our choir was ready to leave on the tour, we might not have been so excited to be home.

7

One of the first things I did after returning from the planning trip was to contact Tony Bohlin and make arrangements to produce a video of our trip. We were able to finish the video, "Journey to Macedonia," in less than two weeks and had it ready to show the choir at our fall retreat the weekend after Labor Day. Even though the choir had given its approval for us to move ahead with the tour, we realized that some choir members were still anxious about venturing behind the Iron Curtain. We hoped that hearing from "three spies" and seeing the video about the planning trip would encourage them to go. We believed that the words from Isaiah 6:8 (NIV) were meant for us:

> *"Then I heard the voice of the Lord saying,*
> *'Whom shall I send? And who will go for us?'*
> *And I said, 'Here am I. Send me!"*

Daniel Schutte wrote a popular hymn in 1981 based on the above verse, which expresses the same sentiment:

> *"I, the Lord of sea and sky, I have heard my people cry.*
> *All who dwell in deepest sin My hand will save.*
> *I, who made the stars of night, I will make their darkness bright.*
> *Who will bear My light to them? Whom shall I send?"*
> *"Here I am, Lord. Is it I, Lord?*
> *I have heard You calling in the night.*
> *I will go, Lord, if You lead me.*
> *I will hold Your people in my heart."*

These words spoke to my heart in a special way. I knew we were being called to something far greater than anything we could imagine. God's heart was breaking for His people locked behind the Iron Curtain, and He wanted us to be His messengers of love, hope, and peace in this dark part of the world. It was my prayer that our choir would catch this vision, respond to God's call and say, "Here I am, Lord. Send me."

In the remaining ten months before our trip, we had several tasks to accomplish. One was to obtain commitments from all those in the choir who had been called to go. The ministry tour would take place, Lord willing, from Thursday, July 27, through Saturday, August 19, 1989, a 24-day trip. This was a daunting prospect for many in the choir. Most people normally got only two weeks of vacation time, so they would need to save up extra time or take time off without pay in order to go on the trip. As for concerns about going behind the Iron Curtain, our planning trip seemed to have assuaged some of those fears. Finally, there was the matter of cost. While we did not have our final bid from Icontas Service, we knew the cost of the trip would be about $4,000 per person. It would require a great deal of prayer and planning before we had the balanced choir we believed God was calling to the ministry.

The second remaining task was to get the support of the church leadership. We had received their provisional approval to proceed with the planning, but we needed their final approval now that we knew our itinerary and how much the trip would cost. Mike Maduras and I were invited to present a report on our planning trip to the Board of Nurture and to explain what we believed our ministry would include. As a part of our presentation, we showed them the video, "Journey to Macedonia." When the meeting was over, the chairman told us he had previously questioned the ministry tour, but after seeing the video he was convinced that God's hand was on the trip. He mentioned in particular that our ability to get an appointment with the Polish cardinal and receive his permission to minister in Wroclaw had convinced him this was God's plan for the choir.

We received the final bid from Icontas Service toward the end of October, which confirmed that the cost per person would be $4,000. Because we had planned a trip five days longer than the 1984 tour, it was not surprising that this trip would be more expensive. When we added up all the travel and ministry expenses for the trip, the total came to about $500,000, depending on the exact number of people who ended up going. When we presented this information to the Board of Trustees, they gave their approval, with the stipulation that we must raise all of the money on our own.

Betty, the new chairperson of the Board of Nurture, later told us an unusual story. She had attended a rather contentious church meeting, during which the ministry tour was discussed. On her way home after the meeting, she prayed the Lord would give her a sign if our tour was really His plan for the choir. Betty said that as she turned onto the road leading to her home, she clearly saw a brilliant cross in the sky directly ahead of her. It was as if God were saying to her, "This is my plan for the choir to bring the message of hope to my people in Eastern Europe." Betty concluded, "I had never had an experience like that before, so from then on I knew God's hand was on the tour."

We put together a document which proved to be extremely valuable: a prayer calendar. This was a detailed day-to-day list of specific prayer requests for the ministry tour, along with maps of the places the choir was scheduled to visit. Four thousand prayer calendars were distributed to people throughout the congregation, as well as to many others who had committed themselves to pray for the ministry. One cannot overstate the positive effect which concerted prayer had on the success of the ministry tour.

A couple of weeks before we were to leave on the trip, we received a phone call from Joe Leonards in Germany. He had been talking with Peter Wisst at Icontas Service about problems we might face in crossing the borders into Communist countries. Joe told us we needed to obtain a "Carnet" for all of the equipment we would be bringing with us. Not knowing what a Carnet was, I called Wilma Webb at Koopman's Travel, who was handling our transportation to and from Europe. She told me she had never heard of a Carnet and that no travel group she had worked with had used one.

We eventually found out that a Carnet, commonly known as a "merchandise passport," is a detailed international customs document which guarantees that all items listed in the Carnet will be returned to the United States. It was designed to facilitate the smooth transit of equipment at border crossings. The Carnet required us to list every box, including its specific contents—down to the last wire and cable. Completing this list would be quite a task, since we were taking seven sets of choir risers, five octaves of handbells, handbell tables and foam, and extensive audio and video equipment. Ed Fischer made a list of all of the handbell equipment and Tony Bohlin did the same for the audio and video equipment. Amazingly, all of this was accomplished in less than a week.

After completing the detailed Carnet, we had to take the forms, along with all of the listed equipment, to the U.S. Customs office at Los Angeles International Airport. In 1984, we had taken the handbells as personal luggage, but this time—because of the Carnet—we had to ship all of the equipment together. Fortunately, a choir member had a large truck he used in his business, so he, Tony, and Ed loaded up all of the equipment, transported it to customs, and got the Carnet properly stamped. The equipment was then loaded into an air freight container and would be waiting for us when we arrived in Frankfurt two days later.

On the eve of our departure for Frankfurt in July of 1989, we could report that the choir had raised $560,000 for the tour. Unlike in 1984, we did not have to make a special appeal to the choir in order to meet our financial goals because so many people had given sacrificially to make the tour possible. Our prayers were also answered regarding those called to participate in the ministry tour. We ended up with a total of 139 people, including a balanced choir of 111 singers; four additional bell ringers; 22 spouses, children, and other Lake Avenue members; and, of course, Dan Bird, our choir director, and David Dalke, our accompanist. This was the largest group ever to be commissioned by Lake Avenue Church for a ministry or missionary venture.

One final "salvo" threatened to torpedo a major aspect of our ministry. Just eight weeks before we were to leave, Tony Bohlin descended into the audio-video rooms below the new church sanctuary to do some work. Unfortunately, someone had left a ceiling trap door hanging down. As Tony went to turn on the lights, he ran head-on into the edge of the trap door and was knocked flat on his back on the hard cement floor. Tony was taken to the hospital and had to undergo back surgery. The doctors said he would be paralyzed without the surgery.

I remember visiting Tony in the hospital, only to find him talking on the phone taking care of details for the tour! He would not let his surgery and hospitalization keep him from doing what he felt was necessary to prepare for the trip. Dr. Moline, Tony's neurosurgeon, said Tony faced six to eight weeks of recovery from the surgery. He was not allowed to lift anything and would have to undergo weeks of physical therapy, but there still was no guarantee Tony would not become paralyzed. It was under these conditions that Tony made sure all of our equipment was packed, taken to customs, and transported to air freight.

Earlier, Dr. Moline had told Tony, "I don't have the kind of belief in God's healing power that you have, so I cannot recommend that you go on the tour." However, when Dr. Moline saw how well Tony was able to recover from the surgery and participate in the trip, he said to Tony, "A Higher Power has definitely been involved in your recovery!"

Planning for the 1989 European Ministry Tour had taken the choir totally out of its comfort zone. Our itinerary had been through a major change requiring the addition of a new land provider, Icontas Service; Dan, Mike, and I had gone on a planning trip behind the Iron Curtain; major problems with the church leadership had been solved just five months before our departure; and we had been required to develop a Carnet at the last minute. In spite of all of those problems and changes, the Lord, in His own time, had brought together His called choir to minister to His chosen people in Eastern Europe. I had to believe the ministry tour would hold blessings unimaginable. Though there would be unexpected challenges, we had the assurance that God was still in control. I could not wait for tour to begin.

On the face of the program we took with us was a drawing of the huge cross rising tall over our new sanctuary. Below it were the words of the refrain from a hymn the choir had come to love:

> *"Lift high the cross, the love of Christ proclaim,*
> *Till all the world adore his sacred name."*
> Words by George W. Kitchin (1887)

CHAPTER FOUR

Out of Despair, HOPE!

> *"May the God of hope fill you with all joy and peace as you trust in Him, so that you may overflow with hope by the power of the Holy Spirit."*
> Romans 15: 13 (NIV)

Thursday, July 27, 1989, was the beginning of a once-in-a-lifetime adventure which would take us behind the Iron Curtain into East Berlin, Poland, and Hungary, as well as to West Germany and Austria. There was great anticipation as 139 tour participants, along with family and friends, assembled in the new sanctuary before setting off on our second European Ministry Tour. Dan Bird led us in a meaningful time of celebration, prayer, and praise. Many of those going with us had been a part of the 1984 European Ministry Tour, but this tour would be completely different for all of us.

As we boarded the buses, we noticed they were a definite upgrade from the buses that had taken us to the airport in 1984. These were comfortable, air-conditioned tour buses, not the school buses with hard seats and no air conditioning which had transported us to the airport five years earlier. Already, we could see how much better Wilma Webb at Koopman's Travel had prepared for our group. We encountered the same professional expertise when we arrived at LAX. Wilma and her husband Bob, along with their son David, met us at the terminal entrance. They proceeded to hand a plane ticket to each of us and directed us to two special check-in lines they had arranged for our group at the Lufthansa Airlines counter. Before we knew it, everyone was checked in and had time to relax before our 3:30 p.m. flight to Frankfurt.

When we arrived at the Frankfurt airport, my major concern was recovering all of our personal luggage and the boxes of LP records, audio cassettes, and English language programs we had brought with us. Joe Leonards met us in the baggage claim area and helped us get everything out to our three buses. Tony Bohlin had prepared color-coded luggage tags which identified the bus to which each person had been assigned. He had also made identifying signs for each of the three buses. Tony's efficient planning enabled us to leave the airport in record time.

Once again, we were staying at the Mainz Hilton Hotel overlooking the Rhine River. Everyone seemed to enjoy the free time they had in the city during the afternoon. The "welcome banquet" Icontas Service served us that evening was superb. During the dinner, we had an opportunity to become acquainted with our three tour escorts—Helga, Christl, and of course, Joe Leonards. Joe shared his insights about what we might experience on the trip, especially when we crossed the Iron Curtain into East Germany and the other Communist countries. We did not have a rehearsal on our first night in Europe, as we had in 1984. We had learned from the 1984 tour that most choir members wanted to go to bed early after the long flight.

Before we could leave Mainz, however, a problem arose with the equipment listed on our Carnet, which had been shipped separately. Our equipment was waiting at the air freight terminal in the Frankfurt airport. Icontas Service had provided us with a truck to carry our equipment, and we provided the driver, choir spouse Chuck Gilbert, who was ably assisted by Ernie. When Chuck and Ernie arrived at German Customs at the airport, they were told the equipment could not be picked up because a number of cases were locked and could not be released until their contents were verified. We soon learned that the cases contained handbells and that the person with the key to the cases was Ed Fischer, the director of the Son-Light Bells. We asked Tony Bohlin to get the key from Ed and take it to the airport. Tony was a logical choice, since he had been one of the signatories on the Carnet and was responsible for all of our audio and video equipment.

Later, Tony told me what happened when he arrived at German airport customs. He was met by two armed guards with their automatic weapons aimed right at him! Tony thought, "This looks like a scene from a movie about the Mafia!" The guards led him into the office and introduced him to the customs agent. Tony tried to tell the agent that the cases contained handbells, but he could not think of the German word for "bells." So he tried to imitate someone ringing a bell while he repeated, "Ding, dong, ding, dong." The officer in charge of customs looked at Tony as if he had lost his mind!

Tony then took the key and started to open one of the cases. Again, automatic weapons were pointed at him—just in case guns, bombs, or drugs were hidden in the cases. Tony slowly opened the lid of the first case and took out one of the handbells, giving it a hard ring. The agents jumped back, startled by the loud sound. Then they realized what was in the cases and asked Tony to open all of them. He had to carefully open each case to show he was not a drug or arms dealer, just a musician! The customs officer finally signed off on the Carnet and let Chuck, Ernie, and Tony load the truck. The three of them arrived in Pohlheim in the middle of the afternoon, having totally missed the welcoming reception in the Volkshalle.

It is difficult to describe our feelings as we drove from Mainz to Pohlheim. As we approached the village, we could see the spire of the Christus Kirche across the fields and our hearts began to beat faster in anticipation. Then, as we turned a corner and drove up to the Volkshalle, we saw a large crowd of people cheering and waving to us in welcome. On the Volkshalle was a huge sign saying, "Welcome LACC Choir" with the West German and American flags painted on it.

Those of us who had been there before grabbed our belongings and raced across the street to friends we had not seen for several years. Everyone was hugging, laughing, and crying with joy. Roger Bosch, Lake Avenue missionary in Pohlheim, was trying—not too successfully—to get everyone inside the Volkshalle so he could match our people with their host families. Pastor Maschmann, who got us all singing the chorus, "Allelu, Alleluia, Praise Ye the Lord," gave us a warm welcome. Finally, everyone embarked upon one of the grandest experiences of the trip.

June and I had stayed with the Wehrenfennig family in 1984 and had been close to them ever since. However, we had also developed a close relationship with Erhard and Edith Jung, who were our guests for ten days when the Pohlheim group visited us in Pasadena. Unfortunately, a difficulty arose: both the Wehrenfennigs and the Jungs wanted us to stay with them. June and I loved both families dearly, so we were not about to decide which family would have the "honor and privilege" of hosting us for the weekend.

A number of other choir members were having the same problem. It almost required a Solomon to resolve the "tug-of-war" between some Pohlheim families; our Solomon, Pastor Maschmann, had to resolve some cases by making the decision himself. The situation would have been comical if there had not been the danger of deeply hurt feelings. After all, the host families had gone to a great deal of trouble for us; many of them had even changed or canceled vacation plans in order to be there for our visit. Eventually, some families reached a compromise by deciding to share choir members for meals and other activities with one, or even two, other families. Believe me, no one could complain about not feeling welcome in Pohlheim!

Sunday was a special day for everyone. The church was packed that morning. Pastor Maschmann spoke in English for his American guests, while the assistant pastor translated the service into German for their regular congregation. A very special treat was the decision by Pastor Maschmann to serve Communion that Sunday in order to demonstrate our unity in the Lord.

June and I stayed with the Jungs, who could not have treated us more royally. After church on Sunday, they served us a huge dinner. Then at 3:00 p.m. we all went to the Wehrenfennigs for *Kaffee Trinken*, the German equivalent of the English "afternoon tea." Our time together that afternoon was a wonderful reunion as we caught up with what Günter and Adelheid and their four children had been doing. Of course, since no German family wants their guests to go hungry, they served us not only coffee, but also five different kinds of cake, urging us to try all five of them—even though we had eaten a big meal just a couple of hours before! The Pohlheimers were doing everything in their power to make sure we put on at least five pounds during the weekend.

The first concert on our ministry tour that evening started late—not because we were still eating, but because the ushers were having great difficulty trying to find places for all the people who kept streaming into the Volkshalle. It was designed to comfortably hold 800 people, but the crowd that night, according to estimates, was close to 1,300 people—the most to ever attend any program in the history of Pohlheim! Following the Spirit-filled concert, Pohlheim Mayor Hermann Georg told the packed-out audience, "The Americans came to Western Europe with one message: that of democracy. The message of Jesus Christ which the choir has brought us, however, is even more needed and meaningful."

A description of the concert, written by an unbiased reporter, later appeared in the Giessen newspaper, the <u>Giessener Allgemeine Zeitung</u>: *"On Sunday evening, the audience was very receptive to the choir's program. The choir has the reputation of being one of the best choirs in America, and it must be said that no one's expectation was disappointed. What the 110 singers presented was "mouth-watering" for knowledgeable choral music fans. Both the precision and the blend of voices were equally convincing. The constant jubilation was certainly not in their voices because the musical score required it, but simply because of the choir's joy in their faith, which was clearly visible in the singers' facial expressions. The U.S. choir places a great emphasis on the text of their songs because their European tour has an evangelistic design that places the Gospel of Jesus Christ in the middle of their musical expression. The desire of the choir that Jesus, and not the singers, would be in the spotlight was indicated during the concert by conductor Dan Bird, as he repeatedly pointed the audience's applause toward heaven."* (Translated from German by Roger Bosch)

On Monday morning we enjoyed a leisurely breakfast. Then at 8:30 our group joined the Pohlheim host families at the church for a time of singing and praying together before we left. Back on the street, we found it was tough to say "good-bye" to our hosts. Shakespeare was right: "Parting is such sweet sorrow." The bonding process, which had started in 1984, took a quantum leap in 1989. One would truly have had to be there to fully comprehend the sharing of lives, love, and the Lord which took place in the village of Pohlheim during those all-too-brief 48 hours. Our stay in Pohlheim had set the tone for the rest of the tour. We had been privileged to share the Lord in music and word with His people, which would continue to be our mission for the next three weeks.

2

After we left Pohlheim, we had devotions on each bus, as we did every morning we were on the road. Dan and Linda Bird had prepared the devotions for us, which included scripture verses, thoughtful applications of these verses to our lives, a prayer, and a hymn for the day. The whole series of devotions was based on the theme of relationships: our relationship with God, our relationship with one another, and our relationship with those we were trying to reach for Christ. It was a great way to begin each day. These devotional times were vitally important for a group of 139 people who would live and travel together for 3½ weeks in close, not always harmonious, relationship!

The glow from the weekend in Pohlheim carried over as we traveled toward the university town of Göttingen. This town had become a part of our itinerary as a result of the special relationship the choir had developed in 1984-85 with Birgit Hegerfeldt. Her strong desire to have her adopted choir come to Göttingen had resulted in our adding her city to our itinerary. Because many Göttingen residents would be leaving on vacation before we arrived, Birgit and others were worried we might not get much of a crowd.

Having come off such an outstanding experience in Pohlheim, many in the choir were expecting our concert in Göttingen to be somewhat of a letdown. It had also rained off and on during the day, which had a dampening (no pun intended) effect on our spirits. Then God stepped in and showed us that each concert is important, no matter how many people are there. While the choir was having its pre-concert time of prayer, people poured into the church, including many young people. When we began the concert, every seat in the church was filled, including those in the balcony. Even the large narthex was filled with people. The audience continued to clap until we had sung two encores. The prayers which had been lifted to the Lord for this concert were most evident. We would no longer take any of our concerts for granted or expect less than all that God desired for us. It was an important lesson for us to learn.

Fritz, a choir member with MS who had fallen and broken his collarbone on our 1984 tour, had more problems this time. Each choir member was responsible for bringing his or her own choir robe on the tour. Since we were going behind the Iron Curtain, we wanted to display our identity as a church choir, so we wore choir robes in place of the "tour outfits" we had worn on the previous tour. Unfortunately, Fritz forgot to pack his robe, so he had to wear his dark blue suit for our performance in Pohlheim. However, God provided for him. One choir member who could not join the tour until after we left Pohlheim picked up Fritz's robe and brought it with him.

The next morning as we were preparing to leave Göttingen, Fritz fell in the bathtub and badly cut his arm. We got him taken care of at the hospital. Then he was put under the care of Marlene, the designated RN for his bus. Marlene checked and changed his dressings daily. She took superb care of him—even with the rudimentary medical services available behind the Iron Curtain. Marlene proved to be Fritz's "guardian angel."

We arrived in Hamburg in the late afternoon and checked into the modern and comfortable Ramada Renaissance Hotel. One of Germany's largest cities, Hamburg has always been a leading center for trade and is Germany's number-one port. It is a scenic place with many lakes and parks. It is also a city of spires—church spires. In every part of the city, one can see an horizon lined with church spires pointing to the heavens.

August 1st, the day we arrived in Hamburg, was also an important day for two special people on the trip. It was Dan and Linda Bird's 25th wedding anniversary. That evening the choir held a big celebration for them. The hotel prepared a magnificent dinner, Dan and Linda were properly feted and toasted, and each bus presented them with all kinds of gifts, cards, and honors. To cap off the evening, a huge multi-tiered decorated cake surrounded by lit sparklers and a gorgeous wreath of flowers was wheeled into the banquet room. The whole affair was a complete surprise to the two "love Birds," who soaked in the outpouring of love. Dan and Linda graciously responded, "Other than our immediate family, there is no one we would rather celebrate with this evening than the choir." I guess you could call that evening a real "love fest!"

The traditional landmark in the city of Hamburg is the Hauptkirche St. Michaelis, Northern Germany's beautiful Baroque church built in the 1700s. The Hauptkirche was a well-known center for concerts, their church choir had an excellent reputation, and the music program there was considered a major training ground for church and professional musicians. It was not, however, known as a place to which people came in large numbers to worship the Lord. How sad that it served as a concert center and not a worship center! Rainer Haak, who was responsible for all Lutheran church youth ministries in Hamburg, was our contact person. He had chosen St. Michaelis as the site for our concert because he and other church leaders wanted our music to be an outreach to the entire city.

When we arrived at this magnificent church, we began to wonder if we would be able to sing there at all. The church custodial staff had not been informed that we would need to set up our risers or that we wanted to use one of their three organs. Rainer Haak talked with the church leaders at St. Michaelis and worked out all the details. In the end, we were able to set up the choir risers and bell tables, the church provided microphones, and David Dalke, our organist, was given permission to play the organ in the side balcony.

Almost 2,000 people filled the church sanctuary for the concert. During the first section of the program, there was a polite silence after each choir number. Then the Son-Light Bells took over, and the people's reserve was completely shattered. At the end of the bells' first two numbers, the audience simply exploded. We were used to hearing the rhythmic clapping of European audiences, but we were not prepared for the thunderous noise which came forth as the people stomped on the wooden floors with their feet. The entire edifice shook like thunder. From that point on, every number was equally well-received, as choir and congregation became one. The people demanded several encores, which the choir was happy to give.

After the concert, Harold and Karen, a young Lutheran pastor and his wife, wrote to us: "*Your choir was gorgeous! . . . You know we never had experienced such a sacred concert or seen such a unity within so many very different persons' faces. It was fascinating, also, that you didn't want any money.*"

Thursday, August 3rd, began our venture into Eastern Europe and behind the "Iron Curtain." For the next twelve days, with the exception of our time in West Berlin, we would experience a kind of life to which we were totally unaccustomed. We were not quite sure what to expect. As we headed east on the autobahn from Hamburg, we fervently prayed for safe travel and for the people we would minister to. We also praised God with great rejoicing for giving us the opportunity to enter our "Macedonia" in response to His special call. We traveled through a long "no-man's land" after leaving the West German border before we reached the official DDR border crossing. (Names were very significant to the "East Germans." Their capital city was simply "Berlin," not "East Berlin," and their country was referred to as the *Deutsche Demokratische Republik* or the DDR.)

As we approached the border we saw tall barbed-wire fences, observation towers, and cleared fields, which were probably mined. Then for the next two hours we sat in the buses as border guards collected all of our passports and checked the bus luggage compartments and the equipment van. It was clear the authorities already knew all about our van and three buses and were aware we were going to (East) Berlin, in which we would be staying and performing a concert. Several times along the transit highway, the only available route from Hamburg to Berlin, we would see a police vehicle parked along the side of the road, which would then pass us after all of our vehicles had gone by. We were indeed being monitored along the entire route.

One rather comical incident illustrates how closely we were being watched. Westerners were allowed to get off the "transit autobahn" at only a few, specifically-designated rest stops. We had placed the equipment van, driven by Chuck Gilbert, between Bus #2 and Bus #3 in case there were any emergencies. There turned out to be one, but not the kind we expected. It seems that Chuck had drunk several cups of coffee that morning and was now feeling the need for a pit stop. He was hoping to make it all the way to Berlin, but realized that he would have to stop before then. He finally saw a rest stop (which was unauthorized) and made a quick turn off the autobahn. Our bus, which happened to be the second in line, did not notice his departure behind us, so we drove right on. The third bus, however, saw the van turn off the road and decided to follow it to see what the problem was. Chuck quickly returned, and the van and Bus #3 got moving again as fast as they could.

Meanwhile, the first two buses went merrily on their way, unaware that they had become separated from the other two vehicles, and entered the highway which led directly into (East) Berlin. We had not traveled along that highway more than a half-mile when the police stopped us dead in our tracks. They boarded the bus in front of us and explained something to them. Since we were not allowed to use our radio communications between buses while in the DDR, we had no idea what the problem was. Thankfully, after a few minutes the authorities allowed both buses to proceed. Those of us in Bus #2 did not know what the first bus had been told, so all we could do was follow it.

Later, we pieced together what had happened. The police had stopped the first two buses because the guard in the tower at the last highway intersection had noticed we were missing one bus and one van. The police evidently decided to punish us for not staying together and also possibly tried to make us late for (or miss entirely) our concert at the church. For the next hour or so, Buses #1 and #2 went on a "wild goose chase" to find the third bus and the van. We finally arrived at our assigned meeting point a full forty-five minutes after the other vehicles.

The first impression we had of Berlin was of a city lined with row upon row of drab, sterile apartment buildings. Berlin seemed to be a city without color. All of the West German cities we had visited had gardens and flowers everywhere, but none could be seen in Berlin. We were surprised to see only a small number of people walking along the streets and shopping in the stores, even along the famous Unter den Linden.

When we arrived at our hotel, we were met by two women who said they were in charge of the hotel's "public relations." They were accompanied by a photographer who was busy snapping pictures of our group as we entered the lobby. They arranged to interview Dan, David, and Mike about our choir and about the concert we planned to give that evening. I may have been a little cynical, but I wondered if they were part of the ongoing surveillance of our group. However, the two women were genial and eager to help. They even attended the concert that night and told us how much they enjoyed it.

We had selected the Gethsemane Kirche (Church) for our "musical worship service" because of its size and location. We did not know until later that this church was the center for the peace/prayer and pro-democracy movement in (East) Berlin; the church later appeared in pictures and TV news programs about the fall of the Berlin Wall. While we were there in August of 1989, however, everything was relatively quiet and we had no idea of the turmoil which would soon be rocking the DDR. Relations between the church and the DDR government were already so strained that, had we not gone to Berlin when we did, we probably could not have visited the city, let alone have sung a concert there.

When we arrived at the Gethsemane Kirche, we noticed there was a cordon of police armed with automatic weapons positioned on the streets all around the church. This probably meant that not only the choir, but also those who attended the concert, were under surveillance. Despite the fact that the churches which sponsored our concert had not been allowed by the government to do any advertising for the event, over 1,000 people came to hear us. The audience was initially reserved and polite. However, they soon "caught the spirit" and began applauding enthusiastically after every song. When we finished singing the Negro spiritual, "Here's One," a man ran onto the stage to give a red rose to Anna Giles, who had sung a solo during the piece. Anna, who was then close to 80, never forgot that moment. The audience was animated and many of the people stayed long after the concert to talk with individual members of the choir.

It had been our practice after every concert to present our choir recordings (LP records and audio cassettes) to the audience free of charge. When we arrived at the church that night, the pastor told us that "the authorities" had notified him we would not be allowed to hand out our recordings. The boxes of recordings had already been brought into the assembly room which the church had set aside for the choir. After the concert, everyone was so occupied with talking to various attendees that we actually "forgot" all about those recordings. Can you believe it? What a shame! We had not handed out the recordings to the audience as we had planned; instead, the pastor now had found several boxes of recordings he could do with as he pleased. Life behind the Iron Curtain had all kinds of surprises.

One young man, who had been busy throughout the program taking pictures, came up to me and asked if we would be giving any more concerts in the DDR. I told him that unfortunately we were not, but I mentioned that we were leaving the next morning for West Berlin and would be singing at the Kaiser Wilhelm Memorial Church on Saturday evening. He was elated, saying he wanted his mother to hear the choir and experience the same joy he had felt that evening. Evidently, because of her age she was eligible for a pass permitting her to go into West Berlin.

A couple came up to Dan after the concert and invited him to visit them in their apartment a short distance from the church. Dan was not quite sure what he should do, so he spoke to Joe Leonards, who said it was probably all right. Dan decided to take the chance, but he also decided to take Mike Maduras with him. They could barely fit into the couple's little "Trabi" (the East German automobile, Trabant), which many Berliners drove. It proved to be a fascinating visit even though Dan was sure the couple had been a "plant." However, a postcard they later sent to Dan said how much the evening had meant to them.

The East German guide on our bus, a young man in his early 20s, was honest as he described various points of interest in East Berlin. For example, he pointed to a particular statue and said, "There is a typically ugly statue of Lenin." He told us he had never been to West Berlin and doubted that he would ever get the opportunity. We found out he would be celebrating his birthday on August 4th, the day we were leaving East Berlin, so someone on our bus bought a large birthday card and had all of us sign it. We gave it to him that morning as we all sang "Happy Birthday." He was moved to tears and wished us well on the rest of our tour. God had given us the privilege of supporting this fine young man on his birthday! We then said "good-bye" to our East German guides and headed for Checkpoint Charlie and West Berlin.

After we cleared Checkpoint Charlie, we picked up our West Berlin guides. The guide on our bus was a woman who had been born in Berlin in 1934, the same year I was born. She grew up in a Berlin devastated by the war and the occupation that followed. She told us how the years from 1943 to 1949 were so horrible in Berlin that it was impossible to describe what it was like. She saw her sister killed in one of the bombing raids. She lived through the rape and pillage that took place when the Russian troops overran the city in 1945. She also experienced the starvation and cold of those first post-war years when there was no food or fuel as a result of the war's destruction and later as a result of the Berlin Blockade. I had never felt so personally the physical, emotional, and spiritual ravages of war. It was a lesson I hope I will never forget. But for the grace of God, I could have been born into that horrible situation.

The contrast between East and West Berlin was stark. After passing into West Berlin, one immediately sensed the vitality and excitement of a thriving city. West Berlin had more land set aside for parks than any other German city. The business districts were jammed with shoppers going through stores filled with every conceivable kind of merchandise. In spite of its appearance of wealth and well-being, however, an invisible cloud hung over the city. Its citizens were living on an island totally surrounded by Communist East Germany. West Berliners could not just drive out of the city and go wherever they liked. Unless they possessed the proper visas, they either had to stay on one of the three transit routes connecting Berlin with West Germany or fly out to the West.

It is no wonder that when their holiday time arrived, West Berliners left the city en masse for Western Europe, where they were not caged in by their city limits. Perhaps because of this, we detected a dryness of spirit in the people. Life for them was concerned only with the present, and material possessions and worldly pleasures had become their gods. We could see why the Lord had wanted us to go to West Berlin to share a message that could bring West Berliners the kind of freedom that city boundaries can never take away.

Our first concert in West Berlin took place at Dieter's Wunderlich's church, the Baptist Church of Berlin-Schöneberg, on Friday evening. The concert was a family affair, much like our time in Pohlheim. On Saturday night, we sang at the Kaiser Wilhelm Church, an elite place of worship in Berlin before World War II. It suffered severe damage from the Allied bombing during the war and only the damaged tower of the edifice was left standing. After the war, the city decided to leave the tower as a reminder of the war's devastation. However, the church eventually built a new sanctuary next to the ruins.

Having a concert at the Kaiser Wilhelm Church was designed to be an outreach to the Berlin community at large and to the hordes of visitors from all over the world who flock there every summer. The church was packed with over a thousand people, many of them standing along the back and sides of the building. A number of people came simply because the church is located in the center of the city; they were just passing by, heard the choir singing, and wandered into the church.

After the concert, an older woman came up to me and introduced herself in fairly broken English. She said she was from East Berlin and that she had come because her son had heard us at the Gethsemane Kirche and had urged her to attend the concert. She then handed me an envelope full of pictures her son had taken at the concert in East Berlin. She thanked me profusely for the inspiration and joy we had brought and then gave me a big hug for good measure. I could not have asked for a more meaningful "thank you."

When I think back on the time we spent in Poland, the word that comes to my mind is "poverty"—economic poverty and poverty of spirit. Of all the places we visited on the 1989 ministry tour, the Poles were the worst off when it came to the basics of life: food, shelter, and clothing. Even more significant was their lack of hope. A complete resignation of spirit overpowered even their economic deficiencies. It was as if they had struggled against insurmountable odds all of their lives (if not for their entire history) and had given up any hope that conditions would ever improve. If ever a people needed the message of hope, it was the people of Poland. All of us sensed this great need and were touched by it.

The lesson we learned our first day in Poland was the importance of trusting God. The concert in Wroclaw was set for 4:00 on Sunday afternoon, since the church held regular Masses at 6:00, 7:00, and 8:00 p.m. every Sunday. During the 1988 planning trip, our drive from Wroclaw to West Berlin had taken us five hours, leading us to believe that an 8:00 a.m. departure from West Berlin would get us to Wroclaw in plenty of time. Obviously, we miscalculated.

Entering the DDR from West Berlin took us about 1½ hours; the Polish officials had decided we should pick up our Polish guides at the East German city of Frankfurt-an-der-Oder. This took us on a longer route which almost doubled the distance we had to travel. Upon reaching the DDR-Poland border, we met our three Polish guides, who seemed totally incapable of speeding up our processing time. It took almost three hours to get our passports and visas cleared and stamped. By this time it was almost noon, so we decided to eat the box lunches which had been prepared by our hotel in West Berlin. Unfortunately, a swarm of bees was attracted to our lunches. By the time we finished eating, six people—two of whom were allergic to bee stings— had been stung by the bees. Therefore, it was after 2:00 p.m. when we finally cleared Polish customs and border control.

It was frustrating to see the time tick away toward our 4:00 concert time, knowing there was no way we were going to make it. With the Polish phone system in continual disarray, it was also impossible to let the priest at St. Elizabeth's know that we would be late. All we could do was keep moving along the two-lane roads, which we shared with the tiny, gutless Polish cars; horse-drawn wagons and carts; and pedestrians.

I described in the introduction to this story how we arrived at the church at 5:45 p.m., nearly two hours after our concert had been scheduled to begin. We were sure we had completely missed the chance to present a concert at the church. We also did not know whether we would be able to communicate with St. Elizabeth's priest, since no one in our group spoke Polish. God answered our problem when a young lady, Niusia, came running up to us just after we arrived at the church, breathlessly identifying herself as the interpreter for our concerts in Poland. Niusia had stayed at the church long after the scheduled 4:00 concert time. Finally, thinking that the concert would not take place, she had decided to go home. But when her cousin saw our three buses, he found Niusia at the bus stop and brought her back to the church.

Even now, I am humbled by how God's hand was upon us that evening. When the priest told us we could present our program at 8:30 p.m. after the abbreviated 8:00 Mass, I did not see how we could get ready. Yet, we believed God had called us to minister in this church and that somehow He would bring it to pass. And that is exactly what He did. This is an example of how God was teaching us to trust Him. We realized we could never be in total control of our circumstances, even in ministry.

The concert was presented in God's time, not ours. If we had arrived on time, we would have ministered to a half-filled church. Instead, at

8:30 p.m. the church was filled to capacity. God allowed us to minister to those dear people and to their priest with the message of joy and hope, a message they desperately needed to hear. Since we had said "yes" to God and had trusted him for the result, God enabled us to serve as his ambassadors of reconciliation. The apostle Paul describes this ministry in his second letter to the church at Corinth.

"All this is from God, who reconciled us to Himself through Christ and gave us the ministry of reconciliation: that God was reconciling the world to Himself in Christ, not counting people's sins against them. And He has committed to us the message of reconciliation. We are therefore Christ's ambassadors, as though God were making His appeal through us." (2 Corinthians 5:18-20a – NIV)

The events of that day in Wroclaw turned out to be one of the greatest blessings of our trip! After we returned to Pasadena, the choir received a note from a young woman, Sophia, who had attended the concert. In the note she said, *"Dear brothers and sisters in Christ of Lake Avenue Church in Pasadena in United States of America: Permit us to express our deep gratitude, and we thank you from whole our hearts, for the God's gifts you were able to bring to Wroclaw, which remains constantly on our minds and hearts."* Her note was heartening to all of us.

During the three days we were in Poland, we got to know Niusia, our interpreter, quite well. We discovered she was a deeply committed Christian who was very involved in the small Baptist church in Wroclaw. She shared with us that she was planning to be married in September to a fine young man of Sri Lankan descent and the two of them had a strong calling to serve as missionaries in Sri Lanka. Niusia was God's special gift to us during our stay in Poland, as she found numerous ways to assist us in our ministry. Shortly after we got back to Pasadena, we received a wedding invitation from her, along with the address of the place where she and her husband would be staying in Canada for three months. Niusia is just one example of the bonding process which took place throughout the tour.

Upon arriving in Krakow the next day, we found that the Lord had not finished testing us. After we checked into our hotel, we contacted Stanley at the Christian Society, our contact in Krakow. We thought we were simply reconfirming the time of our concert at the Philharmonic Hall, but Stanley informed us that he had changed the site from the Philharmonic to the Krakow Sports Arena. We could not believe it! He also told us he had moved the time of our concert from 8:00 to 9:00 p.m. On top of that, instead of giving our own concert, we were now scheduled to present our program as part of a "Love Europe" city-wide crusade, and our program would be the last event in a series of day-long activities and talks.

We felt crushed. We had major concerns about the acoustics in the sports arena, the lack of a piano and organ, and the late hour the concert was scheduled to begin. We wondered how many people would be willing to stay for a concert after sitting all day long in a series of meetings. Dan Bird, David Dalke, and Ed Fischer went over to the sports arena to check out the place and discovered that the only instrument available to accompany the choir was an "electronic" piano. They were also discouraged to hear that the day's attendance at the meetings had been poor.

When we arrived at the sports arena to set up for the concert, we had to wait around outside because the sessions were running over 30 minutes behind schedule. When the speaker finally finished his message and "altar call," it was after 9:00 p.m.. Those remaining in the arena got up and left. As we were setting up, we could not help but wonder if any of them would return for the concert. Nothing seemed to be going right. The Christian Society had even failed to print the programs which had been translated into Polish, so the only programs we had available that night were in English.

It was 9:40 p.m. before we were ready to begin the concert. To our surprise, not only did many people come back in, but the size of the audience was far greater than the number of people who had attended the first two days of meetings. When we finished our first number, the entire arena exploded with clapping, stomping, and shouting. Nowhere on the tour did we witness a greater outpouring of joyous enthusiasm after every number we sang than we experienced in the Krakow Sports Arena that night. In spite of the late hour, the people kept asking for encores.

The sharing time after the concert was also heartwarming. We met people from all over Eastern Europe, including the Soviet Union; people from the West, even a couple from Orange County, CA; a mixture of youth and older people, believers and seekers. When we were loading the buses to return to our hotel, David Dalke leaned over to Dan and asked, "When are we going to simply trust God?" The idea of trust was the essence of our Polish ministry.

Earlier in the day, we took a trip that is permanently burned into our memory. We drove to the Polish town of Oswiecim and spent two hours touring Auschwitz, the World War II German concentration camp. One cannot walk inside the once-electrified barbed wire fence and see the evidence of years of cruelty and death without being deeply moved. Auschwitz is a dreadful example of man's inhumanity to man. While not pleasant to see, it is something we should all experience, since places like Auschwitz bring us face-to-face with the truth that all human beings, apart from Christ, are totally depraved. If there ever were a hell on earth, it surely would include life at Auschwitz.

5

With our stay in Krakow, we passed the halfway point in our ministry tour. As we began the long drive from Poland through Czechoslovakia to Budapest, Hungary, we felt great anticipation. Our original call to Eastern Europe had come from Hungary, so it had always been the central focus of our 1989 tour. We were looking forward to our five days there.

Ildikó Barbarics met us the next morning in Budapest. We had gotten to know and love Ildikó while she was staying with Bruce and Dawn Bell in Phoenix, Arizona, in 1988. It was wonderful to see Ildikó again and to spend several days with her. We were especially grateful that she had laboriously translated the words of all our songs into Hungarian. The choir had four concerts scheduled in Hungary, with Ildikó serving as our translator. Budapest is a captivating city, and we had a chance to see much of it our first morning there. The history of Hungary dates back 1,100 years to the time that the Magyars first settled along the Duna (Danube) River. Hungarians have a zest for life, even though their lives have been difficult. Of all the countries we visited in Eastern Europe, we felt most at home in Hungary.

Accommodations in Budapest were not the best. Budapest was hosting the Formula One Grand Prix race the same weekend we were there, so hotel rooms were scarce. Our choir had to be split up among three different hotels—the Buda Penta, the Hotel Flamenco, and the Budapest Hotel. The first thing the next morning, we heard from those who had been assigned to the Budapest Hotel. They were extremely unhappy, complaining that the hotel seemed far away from the rest of us, that the rooms were small, and that the bathrooms were so tiny that it was difficult for a person to turn around in them. The last straw was that the tub-showers did not have shower curtains!

The group asked Joe Leonards if he could find other accommodations for them, but after hours of searching, Joe had to tell them that nothing else was available. The grumbling which had begun with the group at the Budapest Hotel then began to spread throughout the choir. Some of the choir members who were staying at the Buda Penta also began to complain that their rooms were too small and lacked shower curtains. Our group had already been away from home for a long time, and people had reached their limit – both physically and emotionally.

The choir took a bus tour of Budapest that morning, which concluded with a group lunch at the Fishermen's Bastion Restaurant. Mike Maduras, the choir president, realized that we needed to address the growing unhappiness in the choir before we presented our first Hungarian concert at the Budafok Baptist Church that evening. He therefore asked all choir members to meet right after lunch in a conference room at the Hilton Hotel. Mike knew that if we did not "lance the boil" very soon, the rest of our ministry tour could be in jeopardy.

Mike began the meeting with prayer and then addressed the problems of those staying at the Budapest Hotel. Soon, however, a totally unexpected issue was brought up that evidently had been fomenting since the beginning of the trip: the fact that some people had been upgraded to business class on the flight from Los Angeles to Frankfurt. Choir members wanted to know who had decided which people would be upgraded and how that decision had been made. Our travel agent, Wilma Webb, who had decided to attend the meeting, then addressed the choir. She explained that she was the one who had done the upgrading and—without consulting anyone in the choir—had given the upgrades to those who had played a major role in organizing the tour. Wilma was almost in tears as she apologized for anything she had done to cause bad feelings.

The meeting continued for almost two hours, but after much prayer, the "boil had been lanced." I might add that if airline upgrades are ever available to us in the future, either no one will be upgraded or we will simply hold a lottery to select the "winning" people. This incident was also a reminder that divisive issues need to be addressed quickly and directly, but lovingly.

Our first concert at the Budafok Baptist Church was special for us; we had the same feelings about this church that we had about the Christus Kirche in Pohlheim. Leaders from the Budafok Church had been the first ones to invite us to Hungary, and Dan, Mike, and I had made many friends there during our planning trip in the summer of 1988. The choir had been praying for the Budafok church while it was seeking a new pastor to replace Géza's father, who wanted to retire. We looked forward to seeing Pastor Kovács again, as well as meeting their new pastor, Tibor Kulscar, who had come to the church just a month before.

When Géza had met with the choir at Lake Avenue in February of 1989, he had shared what he believed God wanted to do at each place we would sing in Hungary. He said that Budafok Baptist Church loved the Word of God and sought to put it into action, but he longed for the people of the church to learn to love and experience the joy of worship. From the moment we stepped inside the church, we were welcomed like long-lost friends and family. We were greeted by Géza's father, Pastor Géza Kovács; his uncle; his brother Zoltan; Olga and Ferenc Barbarics, Ildikó's parents; and Gabor Hellinger, the Budafok choir director, with his wife Kati and their three boys. It was an honor to be with these wonderful friends!

While Budafok was not a huge church, it was the fastest-growing and most active Baptist Church in Budapest. That Thursday night the church was packed all the way up to the second balcony high above the choir. Singing and sharing our music with the audience filled us with joy. We all felt a special bond that evening. The worship chorus said it best:

> *"We are one in the bond of love*
> *We are one in the bond of love*
> *We have joined our spirit*
> *With the Spirit of God*
> *We are one in the bond of love."*

When the concert finally ended and we had sung our last encore, Pastor Tibor emphasized how we had expressed great joy through our music and our facial expressions. "Why," he asked his congregation, "do we Hungarians always worship in such sadness?" He vowed that this was going to change. He then invited all of us to join in singing the hymn, "Praise Ye the Lord." He added, with a smile, that we would sing all five verses while they took up the offering.

During the reception after the concert, we met many people, including a young East German girl, Steffi, who told us she had decided not to return to the DDR. Steffi was only one of many refugees from all over Eastern Europe whom we met during our time in Hungary. We also met a Bulgarian couple and their children. He was a Baptist pastor from Sofia, the capital of Bulgaria, and his family had, for the first time, been allowed to spend their vacation in Hungary. He said that the opportunity to attend the European Baptist Convention in Budapest, the Billy Graham Crusade, and our concert had helped him to face going back to one of the most repressive countries in Eastern Europe.

Our Friday night concert at the Varosmajor Roman Catholic Church was scheduled for 8:00 p.m. This church was one of the most active Catholic churches in the area and was unusual in allowing Protestant groups to sing there. The priest welcomed us graciously when we arrived. We discovered that the church had planned a full-blown reception for the choir, including a buffet of sandwiches and pastries. Unlike in Western Europe, we had not requested, nor did we expect, the people of Eastern Europe to provide any kind of food. But they did it anyway, with great joy and hospitality. We in America, who have been blessed with so much, can learn a great deal from our East European brothers and sisters.

Géza Kovács had previously told us that the people of Varosmajor Church loved to worship, but lacked the assurance of their salvation.

Because of this, we stressed the songs in our program which spoke of Jesus and His gift of salvation. We also talked about salvation as we shared one-on-one with people after the concert. Bolla Arpad, the pastor of the Lutheran church in which the choir would be singing Sunday afternoon, came to hear our concert and spoke with Dan afterwards. "In my church," the pastor said, "clapping is not considered appropriate. In fact, we have never had clapping in our church." Since the pastor had seen the joyful response and applause of the people at Varosmajor, he felt he needed to advise Dan that clapping should not take place in his church. Dan assured him that we would not say or do anything to encourage such a response.

Saturday offered "no rest for the weary" unless one was good at sleeping on the bus. We left Budapest right after breakfast for the three-hour ride south to the city of Pécs, which is near the Yugoslav border. Even though Pécs is only 125 miles from Budapest, it was a slow trip on the narrow two-lane roads. The Baptista Templom in Pécs had been without a pastor for about a year and a half, so their first elder, Dr. Ferenc Melath, had been in charge of the church during that time. Géza Kovács told us that under their previous pastor the emphasis had been on the cultural aspects of Christianity and not on a strong proclamation of the Word of God. Géza's desire was that many would come to the concert because of their love of music and then be confronted with the truth of the Gospel proclaimed in our songs.

Since the concert was scheduled on a Saturday during the vacation season, Dr. Melath was not sure how many people would get back in time for the program. He need not have worried. Not only was the sanctuary filled, but also the room they had set aside for the reception and the church narthex were packed. It was an extraordinary evening. The new pastor was thrilled by the response of his congregation to our singing. A touching scene unfolded just before we boarded our buses. The choir was still circulating outside talking with many people. As we started to say good-bye, the people joined hands and sang, "Until we meet again"—they in Hungarian and we in English. Their love warmed our hearts as we pulled away from the church for our long trip back to Budapest.

We were not sure what to expect that Sunday evening at the Evangelikus Nagytemplom Lutheran church in the Rakospalota district of Budapest. Pastor Bolla Arpad was a dear man of God who had a great burden for his congregation. His church was located in a more rural section of the city and served working-class people. Most of them, according to Géza, were "traditional" Christians who lacked a personal relationship with Jesus Christ. Géza was praying that the reality of Christ in our lives would come through our singing and the sharing time after the service. Since this was the church which did not allow clapping, Dan advised the choir that the lack of an audible response to our music should not be taken as a negative; we simply needed to share the love of Christ through our music with these people who needed to know the Lord.

That night we once again sang for a packed-out church: people were standing all along the sides, at the back, and even on the stairs leading up to the balcony. After our opening number, there was a smattering of applause, much broader applause after the next couple of songs, and loud clapping after the first bell number. Even some of the older women in their traditional black dresses and head coverings joined in the applause, along with Pastor Arpad. At the conclusion of the program, the audience gave the choir a standing ovation.

During the concert we saw tears well up in people's eyes and run down their faces. This was particularly true when we invited the audience to join us in singing their national anthem in Hungarian. At the conclusion of the concert, Pastor Arpad announced that this was the first time in the history of the church that there had been clapping of any kind in one of their services. He confessed, "During the concert the Lord brought to my mind the Bible story about how King David's wife, Michal, laughed at him as David sang and danced before the Lord. I do not want to make the same mistake. I realize now that the applause this evening was not for the choir, but was an outpouring of praise and joy to the Lord."

The reception the Lutheran congregation prepared for us outside the church was a true gift of love and generosity. The people clearly did not have many possessions or a great deal of money, but they shared what they had. That evening was a fitting conclusion to our days of ministry in Hungary. Since we had sung "Battle Hymn of the Republic" as one of our encores, the pastor started singing, "Glory, Glory, Hallelujah" and soon everyone was singing together. As we walked toward our buses, the people gave us hugs, kisses, and fond farewells. They stood on the street waving to us until we departed. Our last sight of the church in the dimming light of that summer evening was of Pastor Arpad and his wife surrounded by many of his parishioners with tear-filled eyes, waving and clapping.

After we returned home, we received in the mail a translated copy of an article which appeared in the September 3, 1989 issue of *Lutheran Life,* published by the Hungarian Lutheran Church. In the article, the writer compared our concert at the Rakospalota Lutheran Church with the Billy Graham Crusade which had been held in the huge Budapest Soccer Stadium earlier that summer. The article mentioned that after a massive publicity campaign, over 70,000 people attended the Graham Crusade. He contrasted this with our concert, for which there had been no publicity except for an announcement from the church pulpit a week in advance.

The article continued, "*This [concert] was truly Christian, a rejoicing in Christ. Their faces were not only golden by the rays of the sun flooding through the windows, but by the recognition that through their songs of joy and love they had raised up the Lord and praised Him. At the end of the concert, as the choir sang with beautiful Hungarian pronunciation our national anthem, we realized that something had touched our hearts, that something had started within us: and now it is our earnest hope and prayer that we will be able to continue as we have seen and heard the call from the Pasadena Choir Ensemble."*

When God promises He will do above and beyond all that we could ask or think, He is faithful to His Word. Our ministry in Hungary, which had always been the cornerstone of our European tour, was far more effective than we could have anticipated. God poured out his Spirit upon us and the four churches in which we sang. We developed relationships with many people, energized the Hungarian churches, and became part of God's mighty plan for the nation of Hungary. If nothing else had been accomplished on the tour, our time in Hungary would have made it all worthwhile.

6

We had mixed feelings as we left Budapest on Monday morning and headed for Austria. We were exhilarated as a result of the ministry God had allowed us to experience in Hungary, but at the same time we were happy to be returning to Western Europe. As we rode, Joe pointed out two small East German Trabis. He told us the cars had probably been left there by people who had walked to the Austrian border in the hope of sneaking across the border to freedom. As we watched, some Hungarians were already taking things out of the cars left behind by the East Germans. The sad part, Joe explained, was that if the East Germans were unsuccessful in getting across the border, they would come back to find their cars totally stripped.

It was with a great sense of relief that we made it across the Hungarian-Austrian border back into the free part of Europe. We had lunch in the Austrian town of Eisenstadt, not too far from the border, and then took a tour of the Esterhazy Palace. Joe Leonards had arranged for us to give a short recital in the Haydnsalle of the Palace, the very hall in which Joseph Haydn performed so much of his music for Count Esterhazy back in the 18th century. What a thrill it was to sing in that splendid hall with its outstanding acoustics! One could almost imagine the hall in the 1700s, filled with ladies and gentlemen enjoying the exquisite music of Haydn, directed by the composer himself. This peek into history was one of those little serendipities which added so much to our tour experience.

Vienna has stood at the heart of European history and culture for centuries. One cannot see and experience Vienna in one or two days, but we tried! Since the choir was coming off the heavy and stressful ministry in Eastern Europe, we had arranged to give the choir as much free time as possible. We stayed at the Vienna Marriott Hotel, directly across from Vienna's Stadtpark. After our experience with the three hotels in Budapest, this was pure luxury. From the moment we checked into our hotel until we had to prepare for our concert the next evening, we had leisure time. Unfortunately, our "free day" turned out to be one of Austria's major religious holidays; thus, all of the stores outside of the hotels were closed. Alas! There would be no shopping! However, we were able to visit the many historic sites in Vienna and enjoyed stopping at one of the delightful Viennese coffee houses.

One place we visited was St. Stephan's Cathedral, located in the historic center of Vienna. While Don D. and his wife, Eulene, were in the cathedral, they were shocked to see Joseph, our bus driver, talking to Steffi, the young woman from East Germany we had last seen in Budapest. Steffi told Don how excited she was about having found a way into the West. She did not say how she had gotten to Vienna, but Don surmised that somehow Joseph had smuggled her onto our bus—perhaps hiding her in the bus WC. It had seemed strange when, as we were leaving Budapest, Joseph had told the people on Bus #1 that the WC was inoperative, but would be fixed when we arrived in Vienna. We never solved the mystery of how Steffi managed to get to the West, but she is just one example of how much the people living behind the Iron Curtain longed for freedom. They never dreamed that the Communist stranglehold on Eastern Europe would collapse in just a few months.

Other than the Volkshalle in Pohlheim, the Lutherische Stadtkirche, Vienna's oldest Protestant church, was the only "repeat venue" from the 1984 tour. There had been a small turnout when we sang there on a Sunday night in 1984. This time we were presenting a 6:00 p.m. concert on a major holiday, so the chances of having a large audience were not very promising. To make matters worse, we could not find the thousand fliers in German and English which had been printed to advertise the concert. Distributing similar fliers had been very successful in promoting our concert in the Kaiser Wilhelm Memorial Church.

Just as in 1984, a major drawback of the Stadtkirche was that the only place with room for the choir was the second balcony. This required the choir to be divided into two halves, each singing from opposite sides of the church. David Dalke played the organ in the rear balcony, from which Dan directed the choir. Each of the three sections of the upper balcony was totally separated from the others, and it took 93 stairs to get there from the main floor. Thankfully, the bell choir was able to set up downstairs on the chancel, but David had to climb down the stairs to play the piano for our final numbers.

Someone finally found the fliers, so we asked our choir associates to take a stack and hand them out to people in the area outside the church. We did not know if we would have even twenty people at the concert. However, people started to file in, the downstairs was soon filled, and many people were making their way up to the first balcony. What a blessing it was to see so many people at the concert! The audience represented not only people from Vienna, but also visitors and tourists from all over Europe, both East and West. It was our responsibility to sing where He had called us and He would take care of the rest.

A boat trip on the Danube River had been one of the highlights for a number of people in 1984, so I was happy that Icontas Service had arranged for our whole group to take a similar boat trip on our way from Vienna to Munich. We caught the boat at the medieval town of Durnstein and took it through the beautiful Wachau region of Austria to the city of Melk. Many castles dotted the hillsides, including the castle above Durnstein in which, according to tradition, the Duke of Austria held English King Richard the Lionhearted as a prisoner. The delightful interlude in the boat helped break up the long drive to Munich.

Peter Wisst of Icontas Service had arranged a special treat for the choir the evening we arrived in Munich. We would drive to Keferloh, a small village on the outskirts of the city, and spend the evening at the Gasthof Kreitmair, a German beer garden and restaurant. There we would enjoy a four-course dinner and be entertained by a group of Bavarian folksingers and dancers. It was a place people could relax, enjoy wonderful food and drink, and experience the traditional music and dancing of the region. After spending the last twelve days behind the Iron Curtain, everyone seemed to love the evening. Only later did we discover that this feeling was not unanimous.

All of us were looking forward to visiting Munich, Germany's third largest city, with its many places to see (and shop)! Munich was the hometown of our three guides and drivers, so they loved being able to show off their city. The choir had the morning free, and then we all had lunch at the famous Rathskeller in the heart of Munich. The concert that night was in the Paul Gerhard Kirche, probably Munich's most active evangelical church. Their assistant pastor, Kurt Jung, was an American who had ministered in Germany for over thirty years. Coincidentally, he grew up in the same town as Dan Bird—Kenosha, Wisconsin.

The people in the Paul Gerhard church were hospitable, providing us with a typical Bavarian dinner, with more food than we could eat. A special delight was seeing Hal and Liz Leaman and their two daughters in the dining hall. Back in 1984 they had made all the arrangements for our concert in Salzburg, and this time they had provided our contacts in Munich. Hal and Liz told us how much they had been looking forward to having "their own church choir" sing in Munich; it was clear that our visit was an encouragement to them.

From a technical standpoint, our Munich concert was probably our finest. Everything seemed to come together to make it an outstanding program. Our guides, who had brought their families with them, as well as Peter and Maria from Icontas Service, were enchanted by the concert. They expressed how proud they were of "their adopted choir." Several people who had entertained us the night before also came to the program. The band leader at the restaurant had been so impressed by the choir that he came to the concert that night, as did the young lady who had played Swiss handbells for us. Our handbell choir and the English handbells enthralled her.

At the end of the concert, Senior Pastor Wilfried Kunneth told the audience that our concert was one of the two most significant events ever to take place in their church. "The first event revolutionized our whole approach to ministry and outreach within the city of Munich. The second event, tonight's concert, is the embodiment of a dream I have had for the past ten years. I have been praying that God would give us a clear vision of the kind of worship and praise He desires from us when we come together on Sunday morning. This is it!" Pastor Kunneth closed by imploring us to please come again.

The next morning I began to hear rumblings that not everyone had been happy with our evening at the Gasthof Kreitmair. Several choir members were upset that beer had been served and suspected that a few people in the choir had imbibed too much. I thought that these concerns would blow over, not realizing that some choir members had been so upset about the previous evening that they had not wanted to sing at the Paul Gerhard Kirche that night. But that concert had gone well, so I thought the problem had taken care of itself. However, after we returned home, complaints about the choir's use of alcohol came up again. This incident reminded me that Christians must be very careful when dealing with this controversial issue.

On our last full day in Europe we had a long drive, but it was broken up by a visit to the fascinating medieval walled town of Rothenberg-ob-der-Tauber. Walking into the town was like walking back in time to the 15th and 16th centuries. Rothenberg is probably the best-preserved town from the Middle Ages to be found in Germany. What fun it was to roam and explore the narrow streets and intriguing shops! For me, it was a perfect day: gorgeous weather, immersion in historical settings, and all of it on my 55th birthday.

Our group stayed in the city of Ludwigshafen, which happened to be Pasadena's "sister city." The city officials met us at the hotel and welcomed us to their town. The people of Overseas Crusades (now called OC Ministries), our official sponsors for that concert, had not found a church in Ludwigshafen which was large enough, so they had arranged for our final program to take place in the nearby town of Speyer.

The Gedachtniskirche (Memorial Church) in Speyer was built at the end of the 19th century in the neo-Gothic style as a special memorial to the Protestant Reformation and Martin Luther. In the center of Memorial Hall at the entrance to the sanctuary stands a bronze likeness of Martin Luther on a pedestal made of Swedish granite, which was donated by a group of German-American Lutherans. In his left hand Luther is holding an open Bible and his right hand is formed into a fist. With his right foot he is stamping on the papal bull of excommunication.

Sunk into the ground are the final words Luther spoke in his own defense before the church leaders at the Diet of Worms in 1521: *"Heir stehe ich, ich kann nicht anders, Gott helfe mir. Amen!"* The following is Luther's full concluding statement: *"Unless I am convinced by the testimony of the Scriptures or by clear reason (for I do not trust either in the pope or in councils alone, since it is well-known that they have often erred and contradicted themselves), I am bound by the Scriptures I have quoted and my conscience is captive to the Word of God. I cannot and will not recant anything, since it is neither safe nor right to go against conscience. Here I stand. I can do nothing else, God help me. Amen."*

The senior pastor of the Memorial Church was also the superintendent of all Lutheran churches in that part of West Germany. Ralph Foster and his OC colleagues hoped our concert would give them an opening to talk more with the superintendent, who was very liberal in his theology. We were excited about singing in that breathtakingly beautiful church, but we were also saddened to realize that this would be our last concert of the trip. According to reports we later received, more than 2,100 people poured into the church that evening to hear "the choir from Pasadena, California."

It was a Spirit-filled evening. One person told us that our concert was the first time in twenty-seven years that the Word of God had been proclaimed in such truth and power in their church. As in many other European churches, the church's regular attendance was poor: this huge church had only 50 to 100 people present on a typical Sunday morning. Their magnificent pipe organ, which David had the pleasure to play, was used no more than once a month. We prayed that God's Spirit, who was so evident in the church that night, would work a miracle in the hearts of the church people and that the church might once again become a beacon to the world.

The next morning, we loaded up our three buses and traveled to the Frankfurt Airport to catch our 10:40 a.m. Lufthansa flight back to Los Angeles. As we approached the airport, we thought about everything our three tour escorts had done for us. For example, it had become a familiar sight to see Joe walk down to the front of the church bringing water for the members of the bell choir and for Dan and David. Our escorts had also caught the vision of our ministry and had done everything in their power to make sure our trip ran as smoothly as possible. Each of them became an integral part of our group.

It was difficult to say good-bye to our tour escorts at the Frankfurt Airport. What happened on Bus #1 could just as easily describe what happened on the other two buses. As we approached the airport, Joe Leonards tried to tell us what the trip had meant to him. He had just started to speak when he began to cry. Picture this big, macho German who had been nicknamed "The Prussian Warlord" now standing before us with tears streaming down his face. He could no longer speak; he just sat down and the heart-wrenching sound of his sobs carried through the bus. The choir, through their own tears, then attempted to sing, "The Lord Bless You and Keep You." It was not a very successful rendition, but the spirit we communicated was genuine.

The choir had no problem getting checked in at the airport, but we received a call from German customs that Chuck and Ernie once again had a problem getting our equipment cleared. When Tony had arrived at customs, he had discovered that the handbell cases were again the problem. This time, at least, he had the key to open the cases. When Tony asked who was in charge of customs, it turned out to be the same man who had helped Tony when we arrived in Frankfurt! Tony opened one of the cases and showed the bells to the men. The customs agent smiled broadly, indicating that he remembered what they were. He quickly stamped the Carnet and cleared all of the equipment for shipping. Our three guys hurriedly got back in the cab and raced to the airport entrance, barely making it to the boarding gate on time. Tony told me later that the customs agent was not supposed to have been on duty that morning; he had been called in to take the place of another agent who was sick. The fact that the same agent who had originally checked in our equipment was there when we left had to be one of those "God things."

For the return flight, several of those who had flown business class on the flight to Germany gave their tickets to others. No one seemed to object.

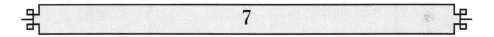

7

After returning from our European Ministry Tour, we heard from many people we had met on the trip. A couple of letters summarize the significance of what God did through our ministry. One letter we received was from Joe Leonards in Munich, West Germany. We had last seen him at the Frankfurt Airport with tears in his eyes. In his letter to the choir, he wrote: *"I hope it is not a secret to tell all of you that my love and admiration for all you did on the ministry tour is great and I am very proud to have been part of it. With all the hard work and the stress, it is by far the most memorable journey for me in all of my travels. It has and will give me a source of energy and will do so for the rest of my life. The privilege to be with all of you, to help and assist you, and to hear you over and over again still fills my heart and soul. In no way am I ashamed of my tears at the airport because feelings like that are only for true friends and I felt and feel that all of you are my true friends and that is rare in these days and I can cherish the feeling and thought. Joe Leonards"*

A short time after Joe's letter arrived, we received a poignant letter from Dorothy, one of our Polish guides. Dorothy had developed a strong bond with the people on her bus. The four days she was with us in Poland had a tremendous impact on her life, as she shared in a letter she wrote the choir: *"How difficult it is in Poland only we, the Polish people, know. Do you know, that today I searched out a lot of bakeries by three hours in order to buy a piece of bread for my family? But I must tell you the truth, something happened in my life. I don't know what, that I'm already not angry, not nervous, that I'm already still smiling. I don't know why, maybe to you, maybe to your songs, to your art. . . . Maybe we'll meet in Poland again, and maybe in America, maybe somewhere else—God planned our life and only He knows. . . . Meeting you was an example for me, that on the Earth could exist an easy and happy life in the peace. God Bless all of you, Dorothy"*

Several weeks later, Dorothy again wrote the choir after receiving a letter from us: *"My dear friends: You can't imagine how happy I was, when my mother called me at my school and said, 'Come home very quickly, you have the letter from California' . . . . There, in Poland, you left a delicate impression—the impression of happy, smiling people, like a delicate show of trusting, real trusting. It was only four days, but I feel that I know you very well. . . . God bless all of you – I'm praying every day for it. Dorothy, Polish Guide, Wroclaw, Poland."* Dorothy's letters confirmed that God was at work as a result of our ministry.

We concluded every concert with an American gospel song that conveyed the message of hope we wanted to leave with the people in Europe, especially those behind the Iron Curtain. The song, "Lord, You Are Our Life" by Stuart Dauermann, Director of Interfaithfulness, touched thousands of hearts in both Western and Eastern Europe during the summer of 1989. It still speaks to my heart today.

DON KING

"Lord, you are our life, You are our joy, You are our song;
You are our King, that's why we sing our song of praise to You.
Though trouble may surround us, Your arms are
still around us,
Trusting Your name, we find the strength to carry on.
Though the Devil seeks to harm us, we will not
give way to fear;
With his lies he won't alarm us, for we know that You are near.
Though a host encamp against us, still we will not be afraid
For we know you will defend us, and
Your power will be displayed.
And that is why we just wanna say,
Lord, you are our life, You are our joy, You are our song;
You are our King, that's why we sing our song of praise to You.
Though trouble may surround us, Your arms
are still around us,
Trusting Your name, we find the strength to carry on.
We'll carry on, we'll carry on, we'll carry on!"

CHAPTER FIVE

Ministry Aborted

> *"Many are the plans in a man's heart, but it is the Lord's purpose that prevails."*
> *Proverbs 19:21 (NIV)*

The words of the refrain from the song, "Lord, You Are Our Life," kept going through our heads after we returned from our 1989 European Ministry Tour: *"We'll carry on, we'll carry on!"* We all had been blessed by what the Lord had allowed us to accomplish on the tour and we had every expectation that the "Out of the Loft" ministry would continue to expand. Tony Bohlin and I produced a 15-minute video summary of the trip, which we showed the choir in September. I was feeling, "God is good! All's right with the world!"

The choir's ministry at Lake Avenue did exhibit a greater intensity and purpose, as the size of the choir grew to more than 150 singers. We were also getting used to the new sanctuary and its acoustical challenges. The new 125-rank Casavant organ was dedicated in a celebratory recital in October, followed by a luminous Christmas concert in December.

The years 1990 and 1991 were a time of transition. Tony Bohlin and I had begun working on a two-hour documentary video of the tour right after Christmas, 1989. The catalyst for the production was the fall of the Berlin Wall on November 9, 1989. We all had been glued to our TV sets watching the people from East Berlin stream through the Wall into West Berlin. The previous summer, the choir had stood at that very place: by the Berlin Wall in front of the Brandenburg Gate. We had never expected to see this happen!

We also found out that the church in which we had sung in East Berlin, the Gethsemane Kirche, had become the focal point in Berlin for the peace/prayer movement, the movement which eventually brought about the downfall of the Wall and the Communist government in East Germany. Soon after the Wall collapsed, the Communist governments in Hungary, Czechoslovakia, Poland, and Romania also fell. We therefore decided to call our video documentary, "Out of Despair, HOPE!" The final product, which was completed in March, was powerful. Over five hundred people from the choir and congregation came to see it.

In April of 1990, Dr. Paul Cedar announced his resignation as senior pastor of Lake Avenue Church so he could become president of the Evangelical Free Church of America. Thus began a seventeen-month time of transition. The consistency of the choir during that period did much to maintain the vitality of the Sunday morning worship services. However, the church was struggling under the burden of the huge debt it had incurred during its building program. This, along with a slowdown in the economy, affected church budgets, including the budget of the music and worship department.

In spite of these changes, the choir was able to present phenomenal Christmas and spring concerts at Lake Avenue Church. In addition, we gave a powerful patriotic concert to honor those who had fought in the Gulf War. The Sanctuary Choir also went "Out of the Loft," joining with the choir at the Crystal Cathedral to perform the Brahms *Requiem*, first at their church and then at ours. Another "Out of the Loft" opportunity came when the choir was invited to sing at the National Convention of the American Choral Directors Association (ACDA), which took place in Phoenix in March. (Later, against all odds, the choir was asked for the third time to sing for the ACDA, this time at the Western Convention in Sacramento in 1994. It is a great honor to be chosen once, but being chosen three times is unheard of!)

In September of 1991, Lake Avenue Church called a new senior pastor. At our Christmas concert that year, he publicly expressed great admiration for the choir and for our consistent Sunday worship service ministry. His comments warmed our hearts and led us to believe that he would continue to strongly support the music ministry.

Initially after the new pastor's arrival, the choir's ministry continued to blossom and grow. Dan Bird was able to put together a strong musical team, including David Dalke as our full-time organist, Duane Funderburk as the director of adult instrumental music, and Ed Fischer as handbell choir director. They created new dimensions in our music and worship ministry. Duane organized a chamber orchestra which played in the Sunday morning services at least once a month, and David formed an honor treble choir.

The Sanctuary Choir presented two of our finest Christmas concerts: Ralph Vaughn Williams' "Hodie," with full orchestra, soloists, and honor treble choir in 1992, and Handel's *Messiah* to a packed audience of 3,500 people in 1993. However, we almost had to present the *Messiah* concert without Dan. He had gone into the hospital for surgery on his leg just a week before the performance. Dan, however, was determined to be there, no matter what. He had to be lifted onto the chancel and he conducted from his "rehearsal chair." The choir was so inspired by his presence that we sang with an energy and passion surpassing anything we had done before.

A visit from our friends in Pohlheim in 1993 reignited our call to the "Out of the Loft" ministry. The Pohlheimers began their spring trip to America with a five-day stay in Pasadena. Even though we would celebrate Easter in a few days, we decided to serve our German friends a typical Thanksgiving dinner of turkey, mashed potatoes and gravy, dressing, cranberries, and pumpkin pie. We also told them the story of America's first Thanksgiving. The group seemed to enjoy the evening, even though we had our holidays mixed up! The Pohlheim visit could not have come at a better time. The Choir Cabinet had begun to explore when and where God might be calling the choir for another European ministry tour. The five days we had with our German visitors confirmed our desire to again put Pohlheim on our itinerary.

Now that the Iron Curtain had fallen, we looked for places to minister which would have been closed to us only a few years earlier—the former East Germany and Czechoslovakia. We also wanted to make return visits to Germany and Hungary. Mike Maduras and I were responsible for developing an outline of the proposed tour and presenting it to the Lake Avenue Church Ministry Council, which now oversaw all church ministries. The main concern of the council was the church's huge debt and the impact of the debt on the church's finances. The church leaders therefore urged us to use caution in planning another tour, but they did not restrict us from exploring a new ministry itinerary. Dan and I hoped to take a planning trip during the summer of 1994 to prepare for a possible ministry tour in 1995.

Because of the logistical problems we had encountered during the 1989 tour, we decided to work jointly and directly with Koopman's Travel and Icontas Service. Erhard Jung put us in contact with church leaders in Erfurt, Leipzig, and Dresden—three cities located in what had been East Germany. Dieter Wunderlich provided us with possible contacts in Berlin; Ildikó Barbarics did the same in Hungary. We were also given the name of the president of the Czech Bible Society for possible ministry opportunities in the Czech Republic and Slovakia. (Czechoslovakia had split into these two republics on January 1, 1993.)

When I wrote the Wehrenfennigs that Dan and I were visiting Pohlheim in August, they wrote back with the news that Martin, their oldest son, was getting married just a few days before we were scheduled to arrive. They asked if it would be possible for me to come four days early and participate in the wedding festivities. Of course, I told them I would love to come. The choir's "Out of the Loft" ministry had brought the Wehrenfennig family into our lives, and now I had the privilege to be a part of this special family occasion.

2

Dan and I had planned to fly to Germany on Sunday, July 31, 1994. However, I traveled to Frankfurt by myself on July 27th so I could attend the Wehrenfennig wedding. Martin Wehrenfennig and his bride, Annette, had their civil wedding ceremony the next morning, followed by a lunch for both of their families. A big difference between German and American weddings is that the only "official" marriage in Germany is a civil ceremony performed by the state. Church weddings are not recognized by the government, so couples must hold a civil ceremony before they can have a church wedding. Martin and Annette's church ceremony was scheduled for Saturday afternoon.

On Thursday evening the Wehrenfennigs hosted a special reception and barbecue picnic for over 100 people. Since I was succumbing to jet lag, I went home at 10:30 p.m. for some much-needed sleep, but Martin and his family did not get home until 2:00 a.m.! After a Friday filled with wedding preparations, Saturday dawned bright and hot.

The Wehrenfennigs had asked me to videotape the wedding, so I was honored to be a part of the ceremony. The 2:00 p.m. wedding was lovely, followed by a *Kaffee Trinken* at Arnsburg Abbey, near the town of Lich. I thought this was the reception; family and friends offered toasts, performed skits, and read poems for the newlyweds.

But the day was not over yet! At 6:30 p.m., "Part Two" of the reception began in the Abbey. We enjoyed a lavish buffet dinner, followed by dancing. By 11:00 p.m. I was "fading fast," so Günter asked someone to take me and his 90-year-old father home to get some rest. Talk about feeling old! I found out the next morning that the Wehrenfennigs did not return from the reception until after 3:00 a.m. I do not know how they did it!

Believe it or not, the festivities continued the next day with a Sunday brunch at the home of the bride's parents. When the brunch was over and most of the guests had left, Annette's mother insisted we stay for supper to help finish the food that was left over. Feeling completely bloated, we finally dragged ourselves home at 10:00 p.m. After four days of almost continual eating and celebration, I was not sure I could ever survive another German wedding!

On Monday morning I drove to the Frankfurt airport with Günter to meet Dan's plane. Dan arrived right on time, and the two of us went to rent a car. Thank goodness, we did not need to worry about purchasing unleaded gasoline like we had in 1988. It was now available all over Eastern Europe—a small but significant sign that these countries were no longer under the thumb of the Soviet Union. After we arrived in Pohlheim we met Erhard Jung at the church office. He introduced us to the new pastor of the Christus Kirche and made calls to people at churches we planned to visit in Erfurt and Leipzig. By the end of the day, we were ready to begin our planning trip.

As Dan and I drove east, we could not help but think of all that had occurred since we had last been in Germany. The Berlin Wall and the Iron Curtain had come down and Communist governments had fallen in several countries of the "Eastern Bloc." Germany had become a re-united nation and the Soviet Union had collapsed into a number of independent republics. The border controls, guard towers, barbed wire fences, and mine fields were all gone. Approaching the former border between West and East Germany, we encountered only empty, rundown border control buildings. It was wonderful to drive right over the border with no "Brunnie" to stop us and disassemble our car!

After visits in the cities of Eisenach and Erfurt, we arrived at the Paul-Gerhardt Kirche in Leipzig and met the church cantor and organist. What a fascinating person he was! We had been told that he was blind, but he was such an outstanding musician that we hardly noticed. He played one of Bach's fugues on the church's impressive Schuke pipe organ with such skill that we were mesmerized. It was astonishing that the cantor could play such intricate music without seeing the keyboard! We were gratified when he told us he was interested in having the choir present a concert at his church.

We then made our way to the Alte Stadt, or Old City, and stopped by the Nikolaikirche, the church which had begun the peace/prayer movement. While there, we read some printed information about the history of the church, which I later found on the church website. Dan and I were deeply touched by the following story about the tumultuous events in 1989:

"'Nikolaikirche - Open To All' became a reality in the autumn of 1989 and surprised us all. It united people from all parts of former East Germany—*those who wanted to leave the country and those who were curious, regime critics and Stasi* [State Security Police] *personnel, church staff and Socialist Unity Party (SED) members, Christians and non-Christians*—*all beneath the outspread arms of the crucified and resurrected Jesus Christ. In view of the political reality between 1949 and 1989, this defies all imagination. Exactly 450 years after the*

introduction of the Reformation in Leipzig and 176 years after the Battle of Nations in Leipzig, our city was reborn. However, this dramatic change did not come easily.

On May 8, 1989, the police blocked the driveways to the church. In fact, driveways and motorway exits around the city were often subject to wide-ranging checks and were sometimes closed during the church's prayers-for-peace period. The state authorities exerted great pressure on us to cancel the peace prayers. Week after week there were arrests or 'temporary detentions' of people who participated in the movement. Even so, the number of visitors flocking to the church continued to grow until the church's 2,000 seats could not hold all of the people who wanted to come. The tension between the church and the government increased.

For ten long hours on October 7, 1989, uniformed police surrounded the church, battering defenseless people who made no attempt to fight back and taking them away in trucks. Hundreds of them were locked up in stables in Markkleeberg. The state-run media published an article urging Germans to end what the government called 'counter-revolution.' At last came the memorable day of October 9, 1989. What a day that was! Soldiers, industrial militia, police, and officers in plain clothes made a hideous show of force. Some 1,000 Socialist Unity Party (SED) members were ordered to go to the St. Nicholas Church, and 600 of them had filled the church nave by 2:00 p.m. It is ironic that these Communists were unwittingly exposed to the Word of God and the gospel that afternoon.

Shortly after the prayers, the bishop gave his blessing and appeals were read from Professor Masur, chief conductor of the Gewandhaus Orchestra, and others who supported our call for non-violence. The solidarity between church and art, music and the gospel, was essential in that threatening situation. As more than 2,000 people left the church that evening, they were welcomed by ten of thousands waiting outside with candles in their hands—an unforgettable moment. Then a miracle occurred! Jesus's spirit of non-violence seized the masses and became a material, peaceful power. Troops, military brigade groups, and the police became curious about what was happening, engaged in conversation with church people—and then withdrew. It was an evening in the spirit of our Lord Jesus. This non-violent movement had lasted only a few weeks, but it caused the party and the ideological dictatorship to collapse.

We experienced the truth of the following Bible verses: 'He dethrones the mighty ones and enthrones the weak ones' and 'You will succeed, not by military power nor by your own strength, but by my spirit, says the Lord.' That evening, thousands of people flocked to the city's churches, and hundreds of thousands walked through the streets around the city center. Yet not a single shop window was shattered! This was the incredible power of non-violence. Horst Sindermann, a member of the East German Central Committee, said before his death: 'We had planned everything. We were prepared for everything. But not for candles and prayers.'

The prayers for peace continue in St. Nicholas Church to this day, and the church has developed a program for the unemployed. Thus, St. Nicholas Church remains what it was: a house of Jesus, a house of hope, a place and a source for a new beginning. Rev. C. Führer." (Adapted from the church website: www.nikolaikirche-leipzig.de)

Driving into Berlin that summer brought back many memories from our 1989 ministry tour. Dan and I checked into our hotel and then drove to the place where the Berlin Wall had once stood. Dan had not been in Berlin since 1989, when the Wall still separated the two sides of the city. As we walked through the Brandenburg Gate into what had formerly been East Berlin, Dan became silent. Then I noticed tears trickling down his face. He explained, "Seeing the square open to everyone—for the first time since our 1989 tour when Berlin was still a divided city—overwhelmed me with emotion."

Our last stop in former East Germany was the city of Dresden. We then drove to Prague, capital of the Czech Republic and one of the few cities in Eastern Europe which was not destroyed in the war. The gorgeous drive from Dresden to Prague took us through the eastern end of the Ore Mountains and down into the Vltava River Valley. The next day we took the Metro to the city center for our meeting with Dr. Jiri Lukl, president of the Czech Bible Society. We found Dr. Lukl to be pleasant and engaging, and he was elated that we wanted to share the love of Christ with the Czech people through music. He suggested that we sing not only in Prague, but also in other Czech cities such as Brno, the second largest city in the country. We came away from our meeting with Dr. Lukl with thankful hearts that we had found our primary contact for the Czech Republic. Dr. Lukl even gave us the names of two people to contact in Bratislava, capital city of newly-formed Slovakia.

Jiri Lukl believed that the best place for us to present a concert in Prague would be outside in the Old Town Square in front of a huge stature of Jan Hus, the 15th century church reformer. The statue was erected in 1915 on the 500th anniversary of the reformer's death. Dr. Lukl believed that holding the concert there would attract a large number of the people who flocked to Prague each summer. It would be like our 1984 concert in the center of Salzburg's Alter Markt. After the meeting, Dan and I explored the picturesque city of Prague. As we walked along the Vltava River and the Charles Bridge, through Old Town Square and Wenceslas Square, and past the Prague Castle and St. Vitas Cathedral, we fell in love with everything about the city. We hated to leave, but we were also looking forward to traveling over the Hungarian border to Budapest.

Dan and I were overjoyed to be back in Hungary to spend time with Ildikó and our other friends at Budafok Baptist. We had meetings with Pastor Tibor of the Budafok Church, the church organist of the major Reformed church in the center of Budapest, and a pastor in a town outside the city. Ildikó also took us out to the Word of Life Camp in Tóalmás. This was the first time we had been to the place where Ildikó had ministered since 1989. There we met with Eric Murphy, the director of Word of Life Hungary, who showed us around the grounds and invited the choir to minister at the camp in 1995. We also talked with Géza Kovács Jr. and his wife, Ildikó. Géza was now pastoring a small congregation in Budapest in addition to his work at the Hungarian Science Institute. He wanted the choir to sing in a venue which would attract people from all over the city, so he said he would try to set up a concert for us at the Bela Bartok National Concert Hall in Budapest.

The last part of our planning trip took us to Vienna, Nuremberg, and the city of Ulm. Our final stop was the romantic city of Heidelberg, the setting for the popular light opera, "The Student Prince." Dan and I thought that ending our next ministry tour in Heidelberg would be a special treat for the choir. After an 11½ hour flight from Frankfurt to Los Angeles, we were delighted to be home.

3

Almost as soon as I could get my clothes washed and catch my breath, June and I drove up to Judy and Tony Bohlin's home in the Northern California town of Cottonwood, to which they had moved in 1991. There we produced what I still believe to be one of the best planning trip videos we have ever made. We showed it to the choir at its fall retreat the weekend after Labor Day. The fall of 1994 also marked a huge change for me. After thirty-seven years, I retired from teaching and counseling in the Glendale Unified School District. As a result, I had the time to become Dan's unofficial and unpaid assistant and devoted most of my energy to the choir and our proposed ministry tour.

In September our choir recorded a number of songs for a new Christmas album to be released in November. It was called "Unto Us" and included music by our Sanctuary Choir, as well the Son-light Bells, the children's choirs, and the Saturday night worship team. The album also included two pieces arranged by Duane Funderburk, our director of adult instrumental music. Duane had collaborated with the church organist, David Dalke, in composing a piece written for organ and chamber orchestra. Proceeds from the sale of the recording would be used to help with the costs of our proposed 1995 European Ministry Tour.

David Dalke, our accompanist, had been sick for several months, but he became more seriously ill that fall. As a result, the Choir Council realized that it would be inadvisable for us to go on tour the following summer. We therefore decided to postpone our ministry tour until the summer of 1996. I contacted Wilma Webb at Koopman's Travel and Peter Wisst at Icontas Service, as well as our tour contacts, to let them know of our decision. All of them expressed disappointment that we would not be coming in 1995, but said 1996 would work just as well.

As we prepared for our Christmas concert on December 4, 1994, it was apparent that we had made the correct decision to postpone the trip. David Dalke was so ill that he was no longer able to be a part of the ministry; in fact, we did not know if he would even be able to attend our Christmas concert. One piece on the program that night was Duane Funderburk's arrangement of "Hark, the Herald Angels Sing" for organ and orchestra. Just before the number was performed, Duane went to the microphone to tell the audience that David had collaborated with him in arranging the carol.

Duane then startled all of us by announcing, "David Dalke is in the audience tonight and this song is dedicated to him." David had been determined to somehow make it to our concert! He struggled to rise as the audience gave him a standing ovation. Tears streamed down the faces of everyone, since we knew David's days on earth were numbered. It was one of the most poignant moments I have ever experienced. David passed away less than two weeks later. All of us, especially Dan, felt an indescribable sense of loss for many months afterward.

Now that the ministry tour had been postponed until the summer of 1996, the choir had more breathing room to prepare for the trip. We were well along in the process of putting the ministry tour together and fine-tuning our SCRIP program, our major fundraising project. People earned SCRIP, a form of money similar to gift cards, whenever they shopped at participating stores in the community. These stores then gave a percentage of the SCRIP sales to the choir.

However, we discovered that choir members were slower to commit to the tour than they had been for our two earlier trips. Even so, we entered September with several positives. Members of the choir had been making regular payments into the ministry tour account, and the SCRIP program earnings were "going great guns." The choir had raised over $30,000 through SCRIP, and we still had ten months left before the trip. When we asked the choir to confirm their plans for the tour, seventy-six people indicated they were definitely committed to the 1995 tour, while others were seriously considering it.

We had already paid our airfare deposit to Koopman's Travel and were close to making our first payment to Icontas Service for the land portion of the tour. This deposit, due by September 19th, would be ten per cent of the anticipated land expenses. The September 19th date was also important because it was the last day we could cancel the trip without having to pay a cancellation penalty based on a pre-arranged minimum number of participants. We had decided to commit for seventy-six people, the actual number committed to the tour at that moment. The deposit payment would therefore be approximately $26,000.

We had this amount in our account, so we submitted a payment request to the church business office.

I wrote Peter Wisst of Icontas confirming that we were sending the deposit. The church business administrator told me there should be no problem getting the check drawn and sent. However, I was informed in late September that there had been a delay in processing the check, but that it would be mailed in a couple of days. Then I was told that a "hold" had been placed on the check. Naturally, I felt extremely frustrated and hoped that the problem could soon be resolved.

4

On a Monday in mid-October, 1995, Dan asked Mike Maduras and me to attend a meeting with him the next morning in the senior pastor's office. When we walked into the office the next day, we were surprised to see not only the pastor, but also the business administrator and the church chairman. Whatever was to be discussed, it was certainly serious! The chairman began by telling us that the meeting concerned our planned ministry tour the next summer. Then he asked a strange question: "Could your tour take place if Dan were not to go?" This question came out of the blue and filled us with dismay. After all, Dan was of sound mind, in good health, and was the minister of music and worship at Lake Avenue Church—and he was sitting right there! Why would he not lead the choir on tour? Mike and I breathed a prayer for guidance as we answered, "Dan is our director and ministry pastor, and his presence on the tour is mandatory unless the Lord directs otherwise."

The chairman's next statement was even more disconcerting. He said that since the church leaders could not guarantee that Dan would be able to go on the tour, they wanted us to cancel it. This information took us completely by surprise, but we suddenly realized why the deposit check had not been sent to Icontas. When we asked what possible reason would keep Dan from going on the tour, the church leaders responded, "Certain issues now under consideration by the church leadership may result in Dan's dismissal from his position at Lake Avenue Church." An awkward silence descended upon the room, but the Holy Spirit was not silent. His "still, small voice" clearly directed Mike and me to control our emotions and follow the church's instructions, no matter how upset we were.

I then raised the issue that we were now weeks beyond the penalty-free cancellation deadline date of September 19th. I reiterated that I, on the church's behalf and with its prior blessing, had confirmed in writing our commitment to guarantee the travel of at least 76 tour participants. Based on that commitment and prior to receiving our deposit, Peter Wisst—who trusted us to abide by our contractual agreement—proceeded to make various land arrangements for the tour. The church chairman then responded that he had checked with the church's attorney and had been advised that Lake Avenue Church did not owe any cancellation fee because the deposit had not been sent. Mike and I questioned the chairman carefully to make sure he understood the terms of our agreement with Icontas. Despite our efforts, he reiterated the church's position: Since they had not sent the deposit funds (despite having promised to do so and having agreed to pay cancellation penalties), Lake Avenue Church did not have to pay these fees.

After hours of discussion, I told the church leaders that I would immediately notify the Choir Cabinet, as well as Koopman's Travel, Icontas Service, and our ministry contacts that we had been directed by the church to cancel the 1996 European Ministry Tour. The pastor directed us not to discuss the tour cancellation with anyone at the church before he spoke to the Choir Cabinet on Friday evening. We agreed to notify the cabinet of the meeting and urged every cabinet member to be present. Ironically, Ildikó Barbarics had planned months before to arrive at our home on that Thursday and to stay through the weekend, so she would be there for the meeting.

The Choir Cabinet meeting on Friday was very discouraging. The pastor began by telling the cabinet that since there was a possibility Dan would no longer be at Lake Avenue by the summer, the tour needed to be canceled. He continued, "We hope that it will work out for Dan to remain at the church, since we respect and appreciate his outstanding job as minister of music and worship. I also want to make clear that the situation with Dan has nothing to do with his moral character. We all know Dan to be a man of God who is above reproach." He then repeated a phrase he had said during our meeting in his office: "If you love Dan, you will agree to cancel the tour." He used this phrase to ensure that we would agree to cancel the trip; he knew our love for Dan would supersede any desire we might have to go on tour.

As the meeting continued, Ildikó looked incredulous; she simply could not believe this was happening. She loved Dan and the choir and had come to know Dan as a fully-committed brother in Christ. She had worked hard to help the choir return to Hungary and had arranged all of our ministry opportunities there. Now it looked like everything she had done was falling apart. Dan himself was quiet, responding only when called upon. He looked like his whole world was crashing in on him, which indeed it was.

At the end of choir rehearsal the following Thursday, I handed out a letter to each choir member which summarized the reasons for the cancellation of the tour. The choir was in total shock. They could not believe that we had been directed to cancel the tour or that there was a possibility Dan would not be able to remain at Lake Avenue. It was a somber choir which left the church that evening.

The next day I wrote a letter to the church business administrator, asking him to return all monies which the tour participants had paid directly into their individual ministry tour accounts. I also reminded him that the Icontas cancellation fee would be fully covered by the money we had raised through SCRIP and other fundraising activities. Mike and I then told Wilma Webb at Koopman's Travel to return the choir's air travel deposit, less her legitimate expenses to date. We did this to avoid a fiasco similar to what Icontas was facing. As we requested, Wilma immediately remitted the air travel deposit, minus the expenses she had already incurred. The church leadership later criticized us for allowing Wilma to be reimbursed for her expenses, but by then the issue was moot.

In November I received a formal letter from Peter Wisst in which he reminded me that we owed Icontas Service a tour cancellation fee. He requested payment and enclosed a detailed financial breakdown of their claim. However, the church still maintained that we did not owe anything. Instead of replying to Peter Wisst's letter, they simply ignored it. In addition, I was told that under no circumstances was I to have any further contact with Peter. I felt terrible about the situation because we as a Christian choir had developed a close working relationship with Peter during our 1989 tour, which had encouraged him to work with us again. He had even proceeded with his plans and made commitments based on our word that written confirmation and deposits would follow.

Peter again made a request for payment in a December letter, adding that Icontas would pursue a legal remedy if payment in full was not received by December 30, 1995. I turned this letter over to the church leadership, hoping that it would cause them to honor the agreement with Icontas Service. In January, Icontas formally advised Lake Avenue Church that the matter had been referred to its attorney for collection. The church then retained an attorney to counter Icontas's action. We were told that because this dispute was now in the hands of attorneys, no one in the choir would be refunded the money in their individual tour accounts until all of this was settled.

After twelve months of haggling, Lake Avenue Church paid legal fees in excess of $15,000 to attorneys both in the U.S. and in Germany. In April of 1996 the church agreed to pay $30,000 to Icontas Service to settle the dispute, but they did not pay Icontas until October, a full year after the tour was canceled. The church also eventually refunded all monies paid by tour participants. Thus, Lake Avenue Church ended up having to pay more to settle the dispute than it would have cost them to promptly pay Icontas Service a year earlier. They also would have avoided being a poor testimony to our partners in Europe.

5

The Sanctuary Choir's music and worship ministry during the first months of 1996 seemed fairly normal to the congregation. The choir continued to sing for both Sunday morning worship services, worked on special music for Maundy Thursday and Easter, and began to prepare for a spring concert. But the Sword of Damocles hung over us.

On Wednesday evening, May 1, 1996, I received a call from Dan—a call which I will remember as long as I live. Dan said, "I just attended a meeting of the Church Ministry Council, who informed me that they have dismissed me from my position as minister of music and worship at Lake Avenue Church, effective immediately." I was in anguish as I heard these words. It felt as though an 18-wheeler had just rolled over me from head to toe. How does one cry from pain so great that tears will not come? Dan went on to explain that his keys had been taken away and that he had been directed not to set foot on the Lake Avenue campus for at least two weeks. He was not even allowed to retrieve any personal effects from his office.

The pastor and the church chairman said they wanted to address the choir at our next regular Thursday night rehearsal. I asked the members of the Choir Cabinet to meet in emergency session an hour before the rehearsal, when I advised them of Dan's termination. As choir members arrived, they were surprised to see the pastor, the church chairman, and the church business administrator—but not Dan. The sense that something was terribly wrong immediately swept through the room.

The chairman told the choir that Dan had been dismissed and that the choir would not be singing the next two Sundays. He also informed us that Duane Funderburk had agreed to take over direction of the choir on an interim basis. Someone asked why Dan had been let go, but the three church leaders did not give an answer. When the meeting was over, people remained stunned, obviously appalled about what had happened. They walked out of the room as if leaving an Irish wake—in complete silence.

As I looked ahead, I did not see how I could continue to serve in the music ministry of a church in which such a thing could take place. (In consideration of Dan and his family, I have been constrained from discussing details of Dan's dismissal.) My heart went out to Dan and his wife, Linda. Everything Dan had tried to accomplish with the choir and its ministry had seemed to implode. The "Out of the Loft" ministry had ended with the cancellation of the tour, and the choir's spring concert had been canceled due to Dan's departure. I found myself at a total loss. It was the death of a vision.

As an illustration of the birth, death, and eventual fulfillment of a vision, the Bible refers to the process of planting a grain of wheat. *"Truly, truly, I say to you, unless a grain of wheat falls into the earth and dies, it remains alone; but if it dies, it bears much fruit"* (John 12:24

– RSV). What seemed to be the death of the "Out of the Loft" ministry, the death of Dan's ministry, and the death of my ministry of assisting Dan and the choir were actually the beginning of something greater. God uses the "failure" of our vision to make us depend on Him for the outcome. If we are willing to wait, He often will replace our unfulfilled dreams with plans far greater than we could ever have envisioned.

Spiritually speaking, the next few months were one of the most difficult times of my life. I felt as cut off from ministry as if I had been the one terminated. I could not understand why God had allowed all of this to take place. Yet I knew deep in the very core of my being that the Lord was still in charge. I had to take hold of God's Word, especially the verse which says: *"I know what I'm doing. I have it all planned out—plans to take care of you, not abandon you, plans to give you the future you hope for."* (Jeremiah 29:11 – The Message)

I prayed that Bible verse for Dan as well as for myself. Even though I could not see how the Lord would heal my broken heart and use this situation for His glory, I had to trust Him and believe His Word. I was being called to take another huge step of faith and follow Him.

CHAPTER SIX

Ministry Restored

> *"The steadfast love of the LORD never ceases;*
> *His mercies never come to an end; they*
> *are new every morning;*
> *Great is Your faithfulness."*
> *Lamentations 3:22-23 (NRSV)*

During the twelve months following Dan Bird's dismissal from Lake Avenue Church, I felt totally at loose ends. My involvement in the music ministry had come to an end. As a result of my anger and bitterness toward the senior pastor and the church leadership, I had a hard time attending the worship services. Thus, June and I used the King's Couriers Sunday School class as our church involvement. We had been members of the class since we first began attending Lake Avenue back in 1971. It always had great teaching, and the people in the class gave June and me the fellowship and support we desperately needed.

I knew, however, that I needed to deal with my attitude—the anger and bitterness I held toward Lake Avenue Church. I would never be ready to move ahead with my life as long as I allowed these feelings to consume me. I must say that knowing this truth in my head was one thing; knowing it and living it in my heart was another. Over the following days, weeks, and months, Dan and I got together for "coffee" once or twice a week. Those times helped us to be open about what had happened, express our feelings, and discuss what we needed to do to move ahead. Both of us treasured these healing opportunities to share with one another.

Fortunately, we had experiences which made us laugh. One of these occurred the first week after Dan was dismissed. Dan had been instructed not to set foot on the Lake Avenue Church campus for at least two weeks. However, he was scheduled to conduct a wedding for one of our choir members within a few days, and the notes and materials he needed for the wedding were in his office. Dan asked me to drive him to the church so he could pick up the needed items. He had talked with Mark, Lake Avenue's organist, and Mark had agreed to meet Dan in the church music department.

I picked up Dan at his home and we drove to the church and its underground parking area. The music department is located under the sanctuary and can be accessed from the parking area without going through any other church facilities. As I drove in and approached the door leading into the worship center, I happened to see someone we knew. I told Dan to crouch on the floor so he would not be visible. Then I drove around like I was looking for a parking space until the person could no longer be seen. Finally, I drove up to the door and let Dan out, telling him I would join him in Mark's office as soon as I had parked the car.

When I took the stairs down to the music facilities to join Dan in Mark's office, no one else seemed to be there. Mark contacted a custodian who he felt could be trusted not to say anything about Dan's presence, and the custodian graciously unlocked the door to Dan's office and let us in. Dan quickly found his wedding materials, so we had not been there long when we heard "Bird Alert! Bird Alert!" over the loudspeakers. Evidently someone had seen us and had notified the church office.

I told Dan I would get the car and would wait for him at the door to the parking area, but I asked him to stay put for a few minutes before he left the security of Mark's office to make his escape. In less than five minutes, I had the car ready and Dan dashed out the door and jumped in. I gunned the engine and we went flying out of the parking area. I remarked to Dan, "I feel like we're a couple of thieves trying to make our escape after a bank heist!" At that, Dan and I broke out laughing over the absurdity of the whole situation. It was good to have something to laugh about! I should add that the wedding went off without a hitch.

Dan was not able to retrieve his belongings from his office for several weeks. Finally, he made arrangements to meet the business administrator, who agreed to let Dan into his office and workroom so he could pack up his things. Dan asked me to go along to help him with his packing, but I knew the real reason he wanted me with him—so I could serve as a possible buffer with people who might find out he was there and want to talk to him. He told me to stay close to him whenever anyone entered the music department. Later, the senior pastor did come to see Dan. Even though the pastor seemed to indicate that he wanted to be alone with Dan, I ignored his signals and held my ground. He finally gave up after simply greeting Dan and asking how he was—to Dan's great relief. It took Dan several days to pack up all of the possessions he had accumulated over the past fifteen years.

By the beginning of 1997, life seemed to be returning to normal—whatever that was. Tony Bohlin and I had planned to put together a special documentary video the church could use for its centennial celebration in the fall of 1996; however, we had put that project aside when Dan left. Then we thought of producing a documentary about Dan's fifteen years at Lake Avenue, which we would call "A Celebration of

Ministry." We loved the idea and began to plan what we would include. I now had a new project to which I could devote my energy! I began by developing an outline for the video, writing narration, and selecting all of the music for the production. We eventually chose thirty-six pieces of music which represented all the years of Dan's ministry. June and I drove up to Cottonwood in February so Tony and I could edit and produce the video. We stayed there for almost a month before Tony and I were able to complete the two-hour video project.

We brought the video home and set a date for a "preview showing" to a select group of people. In addition to Dan and his family, we invited people who had been especially close to Dan. Everyone there felt nostalgic as we relived the fifteen years of Dan's ministry, but the video also reminded us of how the Lord had used those years in a powerful way. Since that evening we have shown the video to many other people. Tony and I also produced a two-disc CD of all the music from the video. The video and the CDs proved to be important instruments in the healing process we were all going through.

In the spring of 1997, Dan heard that Solana Beach Presbyterian Church in San Diego County was looking for a full-time person to replace its part-time choir director/organist, who had resigned. The church's new senior pastor, Dr. Roberta Hestenes, was impressed with Dan's musical abilities, as well as his Christian testimony and vision for ministry. In June, Solana Beach extended a call to Dan to become their new minister of music. When Dan phoned to tell me the good news, I was thrilled for him! He officially began his new position on August 1, 1997.

Around this time, June and I began thinking about selling our house and moving to Prescott, Arizona. Several of our Pasadena friends had moved there and we loved the community. In the meantime, we visited Solana Beach Presbyterian on several occasions. Then Dan called and asked me to sing with the Chancel Choir for their Christmas concert.

He said I would know most of the music and would be a great help. I did not have to think twice before answering, "You can't keep me away!"

When I first walked into the choir rehearsal at Solana Beach Church, I felt somewhat uncomfortable, even though several other people from the Sanctuary Choir at Lake Avenue were also there to help out. But it wasn't long before I realized that the Solana Beach choir was a wonderfully welcoming group of people who made me feel right at home. Bob Bates, in particular, made a point of integrating me into their Chancel Choir. I recognized in him the same care and concern for the choir that Ed Fischer had shown at Lake Avenue. In all of the years since then, the love and caring of the Solana Beach choir has been confirmed to us again and again.

While we were at Solana Beach that weekend, we talked with Lorraine and Bob, former members of Lake Avenue Church and good friends of the Fischers. They mentioned that their daughter and son-in-law had recently bought a home nearby. Even though we told her that we were thinking about moving to Prescott, Lorraine suggested that we look at homes in the Solana Beach area. In fact, she put us in contact with Dorothy, the real estate agent who had helped their daughter. Dorothy was also a member of Solana Beach Presbyterian. She showed us several homes in the area, but all of the places we liked were too expensive.

The year 1998 was beginning to look like a much better year for us. Dan was very happy in his new position, which made us believe that life was indeed "moving on." June and I were also looking forward to a month-long visit with our friends from Pohlheim, Günter and Adelheid Wehrenfennig. After having stayed with the Wehrenfennigs several times in Germany, we were delighted to finally be able to return the favor and host them. This would be their first time in the United States, so we wanted to show them as much of the country as possible.

The day after they arrived, we drove down to Solana Beach to attend church and have lunch with Dan. Adelheid told me after the service how much she had loved the worship experience, the music, and the message. Then the four of us went out to lunch with Dan at the Beach House, a restaurant overlooking the Pacific Ocean that had become one of Dan's favorites. Günter and Adelheid were so happy to see Dan again! They had been terribly upset by what had happened to him and were encouraged to see how well he was doing in his new position. The time we had together that Sunday underscored the ongoing impact of the "Out of the Loft" ministry.

Since the Wehrenfennigs would be with us for several weeks, we took two extended trips: a five-day trip to the Grand Canyon and a seven-day trip to Yosemite and the Monterey Peninsula. We visited Prescott on our way to the Grand Canyon and showed the Wehrenfennigs a home we hoped to buy. They loved it and encouraged us to move there. However, by the time they had left and we had a chance to check on things in Prescott, the house had been sold. We then decided to buy a lot and build a new house on it. That summer we put our home in Pasadena up for sale, expecting to have a new house in Prescott within a few months—only to run into major problems with our builder.

Then Dorothy, the realtor from Solana Beach, "happened" to call us to find out where we were in the process of buying a house. She said she had seen some homes in that area we might be interested in. June and I figured that it wouldn't hurt to drive to San Diego County and see what was available. Dorothy showed us several homes, the last of which was in the Laurels development in the city of San Marcos. It was the same development where June and I had almost bought a new home several years before. Dorothy then asked us whether we would mind if she looked at another home in the development which she had been trying to see. We were looking for a one-story home between 1,800 and 2,000 square feet, while the home Dorothy took us to see was a two-story, 2,900 square foot home on a corner lot. It turned out to be the very same model we had almost bought back in 1993.

When we walked into the house, both June and I fell in love with it—even though it was everything we were not looking for. We decided to stop our plans for Prescott and made an offer on the home before we returned to Pasadena that afternoon. Within two days, we were in escrow on both homes and were getting ready to move in a month. Wow! God often makes us wait, but when He wants to move, He moves fast!

I thought I should call Dan to let him know what was happening. He knew about our plans to move to Prescott, so when I told him we had finally sold our home and would be moving, I could hear the disappointment in his voice. Then I added, "We're moving to San Marcos." There was a pause, then a shout of joy, as Dan realized we would be living near him. It looked like our ministry together was not ending after all! Just what it would entail in the future I did not know, but I was excited to find out what God had planned for us.

We moved into our new home on Saturday, October 10, 1998, and attended Solana Beach Presbyterian Church the next day. The following Thursday I joined the Chancel Choir. Incredibly, I was resuming my music ministry with Dan after a two-year hiatus. It felt so good and so right! We missed our many friends in the Pasadena area, but we started to develop new relationships—June with the Christian Women's Club in San Marcos, and I with the Chancel Choir. We were beginning a new chapter in our lives.

When Dan was dismissed from Lake Avenue Church, I felt that everything he and I had worked for had come to an end. However, God restored Dan's ministry, the "Out of the Loft" ministry, and my ministry to Dan and the choir. I believe that this incredible "turn-around" is an example of the principle proclaimed in Joel 2:25 (NIV): *"I will repay for you the years the locusts have eaten."* Other versions translate this verse, *"I will give you back what you lost"* (GNB) and *"I will pay you back for those years of trouble"* (NCV). Only God could have transformed such a great tragedy into a tremendous blessing!

John 12:24 (RSV), the verse I mentioned at the end of Chapter 5, came true: *"Truly, truly, I say to you, unless a grain of wheat falls into the earth and dies, it remains alone; but if it dies, it bears much fruit."* The "Out of the Loft" ministry, on which the Chancel Choir at Solana Beach Presbyterian embarked just a few years after the debacle at Lake Avenue Church, is just one part of the "much fruit" which has resulted from the death of that vision.

In addition, God performed a miracle "beyond what we could ask or think." Several years later, He restored our relationship with Lake Avenue Church. First, John Sutton, Lake Avenue's current choir director, invited Dan and Linda to attend their choir's fall retreat in 2004. Since the retreat would be held away from the church, John assured Dan that only the choir would be present. That weekend was a wonderful time for Dan and Linda as they renewed relationships with former choir members.

In 2006 and 2007, Lake Avenue Church was in a time of transition between senior pastors. In April of 2007, John Sutton arranged for our Chancel Choir to join Lake Avenue's Sanctuary Choir in Pasadena for a weekend. The Lake Avenue choir prepared a dinner for our choir late Saturday afternoon, prior to a rehearsal that evening in the sanctuary. They also hosted about half of our choir members in their homes for the night. (The rest of the choir was able to make their own housing arrangements.)

This was the first time Dan would take part in a worship service at Lake Avenue since he had left in 1996. In the Sunday morning services, John Sutton first introduced our choir and then enthusiastically welcomed Dan back to Lake Avenue. Immediately the entire congregation rose to give Dan a long standing ovation. I cannot describe the emotion of that moment. Tears flowed down faces throughout the choir loft and the congregation. The pain of Dan's separation from Lake Avenue Church and the Sanctuary Choir melted away, and the tension between the two churches was replaced with a joyous spirit of reconciliation and renewal. Among the many people who came over to greet Dan personally was the former church chairman, who welcomed Dan with a big hug. It was as if the huge dark cloud which had been hanging over our lives had been lifted and had been replaced by the love and power of the Holy Spirit. The next month, our choir returned the favor and hosted the Lake Avenue choir at Solana Beach. Our collaboration with them has continued to this day. I am constantly amazed how God lovingly heals broken hearts and broken relationships.

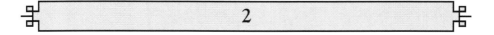

2

When Dan first came to Solana Beach, the choir did not have any formal organization. During his first year he wisely chose to focus on getting to know all of the choir members and letting them get to know him. It was not until January of 1999 that Dan decided it was time to form a Choir Cabinet, a group of choir leaders who would come alongside Dan in carrying out the music ministry of the choir. By that time, he had seen people in the choir display their leadership skills in various church activities. Dan's philosophy was to select choir leaders whose skills would complement his own. Dan asked a multi-talented choir member, Lee Hawley, to take on the responsibility of choir president. Lee had served in a number of church leadership capacities, all of them with great skill. Dan told me he wanted me on the cabinet to oversee an "Out of the Loft" ministry. Since this concept was totally new to the

Chancel Choir, we used the first couple of years to help choir members understand what such a ministry might mean for the choir and the church.

Every church and every choir has its own personality, so we did not expect the Chancel Choir Cabinet to be a copy of the choir cabinet at Lake Avenue Church. For example, cabinet meetings at Lake Avenue tended to be less structured and often went on late into the night, while the meetings of the Chancel Choir Cabinet were much more structured, as is common in Presbyterian churches. During Solana Beach cabinet meetings, choir leaders went straight through the evening's agenda, dealt quickly with each topic, and then moved on to the next item. Someone commented to me after one of our meetings, "Congratulations to the cabinet on completing the meeting in record time!" It had lasted less than an hour! Somehow all of the necessary business was accomplished at these meetings, even though they were different from what I was used to.

In June of 2000 we began a new ministry for the choir: recording choir concerts and making them available to the choir members. Tony Bohlin had been responsible for the audio and video recordings of our concerts at Lake Avenue even after he and his family moved to Northern California. However, bringing him down to the San Diego area to record concerts was just not feasible. Fortunately, Mike Maduras was also capable of making audio recordings. In fact, he had done the recording engineering for Lake Avenue's Christmas CD entitled "Unto Us," which we had been able to sell to the congregation. With Mike's help, in June of 2001 the Chancel Choir made its first recording—a spring concert called "Songs of the Ages." It was a program featuring music in a variety of styles from different periods, with full orchestra. Now that choir members could hear what their singing sounded like, they could not only enjoy the music but also hear how they needed to improve.

Since then, the Chancel Choir at Solana Beach Presbyterian has made over twenty-five recordings, including four which we made available to the congregation. These recordings document what the choir has accomplished musically since 1997. I never dreamed that my collaboration with Mike Maduras and Tony Bohlin would continue after Dan left Lake Avenue, but it has. Mike now records all of our concerts; then I take his raw recording up to the Bohlins so Tony and I can edit and produce a CD of the concert. In fact, the four of us—Dan Bird, Mike Maduras, Tony Bohlin, and I—have been in ministry together for over thirty years. What a testimony to the faithfulness of God!

In March of 1999 the choir received a letter from Ildikó Barbarics in Hungary challenging us to consider a ministry tour in Hungary. Ildikó had been instrumental in getting Lake Avenue's choir to minister behind the Iron Curtain in 1989. That tour had been so successful that Ildikó had tried to get Dan's choir to return to Eastern Europe ever since. Ildikó came to the United States in October and visited our church and choir. At that time, she personally extended the same invitation to the Chancel Choir to minister in Hungary.

About a year later, Erhard Jung and his family also visited us. Erhard brought with him a letter from the church council of the Christus Kirche in Pohlheim, Germany, inviting our choir to sing in their church and stay in the homes of people in their congregation. These two invitations led the Chancel Choir Cabinet to seriously seek the Lord's direction for a possible ministry tour to Europe.

One cabinet meeting, which was held in our home on a Saturday morning in October of 2001, was pivotal in the planning process. This was the first meeting of a new Choir Cabinet with a new choir president, Judy Enns. The most challenging item on the agenda was whether or not the choir should move ahead with plans for a European ministry tour in the summer of 2003. Did we believe God was calling us at this time, or should we delay such plans until a new senior pastor had been called? Roberta Hestenes had recently accepted a call to become "minister at large" for the staff of World Vision in Seattle, so Solana Beach Presbyterian was in the process of finding a new senior pastor.

I had prepared a resolution for the cabinet's consideration which stated that the choir had been called to an "Out of the Loft" ministry. A long and heated discussion ensued, so I was not at all sure that the resolution would pass. Just when it seemed that it might be voted down, Judy Enns expressed her conviction that our choir was indeed being called to this ministry. Judy then asked for a time of prayer.

After we finished praying, we took a vote. Most of the Cabinet voted "yes," setting the choir on a course which would lead to the 2003 ministry tour. When the cabinet meeting was over, outgoing choir president Lee Hawley told everyone that even though she had voted "no" on the resolution, she was a "team player" and that she and her husband, Chuck, would do whatever it took to make the tour a success. Lee's action displayed a depth of character and integrity that I could not help but admire.

Now that the Choir Cabinet had sensed the call, each choir member was asked to pray about his or her own participation in the tour. Responding to God's call was a process which began in the fall of 2001 and was not completed until shortly before the choir went on tour in the summer of 2003. Because the Iraq War had begun, some people were uneasy about traveling abroad. At times, it appeared doubtful that we would have a balanced choir. But God was true to His Word: *"The One who calls you is faithful and He will do it"* (I Thessalonians 5:24 – NIV).

The Choir Cabinet submitted "A Proposal for Ministry" to the church's leaders during their Session meeting in February of 2002 and requested their formal approval for the tour. This approval was given in March. That action by the Session allowed the choir to open a tour account and begin planning for various fundraising projects which had been approved by the Session and the SBPC Finance Committee.

We also let the congregation know about the tour ministry; the official "publicity launch" began in May of 2002. Over the next year, information about the ministry tour was shared from the pulpit, as well as in both the weekly and monthly "Life Together" church publications. Choir representatives also manned a music ministry table in the patio every Sunday morning. Anyone attending Solana Beach Presbyterian Church would have had to be a "Rip Van Winkle" not to know about the choir's upcoming ministry to Eastern Europe.

The response of Solana Beach Presbyterian Church to our proposed ministry tour was completely different from the response of Lake Avenue Church to our proposed tours. At Lake Avenue Church we had received approval for the ministry tours, but no financial assistance. At Solana Beach, on the other hand, the pastors and church leaders were unanimous in their support for the ministry and approved several projects to help us raise a significant amount of financial support. We felt as if the entire church was involved in sending us on the ministry tour—which indeed they were.

As a result of the two ministry tours Dan and I had conducted at Lake Avenue, we had past history and experience to draw upon this time. However, we were determined that this mission would not be just a repeat of what we had done before. We realized that for the Solana Beach Chancel Choir this was a totally new venture.

One of the first things we did was to form the Ministry Tour Planning Task Force. Based on past experience, we knew that the task force should include at least five committees: Travel Planning, Fundraising, Medical Planning, Tour Documentation, and Communications and Prayer Support. At the suggestion of Lee Hawley, we added a Physical Fitness Preparedness Committee. Lee realized that the tour would be physically demanding and that we needed to "get in shape" for the trip. Each of these committees then recruited other church people to serve on sub-committees, increasing the church's level of involvement.

Finally, to coordinate all the committees we added a Steering Committee composed of the chairs and co-chairs of each task force committee. This was truly a monumental project and required the involvement of everyone in the choir, whether or not they were going on the tour. Choir spouses also joined in the tour planning. Without the help of so many people, it would have been impossible to put together a ministry tour.

The two committees which needed to get going as soon as possible were the Travel Planning and the Fundraising Committees. It seemed like a good idea to have two people as co-chairs of the Travel Planning Committee, so I asked Linda Smith, who ran her own travel business, to help me with this huge task. I brought my experience from planning the two Lake Avenue tours and Linda brought her expertise as a travel agent. The committee discussed how we could find the best firm to handle our land and flight arrangements. Linda suggested that it would be best if the two responsibilities were handled separately. We had done this for Lake Avenue's 1989 tour, and the decision to separate the two responsibilities also worked out well for our 2003 trip.

We located the names of tour providers whom we knew from previous experience, who had been recommended to us, or who had expressed an interest in bidding on the tour. On March 21, our committee sent three potential tour providers a 19-page bidding document and gave them two months to submit a formal bid in compliance with the bidding document. As it turned out, only Icontas Service, the company we had used for land arrangements on the 1989 tour, submitted a bid. Dan and I had been pleased with the way Icontas had carried out the 1989 tour's land arrangements and by the personal involvement of Peter Wisst, the president of Icontas Service, so we were happy to work with them again.

To be honest, I wondered how Peter would react to our new tour proposal after the way Lake Avenue Church had treated him when the church canceled the planned 1996 tour. Peter, however, told us he did not hold this against us because it was not the Choir Cabinet who had failed to comply with the 1996 agreement. In fact, Peter said he was looking forward to working with us again. Linda Smith offered to assume the responsibility for our flight arrangements, on the condition that she would receive no compensation for her work to avoid any appearance of a conflict of interest. Linda and the people at Icontas Service did everything they could to ensure that all of our travel arrangements went smoothly.

The second committee which needed to get moving right away was the Fundraising Committee. The smartest thing we did in all of our tour planning was asking Marguerite Walker to serve as the chairperson for this essential committee. Her dedication and organizational skills are unsurpassed. The Finance Committee had to make a number of important decisions. First, they needed to decide how we would raise and collect the money for the tour. They knew the importance of keeping accurate financial records, so they opened a tour account with the church, into which all designated gifts and payments from participating choir members would be deposited, and from which all tour expenses would be paid. An individual account was also set up for each person going on the tour.

The Steering Committee then developed a tour budget based on the best information we had at that time. We also set up a tour payment schedule, the dates when each tour expenditure needed to be paid and the dates when tour participants were required to make a payment. We based the tour budget on several factors—a total of 80 tour participants, a per-person cost for land arrangements of 2,890 euros, airfare costs of no more than $1,050 per person, and money for Dan and my planning trip to Europe in August of 2002.

The Fundraising Committee set a goal of raising $100,000 through a variety of fundraising projects which had been approved by the church

Session at the same time it had approved the tour itself. Marguerite Walker shared what it was like to handle such a daunting task. *"In 2002, when the choir made the decision to go on a European tour, I offered to organize the SCRIP program. Having been a parent volunteer at our sons' schools, I was familiar with selling gift certificates and gift cards to raise money. The next thing I knew, I was chairing the whole Fundraising Committee. It became a full-time job. We had only eighteen months to raise the funds needed to cover the choir tour ministry expenses. Two years was preferable. The committee selected fundraising projects that were appropriate for the choir and its talents: a gala dinner/auction, a musical revue, an all-church cookbook, Christmas caroling, and selling SCRIP. We were uncertain of the amount we needed to raise, so we estimated the income from each project and set a goal of raising $100,00.*

God was good and provided what was needed. Choir members and spouses volunteered and worked tirelessly on each project. A special camaraderie developed among them—those going on tour and those staying home. The congregation generously donated money and auction items, contributed recipes, purchased SCRIP, hired carolers, and attended our events. Dedicated choir spouses, led by Nick Stahl, sold SCRIP on the patio every Sunday morning. Not once in eighteen months did it rain during that Sunday morning time. To our amazement and relief, we met and exceeded our fundraising goal. When all of the fundraising projects were completed, we had raised approximately $107,000! The money covered the ministry tour expenses, and there was enough money to provide scholarships and pay for some unanticipated expenses."

The musical revue involved all choir members and took us out of our comfort zone. It is one thing to sing in a choir of 75 to 90 voices, and quite another to participate in small ensembles, duets, or quartets. Putting together such a complicated show requires a producer. We were fortunate that choir member Karen Troeber had produced similar events in the past, so she assumed that post for the choir. Karen assembled the fantastic group of choir members and spouses who made up the musical revue team.

They decided that the production would portray the progression of popular music in America from 1900 to the present; therefore, they called it "Ragtime to Rock and all that Jazz." Karen's husband, Jeff, wrote a fascinating narration tying together all of the periods of music. Karen was also able to con Tom Theriault, our pastor for mission and outreach, to be the narrator. Choir members learned music for the show, sewed costumes, worked as stage crews and lighting and sound technicians, did artwork and publicity, and helped with just about everything else. This show would not be another "choir talent show," but a full-blown production. We amazed ourselves by what we were able to do. The result was such a success that some attendees said our show should be "taken on the road." More importantly, several key members of the choir were so taken by the revue that they decided to commit to the tour.

While the budget estimates generally proved to be accurate, two factors had a major impact on the actual tour expenses. First, we did not reach the projected number of 80 tour participants; the final total was 75 people, eight of whom would participate in only part of the tour. This made it necessary for Icontas Service to increase the per-person cost. Secondly, the lower value of the dollar resulted in substantially higher costs for our land arrangements. Instead of making payments at an exchange rate of 1$ = 1.02 euros, we ended up making payments at the average dollar value of 1$ = 0.90 euros.

One redeeming factor was that the $100,000+ we had raised allowed us to give scholarship assistance to approximately twenty people who otherwise would not have been able to go on the tour. It also enabled us to keep the per-person cost at $4,200; otherwise, we would have had to increase the amount by several hundred dollars a person. God's provision for our tour expenses confirmed the truth of Matthew 6:33 (NIV): *"But seek first His kingdom and His righteousness, and all these things will be given to you as well."*

3

It had been eight years since Dan and I were in Europe together on our last, ill-fated planning trip, so we were excited about returning there in August of 2002. I contacted many of the people we knew in Europe to see if Dan and I could meet with them to make arrangements for the choir's 2003 European Ministry Tour. We praised the Lord that we were able to schedule meetings in every place we felt the Lord was leading us—with the help of Erhard Jung in Pohlheim, Ildikó Barbarics in Budapest, and Dieter Wunderlich in Berlin. Shortly before we left, June and I took a quick trip up to Cottonwood to pick up a $3,000 digital video camera which Tony Bohlin had agreed to loan me for the planning trip. I was a little nervous about taking such an expensive and complicated camera to Europe and wondered whether I would be able to tape enough good material for our planning trip video. Actually, we came back with the best video we had ever taken, praise the Lord.

On Thursday, August 1st, Dan and I flew from LAX to Frankfurt, Germany on Lufthansa Airlines. Thanks to Linda Smith, we had advance reservations for a rental car and soon picked up an Opal Vectra. After we found our way to the Dorint Hotel in Mainz and had some lunch, we decided to reacquaint ourselves with the city. With our trusty Michelin city map in hand, we took off for the town Marktplatz, the

Dom (cathedral), and the Rhine River. By the time we made it back to the hotel, we were exhausted. Dan was in bed and sound asleep by 6:00 p.m., while I read for a few minutes and then hit the sack myself.

The weather was beautiful the next day as we headed north to the city of Pohlheim, where we would stay with Günter and Adelheid Wehrenfennig for the weekend. Our relationship with them had continued to grow since our the first ministry tour in 1984, so driving back into Pohlheim for the first time since 1994 was like coming home! Several friends were there to greet us: Günter and Adelheid, their son and daughter-in-law Martin and Annette, and Edith and Erhard Jung. We spent most of the day catching up on news about our families. On Sunday we attended the morning worship service in the Christus Kirche and then met with the leaders of the church council and choir. They told us they would translate our tour program and publicity materials into German, print the programs, and then send this material to each of our German ministry sites—which would be a great help to us.

On Monday we began our journey into the eastern parts of Germany, following almost the same route we had taken on our 1994 planning trip, except that the majority of the 2003 ministry tour would be in Eastern Europe. Our first destination was the town of Eisenach. We had an appointment with the cantor—the church choir director and organist—of the Georgenkirche (St. George's Church), the most prominent church in town. Shortly before our meeting with him, I tripped on a step and fell. On the way down, all I could think about was holding onto Tony's $3,000 video camera. Fortunately, I managed to save the camera, but I hit the ground and badly scraped my right knee and the back of my left hand.

The Lord was obviously watching over me that day. None of my wounds became infected and my knee, though quite sore, was not damaged. I attribute my lack of serious injury to the many people who were covering our trip in prayer. Before we left, I had prepared a special planning trip prayer calendar and passed it out to the choir. This incident illustrates that *"The prayer of a righteous person is powerful and effective"* (James 5:16 – NIV).

After stopping in Erfurt, we arrived in Leipzig, one of the great historic cities in Germany. After forty years behind the Iron Curtain, Leipzig had become rather rundown. We had seen a few improvements when we were there in 1994, but now, only eight years later, the city looked much more modern. We were especially happy to see that the Thomaskirche (St. Thomas Church), in which Bach served as organist and choir director for many years, had been completely renovated and restored.

While we were in Leipzig, we met the pastor of the Paul Gerhardt Kirche, which we had visited in 1994. The church's pastor, Reinhard Enders, was an unforgettable person—he had a beard which stretched down almost to his waist! He had struggled with cancer, but that day he was celebrating being cancer-free for one year. Pastor Enders called it "my first birthday." He was delighted that our choir would sing at his church in 2003. Dan and I then drove to the city of Halle, the birthplace of George Frederick Handel. We met with the cantor of the Marktkirche, the city's major Protestant church located on the Market Square. The cantor was a gracious and helpful young man who offered his church as the site for a concert the following year.

Berlin held many memories for us. We would never forget our 1989 concert in the Gethsemane Kirche in East Berlin with the police stationed all around the church watching those who came to hear us. We also remembered the wonderful reception we had received from the East German audience and the encouragement our program had brought to their lives. In 2002, there were no border crossings between "East" and "West," and tremendous building and restoration had made Berlin once again the proud capital of a united Germany. Dieter Wunderlich had set up a number of appointments for us in Berlin. One of them was

As in past tours, we decided to have our program translated into each of the languages we would encounter—German, Czech, and Hungarian—as well as English. We also wanted these programs to be printed in the country where each language was spoken. Erhard Jung in Pohlheim arranged for the translation and printing of the German program. Unfortunately, he did not understand that the words to all of the songs needed to be translated into German. Therefore, when we arrived in Pohlheim for our first concert, we found that the words to the music were still in English. Wolfgang Bluhm, a choir member who was born and raised in Germany, saved the day by translating all of the words into German after we got there—a gigantic task. He then had a supplement printed and inserted in the program in time for our second concert in Eisenach.

We had the same problem in the Czech Republic. The Hungarian programs, however, were flawless. Ildikó Barbarics had translated the program into Hungarian and had arranged for it to be printed by Word of Life Hungary. Many people told us after every concert how much they appreciated being able to read the program in their own language.

During the previous three years, the choir had recorded its spring and Christmas concerts. We had also produced a professional recording called "Sing to The Lord." We decided we would take the best numbers from all of our previous recordings and place them on a new CD entitled "God Is Our Song." Tony Bohlin, who had worked with me on the editing and graphics for our previous recordings, helped us with this project as well, and Audio Outreach produced the 10,000 CDs we would take with us. After every concert, people clutched their choir CDs as they left the church. They were touched that we would give them a CD as a gift, since most other choirs charged for their recordings. We had always considered our complimentary recordings to be part of our ministry, and that is exactly how our CDs were received by the people in Europe.

Whenever a large group of people goes on a long trip and is under a fair amount of stress, the heavy physical demands on them can lead to illness or injury. We had learned from the tours in 1984 and 1989 how important it is to develop a medical team, so we put a great deal of thought into preparing for any medical issues which might arise on the 2003 tour. A choir bass, Dr. Richard Henderson, talked with Tony Bohlin about the medical preparation Tony had done for the two Lake Avenue tours.

"Doc" Henderson immediately caught the vision and began to put together the tour medical team, which consisted of three doctors, one nurse practitioner, and three nurses. The number of medical personnel we had on the 2003 trip exceeded the number of medical professionals on either of the Lake Avenue tours. Everyone going on the trip was required to complete a medical information form and to have a medical clearance form signed by a doctor. Dr. Henderson then asked Sylvia, one of our choir members, to upload the information onto the computer so the forms could be reviewed at a moment's notice.

Three major documents proved to be very valuable for the tour. The first of these was a prayer calendar, a detailed day-to-day list of specific prayer requests for the ministry tour. It also included a map which showed all of the places the choir was scheduled to minister. Fifteen hundred of the prayer calendars were distributed to people throughout the congregation, as well as to many others who had committed to praying for our ministry. One cannot overestimate the importance of the concerted prayer which led to the success of the ministry tour. Tom Theriault, Solana Beach's pastor for mission and outreach, also wrote a devotional guide for each day of the tour, based on the Apostle Paul's letter to the Philippians. The devotional guide kept everyone focused on why we were in Europe: to share the love, joy, and hope of Jesus Christ. The third document was a tour information packet for the tour participants, which contained ideas about how to prepare for the trip, a detailed itinerary, a description of all the places the choir would be singing, and a copy of the tour insurance policy. It also included a personal name tag and individual laminated luggage tags color-coded to each bus. If anything, we were over-organized!

Choosing bus captains was another important task. These people were responsible for making sure that all of those assigned to the bus were there when they were supposed to be. This was not an easy task, especially when a bus was ready to leave and someone was not there. We asked all tour participants to tell their bus captain if they would not be on the bus for any reason. Even though being a bus captain is the quintessential "thankless" job, Charlotte and Mary in the "blue bus" and Ann and Nick in the "yellow bus" did an outstanding job of keeping everyone in line. They also somehow managed to stay friends with the people on their bus!

From the very beginning, the choir leaders believed it was vital to document the ministry tour through audio recordings of every concert and a video of the entire tour. Tony Bohlin had done all of the audio and video work on our previous tours, but he was not able to go with us this time. Similarly, Mike Maduras, who had done the engineering for our audio recordings at Solana Beach, had to stay home because of job commitments. However, Tony and Mike still came through for us. Tony loaned us digital video equipment valued at $3,600, while Mike let us use $13,000 worth of audio recording equipment. I prayed fervently that nothing would happen to any of this marvelous equipment while we were on tour!

However, we still needed someone with audio-visual experience who knew how to use this incredible equipment. The Lord supplied our need in the person of Rich Williams, a 31-year-old young man who had been responsible for recording all events in the San Diego Convention Center for several years. When I contacted Rich, he immediately said he would love to go with us. He and his crew did a superb job of recording all of our concerts, and they caught the heart of the ministry tour. We came back with 80 digital videotapes of the tour and 18 DAT (digital audio tapes) of our concerts.

The Steering Committee brought up one matter which we had not thought about: What would we do if our accompanist, Susie Shick, was unable to go on the tour or got sick during the trip? We agreed that it would be good to have someone who could fill in for Susie if needed, so I contacted Nancy Lewis Davis, a former Lake Avenue choir member who was currently living in Arizona. Nancy had accompanied the Lake Avenue choir several times in the past and was willing to serve as the "back-up" accompanist on our ministry tour. She roomed with Lauren Finalet, Dan's 15-year-old granddaughter. Dan's wife, Linda, was not able to go on the trip due to medical issues, so Dan was pleased and proud that Lauren could be part of the tour. She has an excellent voice and was able to learn and memorize all of the music in time.

God also provided the tenor soloist we needed. Someone told Dan about a talented tenor, Mike Rosensteel, at Rancho Bernardo Community Presbyterian Church. Dan put in a call to the church and talked with Mike about joining the tour. Mike had graduated from San Diego State University with a major in music and was currently directing the youth music ministry at his church. During their phone conversation, Mike told Dan an unusual story. The night before Dan's call, Mike had been watching a TV travel documentary about Germany. Mike, who is of German descent, thought about how wonderful it would be to travel to Germany someday and view the beautiful sights he had seen in the documentary. Then he received the call from Dan the next day! His reply to Dan was an immediate "yes!" It was obvious that having Mike Rosensteel join our Chancel Choir on tour was a match made in heaven.

Only a week before we were scheduled to leave for Europe, Icontas Service advised us that we needed to fill out a "Carnet" for all of our equipment. We should have thought of it earlier, but somehow I had assumed that with the fall of the Iron Curtain, we would not need a Carnet as we had in 1989. Even though Linda Smith, like her counterpart for the 1989 tour, had never heard of a "Carnet," she got right on it. Within three days we had a Carnet listing all of the handbell and the audio-video equipment we were taking with us. That in itself was an amazing feat.

I got another surprise just four days before we were to leave. Erhard Jung called from Pohlheim to tell me that the Christus Kirche had recently been closed due to a problem with termites or some other wood-eating pests in their church ceiling and attic. Since we would not be able to give our concert in their church, we would be singing in the Catholic church instead. "Not to worry," Erhard said. "Everything will work out." Joe Leonards also sent me an email at the last minute saying that due to new security restrictions, he would not be able to meet us in the baggage claim area at the Frankfurt airport to help get our equipment and CDs through customs. Since I have a tendency to be a "worrier," I imagined us delayed for hours trying to get clearance for all of our equipment. However, like most things we worry about, this situation never happened.

One last "wrinkle" concerned our tickets. When the airline tickets were delivered, Linda Smith discovered that Lufthansa had changed our flight. We thought we were leaving LAX at 2:55 p.m., but we had been booked on a flight leaving at 7:00 p.m. instead. It turned out that the later flight worked even better for most of the tour participants. I chided myself for not trusting God with these details.

Neither June nor I slept very well the night before our departure as we contemplated the adventure ahead. I awoke early the next morning, June 26th, eagerly anticipating what the Lord would do in and through all of us on our Eastern European Ministry Tour.

CHAPTER SEVEN

Dawn of a New Day

> *"Greet the dawning, greet the morning,*
> *Greet the Lord with a joyful song.*
> *Day's beginning, start with singing,*
> *Gather with the joyous throng."*
> *From "Greet the Dawning" by Jan Sanborn*
> *Words by Bryan Jeffery Leech*

The 2003 Eastern European Ministry Tour was truly the dawn of a new day. Even though Dan Bird and I had completed two tours with the Lake Avenue Church choir, this was the first time anyone from Solana Beach Presbyterian had attempted such a ministry. We knew the tour would be a unique experience and that God had new blessings waiting for us. Dan said he had been thinking about Isaiah 43: 18-19 (NIV): *"Forget the former things; do not dwell on the past. See, I am doing a new thing! Now it will spring forth; will you not be aware of it?"* Not only were we taking a different choir on tour, but ten of the thirteen places in which the choir was scheduled to sing were completely new venues!

We gathered in the church parking lot on Thursday, June 26, 2003, to begin our Eastern European adventure. As people arrived, we handed them the equipment or CD box they would take as their second checked bag. This arrangement made it possible for us to get most of our items to and from Europe without any extra shipping charge, saving several thousand dollars. As soon as we were able to account for everyone, we met in the church fellowship hall for a final time of prayer and praise with most of the pastors and church staff before departing for the airport.

As we left the room to board our bus, we saw that the staff had set up a corridor of banners for us to walk through on our way to the bus and another corridor of huge orange and red banners for the bus to drive through as we left the church. We felt a little like high school football players as they run onto the field, surrounded by cheerleaders. It reminded me of that passage from Hebrews 12:1-2a (NIV) which says: *"Therefore, since we are surrounded by such a great cloud of witnesses, let us throw off everything that hinders and the sin that so easily entangles. And let us run with perseverance the race marked out for us, fixing our eyes on Jesus, the pioneer and perfecter of faith."* What a tremendous send-off! Once again, the church demonstrated its enthusiastic support of our ministry.

We had asked people to pray for a smooth trip to the airport and a trouble-free check-in, and the Lord answered those prayers. We arrived at the airport in record time and all of our extra equipment was checked through without any hassle. Even after years of preparation, I found it hard to believe that we were actually beginning the Chancel Choir's first "Out of the Loft" ministry tour. We had overcome so many potential obstacles: the events of 9/11 had taken place only two years earlier, so security was tight; the war in Iraq, which had just begun, was unpopular in Europe; and the trip had become more expensive because the value of the euro had risen. Yet God had overcome all these obstacles and we were on our way to Europe!

We boarded our flight with an unrestrained sense of excitement and anticipation. The 10½- hour flight to Germany was smooth and uneventful. Since we were flying east, the night came quickly and morning arrived early. Choir members passed the time pleasantly with meals, movies, conversation, and attempted sleep. It is not surprising that some used the time to "bone up" on their music memorization, since the choir had to memorize twenty different pieces!

Once we were on the ground in Frankfurt, I looked for Joe Leonards, our German tour director. This was the same Joe who had led the two ministry tours for the Lake Avenue Church choir. Joe is a large and imposing individual—some might even say intimidating—but he has a servant's heart and understood what our ministry was all about. He had everything so well-organized that it was not long before all of us, our personal luggage, CD boxes, and handbell and audio equipment had gotten through customs and we were on the way to our buses.

Despite suffering from jet lag, everyone was in a jovial mood that evening as we gathered for our welcome banquet at the Dorint Hotel in Mainz. After stuffing ourselves with wonderful food, we leaned back and listened as Joe told us how our tour would function. He explained the schedule for the following morning: buffet breakfast served beginning at 6:30 a.m., wake-up call at 7:30 a.m., bags out in the hallway by 8:00 a.m., and departure for Pohlheim by 9:00 a.m. Dan then assured the group, "The next few days in Pohlheim will be some of the most significant and memorable days of the entire tour."

Saturday was the true beginning of our ministry, as we drove to Pohlheim to spend the weekend with families from the Christus Kirche. Choir members had mixed feelings about spending the weekend with German families. Some people were a little apprehensive about staying with people they did not know or with whom they might not be able to communicate. Others could hardly wait to see new things and make new friends. As we neared Pohlheim, we noticed that the countryside was filled with lush green farms and long lines of evergreen trees. Pohlheim is in a valley surrounded by low hills, which are covered with dense vegetation. What a lovely setting for our weekend!

As our buses pulled into Pohlheim, many church families were waiting to welcome us to "The Singing Village," as the town has been known for centuries. We gathered in the Volkshalle and listened closely as the president of the Christus Kirche choir, Erhard Jung, warmly welcomed our group and thanked the host families for their hospitality. He then began to connect choir members with their Pohlheim hosts.

June and I were placed with Adelheid and Günter Wehrenfennig, the same family we had stayed with in 1984. We had become such good friends with Günter and Adelheid over the years that we regularly shared prayer requests with each other by phone or via email. Even the choir members who had been anxious about staying with "strangers" quickly bonded with the people of Pohlheim and had a wonderful time that weekend. One of them told us he stayed up and talked with his hosts until the wee hours of the morning both nights we were there!

Dan and I had warned the choir that their time in Pohlheim would be filled with eating, sightseeing, and more eating. We not only were served large meals at noon and in the evening, but our hosts also insisted we drink their rich coffee and eat several different kinds of cake during *Kaffee Trinken* every afternoon. On the Saturday we arrived, the town of Pohlheim was celebrating a special festival, the "Bakhausfest," so we joined in the festivities.

In the main square, many townspeople wore traditional attire, and a group of villagers demonstrated traditional German folk dances in their colorful outfits: the women wore white billowy skirts and bright scarves, while the men wore dark pants, long-sleeved white shirts, and dark suspenders which crossed in the back. They looked like characters from the delightful children's book, *Heidi*. Of course, the town "Platz" was also filled with food and drink! The town's old bakery, the "Bakhaus," was known for making a special kind of bread. Bakery employees brought out huge trays of this bread and other German pastries, which they sold along with Germany's famous beer.

Bill, a choir member, later told us how he had met a 93-year-old fellow World War II veteran that afternoon. The fact that they had fought on opposite sides in the war did not seem to matter, especially when this man began singing and playing his mouth organ. They both knew "Lily Marlene," a German love song that was popular during the war, so they sang it together. Bill's new friend explained that the Nazis had often played this song to make American and Canadian soldiers feel homesick, hoping that the Allied troops would decide to go home! Music is definitely the universal language.

Because the Christus Kirche had been closed due to termite damage in the roof, the Church Council had to find another place for our concert. Unfortunately, the Volkshalle—the place the Lake Avenue choir had sung in 1984 and 1989—was not available that weekend, so the pastor of the Christus Kirche asked the priest at St. Martin's, the Catholic church in town, if the choir could sing there. The priest told him that although we would be there during the church's main festival weekend of the year, he would make their church available "gladly from the heart." His generosity is a testimony to the unity of the Body of Christ.

The congregation of the Christus Kirche was meeting temporarily in their Alte Kirche or "Old Church," which was built in the 1300s. It was much smaller than the regular church building, so the church had wisely set up a closed-circuit television camera with a feed to the nearby Thomashaus, which served as an overflow sanctuary. Some people even sat outside. We discovered that worshiping in the old church was a special gift from God. One could sense the Alte Kirche's seven centuries of worship history and tradition in the intimate setting. At the front of the church, three stained glass windows glowed with rays of sunlight and the large pipe organ towered over the small sanctuary. Outside, we could see the old church cemetery decorated with pretty, multi-colored flowers.

Sunday was a great blessing as we worshiped together with brothers and sisters in Christ. Even though the language and customs were different, we could feel the presence of the Lord throughout the bilingual service. Everyone sang the hymns together in German, our choir sang several numbers in English, and Pastor Hans Übler's message was translated so everyone could understand. His sermon focused on the concept of "reconciliation"—not only the ministry of reconciliation which all believers have in the world, but also the need for reconciliation between believers (Protestants and Catholics) and between peoples (Germans and Americans).

Lola, a member of the choir, later shared her special experience that morning in the Alte Kirche. *"In one of our conversations with Inge, our Pohlheim host, she told us about a woman who had sung there with Dan's choir back in 1989 and had met a gentleman in the village. They had fallen in love and gotten married. Inge told me that the woman's husband had passed away recently. The woman had decided to return to her home in the U.S., so her daughter was there to help her prepare for her trip back to the Pasadena area.*

On Sunday morning we went to the chapel to worship. The chapel was very tiny and very historic, as it was built in the 1300s. The choir lined up in front and we began to rehearse our anthems for the service, 'Sing and Be Not Silent' and 'Grace.' As we were singing 'Grace,' I looked out and saw an older woman sitting there. When I saw tears streaming down her face, I knew that she had to be the widow Inge had described to us. As I saw her tears, I could not hold back my own. I realized that it was God's grace that had brought us to this point after three years of planning. I didn't know how we would be changed over the next three weeks, but I knew it would be profound."

After an enjoyable noon meal with our host families, we departed for St. Martin's Catholic Church to prepare for the evening concert. The preparation time before this concert was especially difficult. Both the Chancel Choir and the choir from the Christus Kirche needed to warm up and rehearse—at the same time that people set up handbell tables and struggled to assemble the totally-unfamiliar choir risers. These risers, which had been rented in Germany, were more like a complicated erector set than the risers we were used to. When I think of that scene, the word "chaotic" comes to mind.

Fortunately, Joe Leonards was right in the middle of everything—helping to bring in equipment, figuring out how to assemble the risers, and even bringing water to the choir during a break in the program. After the concert, he was at it again, helping to take down equipment and pack the truck. I don't know what we would have done without him!

That evening's concert, the first complete program of our tour, was the first time we had to sing all of our songs from memory. As a result, we wondered if we could get through the program successfully. We felt even more uncertain when we did not have time to rehearse most of our pieces. So while the townspeople streamed into the sanctuary, we gathered outside the church and gave all of our concerns and fears to the Lord, asking Him to use us for His glory.

After the choir from the Christus Kirche sang an opening number in German, we made our way up to the chancel. When both choirs were in place on the risers, we sang together in English, "Look at the World," by John Rutter. Singing in a joint choir was a unique experience for both choirs. From that point on, we in the Chancel Choir were "on our own." Even though we were supposed to sing all of the songs from memory, I did spot several people holding small note cards with words written on them. I have a confession to make: I was one of those people. The others shall remain nameless.

That night the church was filled to overflowing, which energized us. Throughout the program the audience was very responsive to our music, especially the selections played by the Bells of Praise. When the choir completed its final number, "My Soul's Been Anchored," choir president Judy Enns presented beautiful plaques from our choir to each of the Pohlheim churches: St. Martin's and the Christus Kirche. Father Schmidt, the presiding priest at St. Martin's, declared, "As a result of your concert in our church, I am now committed to working more closely in ministry with the Christus Kirche." The message of reconciliation which Pastor Übler had proclaimed that morning in the Alte Kirche became a reality that evening in St. Martin's Catholic Church. Praise the Lord!

After the concert, the Christus Kirche gave an elaborate buffet reception in St. Martin's fellowship hall for the choirs and everyone attending the concert. This gave us time to talk with people and share with them the message of hope the Lord had placed on our hearts. Pastor Übler and Erhard Jung presented the choir with an original painting of the Alte Kirche by one of their local artists. During the reception, Erhard Jung confided to me, "The Christus Kirche has been going through troubled waters for the past few years, but the Chancel Choir's weekend in Pohlheim has been a great encouragement to our congregation, our choir, our church council, and our pastor." When the reception finally drew to a close and all of us departed with our host families, our hearts were filled to overflowing with the many blessings the Lord had showered on us that day.

The next morning our Pohlheim hosts brought everyone to the Alte Kirche. After placing all our luggage on the buses, we went inside the church for a final time of praise and thanksgiving. Pastor Übler presented the choir with a large German flag to help us remember our time with them. The German flag consists of three equal horizontal bars displaying the national colors of Germany—black on the top, red in the middle, and gold at the bottom. The colors of the modern flag represent German unity and freedom. To us, they suggested the freedom and unity which we have in Christ.

As we left the Alte Kirche, we felt conflicting emotions: joy and sadness, anticipation and loss. We rejoiced as we thought of the hospitality shown to us by the people of Pohlheim and the memories we had acquired. At the same time, we were sad to say good-bye to new friends who had so quickly become an important part of our lives. Also, it was a little scary to leave the West and move into unknown parts of Eastern Europe. Yet we were excited about the adventure the Lord had laid before us. After many hugs and some tears, we embarked on the next phase of our journey.

The local newspaper printed an account of our visit the next day. The paper concluded the article with the following words: *"The fact that tears were flowing during the goodbyes of the guests in the old church shows that the wishes of the organizing teams on both sides became reality: that this meeting might be considered a cornerstone for a new friendship between Christians on both sides of the Atlantic."* (Translated from German by Wolfgang Bluhm)

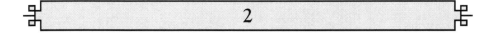

2

The cities of the former East Germany have a strong cultural heritage. Composers Felix Mendelssohn, Johann Sebastian Bach, and George Frederick Handel all grew up in eastern Germany, and their heavenly music was performed in the many breathtakingly-beautiful cathedrals which dot that part of the country. Martin Luther also helped to make eastern Germany famous. His footprints are found throughout the area in homes, churches, and the monastery in which he studied and became a priest. Luther held music in the highest regard. He once said, *"The devil flees before music almost as much as before the Word of God."* It was hard to comprehend that we were bringing our music to Luther's homeland!

The drive from Pohlheim to Eisenach took us through rolling countryside and woods. While the day was somewhat overcast, our spirits were joyful. Shortly before we arrived in Eisenach we were pleased to see that the old East German control tower and former border control checkpoint had been turned into a restaurant and a gas station.

Eisenach is famous for two historical sites: the birthplace of Johann Sebastian Bach and the Wartburg Castle, one of the best-preserved medieval castles in Germany. That afternoon most of the choir toured this castle and saw the very room in which Martin Luther lived and translated the New Testament into German. First built in 1067, Wartburg Castle developed into an extensive fortress complex over many centuries, so it contains Romanesque, Gothic, and 19th century architectural features. Nine hundred years of history are contained within the castle walls, including courtly art from the Middle Ages, St. Elisabeth's life and work, and Martin Luther's translation of the New Testament. Wartburg Castle also attracts a large number of visitors each year because of its art treasures, medieval tapestries, paintings by Lucas Cranach the Elder, and a remarkable collection of European cutlery and arts and crafts from the 11th to the 19th century. The artistic creations we saw were priceless.

The Georgenkirche in Eisenach was the site of that evening's concert. We did not need to set up the risers there (hallelujah!) because the choir could stand on the chancel steps; this made preparing for the concert much less hectic than the set-up in Pohlheim the night before. The Georgenkirche is exquisite, with huge gold chandeliers and a large pipe organ in a loft at the back. It also has outstanding acoustics, which made it an ideal place for a concert. We felt honored to sing in the very church where Bach was baptized and where Luther preached. When the concert was over, the audience—which included many young people—gave the choir a standing ovation.

Inge, the tour escort for the "yellow bus," had not attended the concert in Pohlheim. At the end of the Eisenach concert, I saw her eyes fill with tears. She stated that she had never experienced anything like it before. Another young woman remarked, "It has been years since I have been in a church, but because of your concert I am planning to attend church regularly." As after every concert, many people approached the front of the church to see how the handbells worked. The bell choir members demonstrated the different kinds of bells and hand chimes and let people of all ages play some of the bells themselves. These interactions gave us another opportunity to share the source of our joy, Jesus Christ.

It was a special blessing to have Ildikó Barbarics sing in the choir on the tour. After we returned home, Ildikó wrote some of her thoughts about an encounter she had in Eisenach: *"After the concert I met a Christian lady whom I had known for years from our Word of Life brass tours in that area. Neither of us knew that the other would be there, so it was a nice surprise when we ran into each other. She said that she had come to the concert because she wanted to see what kind of choir was willing to sing in Eisenach for free. As we were talking, she asked, 'Why does this choir come to sing in this town, where nobody comes?' She greatly appreciated that the choir was willing to proclaim the Lord's message even in places where nobody else wanted to go."*

On our way from Eisenach to Leipzig, we stopped in Erfurt, the "spiritual home" of Martin Luther. In early 1505 Luther had just completed his master's degree at the University of Erfurt and was planning to enter law school in accordance with his father's wishes. This changed on July 2, 1505, when Luther was caught in a terrible thunderstorm. Afraid that he would be struck dead by lightning, he cried out, "If you help me, I will become a monk!" Luther survived and kept his vow. He joined the Augustinian Monastery in Erfurt two weeks later, living and studying there until 1511. A British bombing raid destroyed much of the monastery in 1945, but it has since been restored.

Our choir had the privilege of singing several "a cappella" numbers inside the monastery chapel, which dates back to the 13th century. The church's collection of stained-glass windows is over 700 years old and includes a "picture-cycle window" which portrays different scenes in the life of Saint Augustine. Behind the choir loft, on both sides of a tall stained-glass window, stands a restored 1938 Walcker organ, which is available for services and choir performances. I wish we could have performed our whole program in the monastery chapel, accompanied by this organ.

Our next stop was Leipzig, a major city in eastern Germany. The city is noted for its fine music: the Choir of St. Thomas, the Gewandhaus Orchestra, and the Mendelssohn-Bartholdy National College of Music are all found in Leipzig. It is the city in which Johann Sebastian Bach served as church cantor at the Thomaskirche for the last twenty-seven years of his life. Our concert that evening was in the Paul Gerhard Kirche, located in a working-class Leipzig neighborhood. Dan and I had established a relationship with Pastor Enders during our planning trip the previous year and had given him several of our choir recordings. He encouraged his congregation to attend the concert, so many people from the church came to our program even though it was on a Tuesday evening and they had to get up early the next morning to go to work.

People entered expecting to hear fine music; they left praising the Lord for the spiritual encouragement our music had given them. At the end of the concert Pastor Enders told the audience, "When American choirs come to Leipzig, they all want to sing in one of the large historic churches such as the Thomaskirche and Nikolaikirche. This is the first American choir I know that was willing to minister to a local congregation. For that I am deeply grateful." Following the concert, the church held a buffet reception for us in their fellowship hall. As we found in churches throughout Eastern Europe, the congregation obviously was not wealthy, but they graciously extended the hand of friendship to our choir without considering the cost.

We were happy that we had the entire morning free the next day. There were no bags to be put out, no buses to board, no tours or worship services to attend; people could get up and have breakfast whenever they wanted. Most people used the morning to explore the historic areas of Leipzig. Some toured the Mendelssohn House. Most wanted to see the Thomaskirche, in which Bach worked for so many years and where he is buried. Susie Shick, among others, visited the Bach Museum. Some used the time to shop or to have coffee and pastry at a sidewalk café. It was a pleasure for all of us to relax for a few hours without having to worry about a schedule.

That afternoon the choir traveled about 25 miles northwest of Leipzig to the city of Halle, another town known for its musical heritage. George Frederick Handel, composer of the *Messiah*, was born there. Thus, the focal point of our walking tour of Halle was the Handelhaus, Handel's birthplace, an exceptionally interesting and informative museum. It is a grand old house with two garrets, which made it possible for young Handel to practice a small clavichord in the upper garret without being heard in the main parts of the house. Handel's father was so opposed to music that he did not want his son to play an instrument, but his supportive mother sneaked the clavichord into the upper garret.

The Handelhaus contains an extensive collection of centuries-old instruments, including a glass organ, as well as drawings and prints of 18th century London. Each room depicts a different period of Handel's life, with music from that period playing in the background. When we came to the last room on the tour, the music being played was the "Hallelujah Chorus" from the *Messiah*. All of us joined in and sang along with the music.

Our concert in Halle took place in the Marktkirche which, as its name implies, is located on the town's market square. In the middle of the square is a large fountain surrounded by stately old buildings and statues, including a large statue of Handel. The four towers of this huge Gothic cathedral, which has three naves, dominate the town. This is the church in which Handel was baptized; in fact, the church still has the bronze baptismal font, made in 1430, which was used for Handel's baptism. This baptismal font stood directly in front of us as we gave our program! The Marktkirche is also famous because during Holy Week in 1541, Martin Luther preached the first Protestant sermon ever given in that church. It was a rare privilege to sing in this historic setting.

As the choir began to warm up for the concert, we realized that the church was not only historic, but also an ideal place to sing. The sanctuary was very reverberant, which was a great help to us. Susie was in ecstasy about playing its magnificent organ, which Johann Sebastian Bach inaugurated in 1716. However, as in most traditional European churches, the organ in the Marktkirche was located in a loft at the back of the sanctuary. This presented a problem: Susie had a hard time seeing Dan and following his direction. Fortunately, Susie accompanied most of our music at the grand piano located right beside the choir.

At the end of the concert when the choir surrounded the congregation and sang "When I Survey the Wondrous Cross," Nancy Davis stood in the loft at a place where she could see Dan. She conducted his beat, which Susie followed, enabling Susie to be in sync with the choir. It's amazing how "little" things can sometimes become very complicated!

Martin Fritsche, the young cantor at the Marktkirche, was determined to give us a "simple" reception of nuts, pretzels, mints, and drinks after the concert. It was a special treat when the church's youth choir sang a few numbers for us. We loved it! The choir director told us that most of the parents of her singers were atheists, so she felt that working with the young people was a real and effective mission field.

The evening concert ended the first leg of the ministry tour. Although we did not have packed-out audiences in the three eastern German cities of Eisenach, Leipzig, and Halle, we were touched by the warm response the people gave our Chancel Choir and Bells of Praise. We had seen God work in each place we visited, and we knew that God would continue to move in the lives of these German people as a result of our ministry.

3

Thursday, July 3rd, was another "bags out by . . ." day with its pre-determined departure time. The choirs were into the routine by now and were ready to leave on time. As a matter of fact, everyone in the group was very punctual. I was proud of the way they met their various deadlines and responsibilities. Of course, that might have been due to their fear of being shipped to Outer Mongolia by the Prussian Warlord (a.k.a. Joe Leonards), who kept all of us in line.

Our destination that day was Berlin, the capital city of Germany. On the way there, we visited the town of Wittenberg where Martin Luther is said to have nailed his "95 Theses" to the door of the Castle Church. This event in 1517 is often cited as the beginning of the Protestant Reformation. Our tour of Wittenberg began at the Schloss Kirche, or Castle Church. We felt Luther's presence in the church, perhaps because he is buried there. I was struck by the intricately carved wood of the pulpit, situated high above the congregation, from which Luther preached. Our choir had the opportunity to sing several numbers at the front of the church, just as we had in the Augustinian Monastery in Erfurt. As a result, we identified with Martin Luther and could picture the events which had taken place in the church almost 500 years before.

The city of Berlin today bears no resemblance to the war-torn capital of Nazi Germany or even the divided city of the Cold War. Today's Berlin is one of the most vibrant cities in Europe, with a population of over three and one-half million people. Now the capital of a united Germany, Berlin was undergoing a dynamic facelift. The Reichstag, meeting place of the German parliament, was being restored, and a brand new German Chancellery, the equivalent of our White House, had been built. Recently-constructed shopping centers had appeared in the Mitte district of Berlin (formerly part of East Berlin), and a new Adlon Hotel stood across from the Brandenburg Gate, replacing the famous old Adlon Hotel that was so popular in pre-war Berlin, which had stood on the same spot.

We had the luxury of staying in the same place for three nights at the Schweizerhof Hotel, across from the Berlin Zoo and just a couple of blocks from the Europa Center and the Kaiser Wilhelm Memorial Church. We could not have had a finer or more conveniently-located hotel. Unfortunately, as in many large American cities, it was not safe to store our equipment in the truck overnight in Berlin, so we had to unload everything from the truck each night and store the equipment in a room at the hotel. The choir, however, did not feel any danger when walking about the city.

The next day was July 4th, Independence Day in America. In the morning most of us chose to take a guided tour of Berlin. Our buses drove by the Charlottenburg Palace, down the Kurfürstendamm, and to the place where a piece of the Berlin Wall could still be seen. Then we rode through the old Checkpoint Charlie; down the Unter den Linden, Berlin's historic boulevard; and finally to the Brandenburg Gate. I could not believe the changes in that area, which had been empty before the

Wall came down. New buildings stood all around the old square, right up to the sides of the Brandenburg Gate itself.

The guided tour included a special lunch at a restaurant next to the Gendarmenmarkt, one of Berlin's most historic squares. Toward the end of our lunch, Joe Leonards asked for our attention. "The chef had a problem with the dessert, so they had to make a change," he announced. With that, several restaurant employees rolled out a huge sheet cake decorated as an American flag and lit with sparklers. What a fantastic surprise! Joe wanted to honor America on our Independence Day. All of us immediately broke out in singing "God Bless America," and even some Germans joined us.

We had started the ministry tour with concerns about how we might be received by the German people, since many of them were opposed to the Iraq War. I had even put in the prayer calendar for that day: "Pray that this concert which takes place on our Independence Day in Berlin . . . might help bridge and heal the differences that have developed between our two countries this year." We certainly did not expect that the "bridging and healing" would begin at a restaurant in the center of Berlin. The Lord continued to answer our prayers in ways we could never have imagined. What a great God we have!

By 4:30 p.m. we were back in the hotel lobby ready to depart for the "Evangelische-freikirchliche Gemeinde Berlin-Schöneberg." This can be roughly translated as "Evangelical Free Church Berlin-Schöneberg." All German churches are placed in three general categories: the "Evangelische Gemeinde," or Lutheran churches; the Catholic churches; and the "free churches." Churches in the first two categories receive tax support from the government, while those who do not receive any tax support are called free churches. The Berlin-Schöneberg Church is a free church.

The Schöneberg church, located in a modern building with a huge cross suspended in front, had an effective ministry in that part of the city and, unlike most churches in Berlin, had an active congregation. Dan and I first got to know the pastor of the church, Michael Noss, when the Lake choir sang there in 1989, and we had kept in contact with him ever since. That evening we had a particularly meaningful time of prayer before the concert. We took the time before every concert to get our hearts ready for the program and to ask God to do a good work in and through us. We had a good-sized audience that night, even though the official "holiday" for Berlin had begun the day before.

Pastor Noss opened the concert with a hearty welcome, and then we were off with our opening song, "Thank the Lord and Sing His Praise." At the end of our regular program, before we moved down to surround the congregation for our final number, Dan asked the audience, "Would it be O.K. if we sing an encore, 'The Battle Hymn of the Republic,' in celebration of July 4th?" Of course, the audience consented, and they joined us on the final refrain, "Glory, glory, hallelujah, His truth is marching on!" with great gusto. After a time of sharing and fellowship, we sang patriotic songs on our buses all the way back to the hotel. It was a different kind of July 4th celebration than we were used to, but it was an Independence Day we would always remember.

I had always wanted to visit the city of Potsdam, in which the Prussian kings established their administrative center and garrisoned their army in the 17th and 18th centuries. King Frederick the Great built two major palaces here, the Sanssouci Palace and the Neues Palais or "New Palace." The day after our concert in Berlin, we traveled to the town of Potsdam and explored it during the afternoon, beginning with a tour of the gardens which surround the palaces. The Sanssouci Palace is noted for its elegant simplicity and the beautiful terraces leading up to it. By the way, in 1991 Frederick the Great finally got his wish to be buried at the Sanssouci Palace next to his beloved dogs. We saw their gravesites.

Nearby is the Cecilienhof Palace, the English-style country residence built during the First World War for the German crown prince and his wife, Cecilia. This palace is famous because it was the site of the Potsdam Conference, which determined the future of defeated Germany at the end of World War II. On August 2, 1945, the Potsdam Agreement was signed by the leaders of the Allied powers: Winston Churchill of Britain, Harry Truman of the United States, and Joseph Stalin of the Soviet Union. It was awe-inspiring to be in the place where this momentous agreement was signed.

That evening we presented a concert at the Nikolaikirche in Potsdam, an imposing Protestant church located on the Alter Markt. The Nikolaikirche was built in the early 1800s and its condition had deteriorated as a result of World War II and forty years under Communism. At the time we sang there, the church was undergoing a major restoration. Scaffolding covered the outside of the church, and the organ and choir loft were in the process of being rebuilt.

However, the construction could not efface the beauty of the huge domes high above the inside of the Nikolaikirche and the numerous drawings of biblical scenes painted on the ceiling. In 2002, when Dan and I had arranged our concert there, we had told the pastor and church cantor that we would not expect any money from them. Instead, we stipulated that if they wished to take up an offering following the concert, they should use those funds to help rebuild their organ. When this information was announced to the congregation at the end of our program, the people rose with loud applause.

We had been told that Potsdam was a "secular" city, so we prayed that these people, who loved excellent music, might catch the Spirit with which our people sang and rang. We believed that the Lord had broken through that secular barrier and had ministered directly to the hearts of the people during our concert at the Nikolaikirche. One young woman told a choir member, "Jesus was here tonight. . . . You have Jesus in your hearts."

The city of Dresden is just 125 miles south of Berlin, so it was a short, relaxing trip there the next day. Dan and I reminisced about how the two of us had left Dresden the previous summer just before the city suffered one of the worst floods in its history. Our concert that evening was to be held in the Kreuzkirche, the Church of the Holy Cross—an ancient church, its outside walls black with age.

On our way back to the hotel after some sightseeing, June and I stopped by the Kreuzkirche to look over the place. We were shocked when we walked inside the church and found scaffolding all around the sides and back, with pews piled high on top of each other in the aisles and much of the seating in the sanctuary blocked off. This great church, world-famous for its Dresden *Kreuzchor* (Boys' Choir), now had no more than a third of its usual seating capacity. Another problem was the absence of a piano. The assistant pastor, Joachim Zirkler, assured us that he would have their electronic piano ready for the concert. Susie Shick and Nancy Davis had already played on a variety of pianos during the tour, ranging from full grand pianos to small uprights. Now they would get their first chance to play a "pseudo" piano on the tour.

Anyone who has been involved in a musical group knows that the attitude of the performers about a concert is often affected by circumstances. Our concert in the Kreuzkirche is a good example. When we saw all of the scaffolding and renovation in the church, our hearts sank. There was dirt and dust everywhere, and most of the church was a mess. "Why were we not told?" we moaned. Then when we learned that we had to settle for an electronic piano, we became even more depressed. During our prayer time before the concert, we turned the situation over to the Lord. This was not easy from a human standpoint, so we had to remind ourselves that the Lord had brought us here and that

He had called the people who would be in the audience. We needed to trust Him and let the Holy Spirit fill us and pour forth from us through our singing and playing.

When we entered the Kreuzkirche to begin the concert, we were surprised to see that the front part of the church was packed, and that additional people were sitting in the extra pews available at the back and on one side. The audience showed their enthusiasm for our music throughout the concert. The Bells of Praise, as always, was a great hit. At the end of the program Pastor Zirkler said, "Thank you very much for coming to us. At first, at the beginning of your concert, I had to question: 'A handbell choir—what could that be?' Dresden is known as the city of bells, but I have never heard anything like your handbell choir. Now I know that it is music made of the angels. I'm sure that most of the people feel the same. Your voices come directly out of your hearts and so your voices come into our hearts and bring us the message you share with us today. Thank you."

We knew that many people in Eastern Europe did not see a place for God in their lives and that most of the huge cathedrals remained empty. We hoped that our music would bring people back to the church and the message of Christ. One thing we noticed at the Kreuzkirche and throughout the tour is that people would walk into a concert looking skeptical and apathetic. Then, as the concert progressed, their faces began to soften. By the end of the program, these same people were smiling and clapping, radiating a new joy.

Our prayers before the concert asking the Lord to lift our spirits and to use us in a mighty way were answered beyond our expectations. The Apostle Paul wrote in II Corinthians 12:9 (NIV) that the Lord had said to him, *"My grace is sufficient for you, for my power is made perfect in weakness."* This proved to be true for us that night. As we walked back to our hotel, there was a joyous lift in our spirits which comes only from the Lord.

A few days during the 2003 tour turned out to be especially stressful. Monday, July 7th, was one of them. We left our Dresden hotel on time and enjoyed the picturesque drive through the mountains to the Czech border. This would be our first border crossing since we had arrived at the Frankfurt airport some ten days earlier. As usual, we were concerned about getting our equipment across the border, but we did not think this border crossing would be any more difficult than our arrival in Germany. We were in for a surprise, and it was not a pleasant one.

When our buses got in line at the Czech border, Joe Leonards told us to have our passports ready and to stay on the bus until told otherwise. Meanwhile, the customs officials checked out the truck which carried our equipment. They told Joe that our truck would not be allowed to enter the Czech Republic. The problem, they claimed, was that trucks entering from Germany could not be heavier than 3.5 tons. Our truck was rated at 7.5 tons, but obviously weighed much less than that. The discussion went on for almost an hour. Finally, the officials remembered an agreement between Germany and the Czech Republic which allowed trucks from the two countries to drive back and forth over the border. We were finally cleared to go.

People on our buses did not know what was holding us up and were still waiting to show their passports. Czech border officials finally boarded the buses. Then another problem arose. Marjorie Shick, Susie's mother, was carrying a Canadian passport. She had lived in the United States most of her adult life, but she had never acquired American citizenship. The Czech officials told her that Canadian citizens needed a visa to enter the country. Marjorie had not checked with the Canadian consulate before we left the "States" to see if she needed a visa, so she was not prepared for this complication. People from every country in the British Commonwealth except Canada were not required to have a visa, and the Czech government had just added that requirement for Canadians.

Marjorie later related her impression of what happened at the Czech border. *"When the border official boarded our bus and asked people to have their passports out, I proudly held out my Canadian passport and handed it to him. When he looked at it, he said, 'No, VISA! No, VISA!' I couldn't understand what he was saying. The only thing I could think of was that he wanted my VISA credit card, although I couldn't imagine why. So I dug into my purse, found my VISA card, and offered it to the man. He then became angry. He ordered me to get off the bus and told me to follow him to talk with his superior."*

The officials continued to insist that Marjorie could not continue with the group. They said she would have to return to Dresden to get a Czech visa or find a way to rejoin the choir in Vienna, Austria. At this point, Michael Seewald, a professional photographer in our group who had traveled all over the world, volunteered to stay with Marjorie. He said they would return to Dresden by cab, catch a train for Vienna the next day, and meet us in Vienna on Wednesday. People on both buses took up a collection to help Michael and Marjorie pay the extra costs they would incur and gave them 500 euros!

After almost two hours at the border, we were finally able to enter the Czech Republic and head for Prague, its capital city. It is easy to get around Prague by Metro or on foot, difficult to travel by car, and almost impossible to travel by bus because buses can drive on only a few designated streets. The bus drivers managed to find some acceptable streets and we were able to meet our local guides, who took us to a restaurant for lunch.

However, an argument erupted among Joe Leonards, the guides, and the bus drivers about whether we should be required to ride the bus to the hotel after lunch or whether people who wanted to walk to the hotel could do so. The bus drivers claimed it would be too difficult to get the buses into a space near the hotel, while others worried that some people could not walk that far. Everyone in our group could hear this heated discussion, which was upsetting to the choir—especially coming on top of the stressful time at the Czech border. It appeared that our choir was once again "hitting a wall" physically and emotionally, so Monday was not the pleasant day we had anticipated.

Eventually, everything worked out. Most people walked to the hotel and Joe obtained a taxi for the few who could not walk that far. We were pleased to see that our hotel was comfortable and conveniently located just off Wenceslas Square. The choir even had a little time to explore the Stare Mesto, the Old Town section of Prague, before we had to proceed to the Salvator Church for the evening's concert. Dr. Jiri Lukl, president of the Czech Bible Society, had arranged our concert at the Salvator Church, located just off the Old Town Square. However, due to a breakdown in communication between Dr. Lukl and the church, our concert had not been widely publicized. The Bells of Praise decided to provide their own publicity by playing "Joyful, Joyful We Adore Thee" outside the church in the hope of attracting people to the concert.

When the choir walked into the church, the sanctuary was dark, cold, and nearly empty. We felt downcast. But God intervened. Shortly after the program began, the doors flew open and bright sunlight poured in as a large group of people entered the church. We found out later that they were a tour group from Norway who had heard about our concert. Afterwards, Dr. Lukl told us that he was encouraged by the people's response to the concert, even though the audience was not large. After such a stressful day, the choir could have been discouraged; instead, we felt a buoyancy in our spirits. One cannot sing "psalms, hymns, and spiritual songs" without being uplifted by the Holy Spirit.

The next morning, many choir members took a guided tour of Prague. The buses took us up to the Hradcany, the high ridge overlooking the Vltava River and the city of Prague. The Prague Castle, which is still the official residence of the president of the Czech Republic, and the St. Vitas Cathedral are located on this ridge. From this point on in the tour, we had to walk. The good news was that it was all downhill from the Hradcany to the Mala Strana (or the Lesser Quarter) on the west side of the river. From there, we trekked across the 650-year-old Charles Bridge across the Vltava River to the Stare Mesto (or Old City).

As we were walking in front of the St. Vitas Cathedral, June took a serious fall, which resulted in a painful bone and tendon bruise on her left leg. At first she wanted to continue with the tour, but she found it was too painful to walk. So Joe Leonards put her into a taxi to the hotel so she could "ice" her leg. When I arrived awhile later, June was sound asleep. For the rest of the tour, she had to walk slowly and found it difficult to go up and down stairs. Fortunately, Jeanne Striker, wife of choir member Paul Striker, had joined the group the previous day. Jeanne is an MD in the Army Reserves and had just been discharged after a tour of duty at Ft. Lewis near Seattle. Dr. Striker was a great help to June during the last week of our tour.

When we were planning the tour, I had asked Icontas Service to plan a special dinner for the choir in Prague. I felt we could use a fun "evening out" after such a rigorous ministry schedule. That night was sublime. We were bused to a restaurant called the "Koliba U Pastyrky," or Shepherdess' Cottage, in another part of the city. It was a rather rustic place, with a huge barbecue grill in the center of the large dining area.

Our Czech meal began with an Aperitif they call "slivovitz," which is a dry, colorless plum brandy. We then were served a "traditional Slovak Meal - Halusky" which consisted of boiled potato bits with cottage cheese. For the main course, the servers brought in large wooden planks piled high with a mixture of grilled beef, pork, and chicken— along with rice and a mixed salad. The meal concluded with the "the Shepherdess' peach dessert," served with coffee. It was a feast!

While we ate, a group of three musicians played traditional Czech music, as well as popular songs. One played the violin; another, the string bass; and the third a cymbalom, a traditional Czech and Hungarian instrument which looks like a flat harp and is played with different kinds of mallets. In addition, we were entertained by two dancers in traditional Czech costumes. At one point in the evening, the Czech dancers selected two people from the choir to join them in a Slovak dance. Kathy and Ernie were the "lucky" ones chosen—or maybe they were the "unlucky" ones, depending on one's point of view. They were great sports, and Kathy surprised us with her amazing dexterity and skill. We gave the dancers a rousing ovation when they finished. The evening at the Shepherdess' Cottage was the best thing that could have happened to the choir at that juncture in the tour schedule. I was also relieved that, unlike the Lake Avenue choir's dinner at a Munich restaurant in 1989, no one complained about what people had to drink!

A new challenge presented itself the next day. Our schedule called for us to visit the Czech Word of Life Camp in Cerna Hora, about 15 miles north of the city of Brno. We were on the buses ready to leave the hotel in Prague when Joe Leonards motioned for me to get off the bus. The last time he had done this was at the Czech border, which did not bode well. What he told me now was equally disconcerting. Joe said that all of the documentation for our equipment was missing and we would need it when we crossed the Czech-Austrian border. The two bus drivers and the driver of the truck had taken a taxi from the hotel to the place the buses were parked. Unfortunately, the taxi driver took off before Lothar, our truck driver, could retrieve his briefcase containing all of the documents. When Joe heard about this, he contacted the taxi company and asked them to find the taxi driver with the briefcase. As it turned out, the taxi was "unregistered," so we could not trace it. We also tried to get replacement copies of our Carnet and the other documents.

All of this took over an hour and a half. Just as we had completed copying the faxed documents and letters, the taxi driver appeared and returned the briefcase. We were now in great shape for the border crossing, but we were also two hours late in departing for the Word of Life Camp. Therefore, we would be late to the camp and would not arrive in Vienna until several hours later than planned. As a result, Dan and I made the difficult decision to cancel our stop at the camp. I gave the camp director a call to let him know about our problem and he was very understanding.

Once we were on the road, however, Joe had a wonderful thought. He wanted to call the camp director to find out if we could meet him outside Brno before we took the turnoff to Vienna. Joe wanted to give the director some of our CDs to pass out to the campers. I thought it was a great idea, so Joe made the arrangements. We met Rich Hood, the Word of Life camp director, and gave him a full box of CDs—enough for future, as well as current, campers. We also collected all of the Czech coins we had and gave the money to Rich for the camp. He deeply appreciated the choir's generosity.

Rich told the group, "At our camp meeting tonight I plan to give the campers a chance to make a decision for Christ." He continued, "A camper came to me last night saying that he could not wait and wanted to pray right then for the Lord to come into his heart." Of course, Rich immediately stopped to pray with the young man and led him to Christ. This is significant in the Czech Republic, since 80% of the people are atheists. God is at work, even in the midst of widespread unbelief.

When we reached the Austrian border, our truck was quickly cleared and the officials did not even bother to look at our passports. Therefore, we arrived at our Vienna hotel by late afternoon. We had planned the schedule so people could use the rest of the day to explore Vienna on their own. Many told me afterwards that they had a great time in Vienna, but wished we could have been there longer. June and I chose not to do any sightseeing, since she still could not walk without severe pain, but we were able to join another couple for dinner at the nearby "Plachutta," a fine restaurant specializing in traditional Viennese cooking. Our dinner there was a relaxing way to end an otherwise stressful day.

5

We saved the best for last! We would spend the last few days of our 2003 Eastern European Ministry Tour in Hungary. Ildikó Barbarics and the leaders of her church had been the first people to invite our choir to minister in Eastern Europe, so Hungary was a special place for us. We had a packed schedule there during the last four days of the tour, July 10th through 14th.

On our way to Hungary, we stopped in the Austrian town of Eisenstadt to tour the Esterhazy Palace. The choir was scheduled to sing several songs in the concert hall of the palace, the very place where Franz Joseph Haydn performed so much of his music for Count Esterhazy in the 18th century. What a privilege it was to sing in this magnificent hall with its outstanding acoustics! Dan asked us to sing "Achieved is Thy Glorious Work" from Haydn's *The Creation*. The echoes which reverberated through the room made our performance sound heavenly, even though we sang the piece unaccompanied.

Before the buses left Vienna, we had sent our truck ahead of us so it would arrive at the border at least a couple of hours before we got there. Linda Smith rode along in the truck so she could answer questions about our equipment if any problems arose. Earlier in this chapter, I mentioned that a couple of days on the tour proved to be extremely stressful. The first one was the day we left Germany and had to cross the Czech border. We were now about to experience the second.

While we were still in Eisenstadt, Joe received a phone call from Lothar in the truck. Lothar said, "We're at the Austria-Hungarian border, but we haven't been cleared to cross into Hungary. When we first arrived at the border, the Austrian officials stamped our documents and cleared the truck to move on to the Hungarian side. But when we got there, the Hungarian customs officials said the handbell tables that had been shipped separately to Germany did not have the proper Austrian stamp. They told us to go back to the Austrian side of the border, but those officials said they had already approved everything and did not want to have any more to do with it." Thus, Lothar and Linda (and, of course, the truck with all of our equipment) were stuck in a "no man's land" between Austria and Hungary.

Our buses had to wait in line to be cleared by immigration. When we finally made it to the border, the officials entered each bus, looked at each person's passport, and sent us on our way. We stopped at a café just over the Hungarian side of the border to wait for the truck to be cleared. Joe Leonards and Ildikó Barbarics decided to walk back to the truck to see if there was any way to fix the problem, but they returned three hours later, totally frustrated. The officials had reiterated that the truck would have to return to Eisenstadt and unload the bell tables before it could cross the border. This meant we would not have the handbells available for the concert at the Budafok Baptist Church at 7:00 that evening. In fact, we would have to hurry if we were to make the concert at all.

In a letter I later received from Ildikó, she described her frustration about the situation. *"During the entire tour I was looking forward to having the choir in Hungary, especially in my church and at the camp where I work at Word of Life. I knew that my church's congregation was looking forward to the concert very much. When the custom officers would not let all of the equipment across the border, I was ashamed because of the bureaucracy of my country. I was also concerned that we would not have the bells to play for our very first concert in Hungary. I even wondered if we would make it to the concert at all! Thank the Lord, we arrived in time, and what a great blessing the program was for the people of my church! I heard nothing but wonderful comments about the concert. Our church families and all of the guests who came from different churches especially appreciated the CDs they received as a gift after the concert."*

The Lord's presence surrounded us and everyone in the congregation at the Budafok Church that evening. We did not arrive until 7:00, the time the concert was scheduled to start, so Pastor Tibor led the congregation in familiar choruses (with words unfamiliar to us) while we changed into our choir outfits. Since we had no time to warm up, we walked straight into the church about thirty-five minutes after the program had been scheduled to begin. The people had patiently waited for over 45 minutes. It was a shorter program than usual because we had to leave out the five bell choir numbers, but this did not seem to dampen the enthusiasm of the audience. When we surrounded the congregation and sang our final number, the people would not stop clapping. We seldom gave an encore, but that night we sang <u>three</u> encores before their pastor finally gave the benediction!

At the end of the concert we had a joyous time mixing with the audience and handing out our CDs. Then we walked down to the church fellowship hall beneath the sanctuary for a buffet reception. While we were at the church, Joe Leonards received a phone call saying that the truck had made it successfully across the Hungarian border and was on its way to our hotel. Praise the Lord! Pastor Tibor told us we could borrow five of their church's long tables to replace the ten smaller bell tables which had to be left behind in Eisenstadt, Austria. Their generous offer allowed the Bells of Praise to perform in all of our remaining Hungarian concerts.

As I was lying in bed at our hotel that night, I thanked the Lord for what He had done for us that day. It had looked like a disaster at the Hungarian border, but the concert turned out to be one of the most moving experiences of the tour. The Lord had gone before us and had made "the crooked ways straight," even when we could not see it.

The next day we rode our buses out to the Word of Life camp in the village of Tóalmás, about a 90-minute drive from our hotel. After traveling through the rolling Hungarian countryside, we pulled into the camp in mid-morning and were immediately struck by the beauty of the setting. It was originally known as "the Andrassy estate" and belonged to a prominent Hungarian nobleman. Word of Life leased the property in 1989, and eventually it was given to them outright. The main building, which they call "the Castle," was built in the 1800s and used to be the Andrassy family home. It is now the headquarters of World of Life Hungary and contains their offices, rooms for guests, and a Bible college.

Word of Life had constructed many dorms on the estate grounds to house the young people who attend their summer camps, had converted the estate's stables into a large dining hall, and had added a spacious assembly room. The property includes basketball and volleyball courts and a lake in which the campers can swim. In short, their facilities are as extensive as those of any Christian camp in the United States. Word of Life is continuing to "winterize" the dorms and other buildings so they can use all of the facilities year-round.

The week we were there was "Children's Week" for kids ages 7-12. Eric Murphy, director of Word of Life Hungary, told us that young people came to their camps from towns all over Hungary. During each week of camp, many children made first-time decisions for Jesus Christ. After a lunch of Hungarian goulash, we set up in the assembly room as the children filed in with their counselors and other guests to hear our hour-long program, which would include mostly lighter numbers such as spirituals and gospel songs.

Of course, it was the Bells of Praise which really caught the attention of these youngsters; they seemed mesmerized by the handbells. At the end of each song, especially the bell numbers and the gospel songs, they whistled, cheered, and clapped just like kids at a pop concert in America. It was so much fun to sing for those children! At the end of our program, the children sang a Hungarian camp song for us, led by Eric Murphy. Then Eric challenged our choir to sing the same song in Hungarian. The result was so pathetic that I am glad we did not record that particular number!

After the concert we said good-bye to the kids and the staff. We then boarded our two buses for another 90-minute drive to the city of Kecskemét, where we would present a program in the newly-completed Baptist church pastored by Géza Kovács Sr. That week Pastor Kovács was holding a series of tent meetings and revival services in the center of Kecskemét, and our concert that evening was a major part of the week's activities.

The church was completely filled that night and it was very hot, with the only ventilation coming from a few open windows. In spite of the heat and the long program, the audience was one of the most enthusiastic on the tour. We were encouraged not only by the size of the audience, but also by the number of young families who were there with their babies and small children. It was a wonderful climax to a long, but exhilarating day! Even though we were exhausted after singing two programs and were facing another 90-minute bus ride back to Budapest, all of us enjoyed our fellowship with these people so much that no one in the choir wanted to leave. This was just one more sign that we were in the exact place the Lord wanted us to be. It was obvious that we were not doing this in our own strength, but it was His strength which was continually energizing us for ministry.

After two hectic days, the choirs had all day Saturday off. Some of us went on a guided tour of Budapest, a city dissected by the Duna (Danube) River. On the west side of the river, Buda is situated on a number of wooded hills and has a rural, but aristocratic feel with its expensive-looking houses, villas, and well-tended gardens. In contrast, on the east side of the river, Pest is built on a plain which extends to the horizon, punctuated for the most part by old buildings and residential apartments on its outskirts. Today Budapest has a population of over two million people.

The tour took us around Pest, along the Duna River, across the Elizabeth Bridge, and up to Castle Hill. On this famous hill we viewed the Royal Palace; the Mátyás Templom, in which we would present our final concert on Sunday night; and the Fisherman's Bastion, a viewing terrace with many stairs, walking paths, and seven towers representing the seven Magyar tribes that first settled the area in 896 A.D. From Castle Hill we had a fantastic view of the mighty Duna River below and Pest stretching off to the east.

It is a good thing we had a free day on Saturday, since Sunday was extremely busy. We returned to the Budafok Baptist Church that morning to participate in their worship service. Unlike at the Thursday night concert, we now had the handbells with us. The Bells of Praise played four pieces, to the great delight of the congregation. I was especially impressed by an event near the beginning of the service. After the pastor outlined the order for worship, he asked the congregation to break up into groups of three or four to pray for the worship service. What a beautiful way to begin! At the end of morning worship, Pastor Tibor presented our choir with a huge basket of chocolates, all of which disappeared as if by magic within a very short time.

After church Ildikó connected the choir members with families in the congregation who would host us for Sunday dinner. This was something new; except for staying with host families in Pohlheim, Budafok was the only place we spent time with people in their homes. June and I and four other choir members were invited to have dinner at the home of Ildikó's parents. Ildikó's mother is a fantastic cook! She began the meal with delicious homemade soup, followed by the main course of paprika chicken with homemade noodles and salad. She topped it all off with a scrumptious chocolate cake. We were all bursting by the end of the meal! Regrettably, it was not long before we had to get back on our buses and return to the hotel to prepare for our final concert of the tour in the Mátyás Templom (Matthias Church). We had been invited to sing for the 6:00 Mass, after which we would present a full concert.

The 750-year-old Mátyás Templom dominates the Buda Castle area. The church was not named after St. Matthew, as one might expect, but for the Hungarian king, Matthias Corvinus, who Hungarians agree was definitely not a saint! The church was the scene of several coronations, including that of Charles IV, the last Hapsburg king, in 1916. It was also the site for King Matthias's two weddings. (His first wife died.) Following the Turkish occupation in 1541, the church was used as a mosque. Then in 1686 during the siege of Buda, a wall of the church collapsed due to cannon fire. Hidden behind the wall was an old Madonna statue. According to legend, when the sculpture of the Virgin Mary appeared before the Muslim Turks, their morale collapsed and the Hungarian soldiers were able to drive the Turks from the city the same day.

This stunning church was built in the neo-Gothic style around the 13th century and was restored in the late 1800s. The crisp white stone on the outside of the church is a dazzling sight, and the inside of the sanctuary simply takes one's breath away. It is lavishly decorated; every inch of the structure—walls, pillars, and ceiling—is painted. Over the altar is a delicately-designed golden dome, and the church is filled with stained glass windows. The magnificent Mátyás Templom was the perfect place for us to perform our last concert of the tour.

Singing for a Catholic Mass was a novel experience for the choir. We made our way to the choir loft at the back of the cathedral; from there we could look down at the long nave and the ornate chancel of the church, with its elaborately-carved wood paneling. Up in the loft, Susie Shick was trying to familiarize herself with the huge pipe organ. Dan summed up her situation well when he said, "Playing that organ is like going from flying a Piper cub to flying a 747!" The church cantor had asked the choir to sing four numbers at specified places during the Mass, even requesting that we learn and sing a short choral response. After we had sung one of our a cappella pieces, "O Magnum Mysterium" by Morton Lauridsen, the cantor asked Dan if he could have a copy of the music, since he thought it was one of the most beautiful pieces he had ever heard.

When the Mass concluded at 7:00 p.m., we carefully made our way down the narrow staircase from the loft to the sanctuary. Joe and Lothar had already brought our risers and bell equipment into the church so the choir could get them set up quickly. Many people who had attended the Mass remained for the concert, including the priest, while many others came into the church from outside. In the audience were tourists, local residents, and a few people from the Budafok Baptist Church who simply wanted to hear us again. The excitement and anticipation in the church was electric.

We gave our all during the program, since there was no reason to hold back during our final concert of the tour. The audience loved everything we sang and played. Not surprisingly, they absolutely adored the handbells. I believe we were truly inspired by the Holy Spirit that evening. When we finished singing "My Soul's Been Anchored In The Lord" at the end of the regular program, the audience rose in a standing ovation. Then, as we concluded the concert—and our Eastern European Ministry Tour—with "When I Survey the Wondrous Cross," tears were running down the faces of audience and choir alike. The glory of the

Lord had filled the sanctuary of this historic church. What an ending to a ministry tour which had been "more than we could ask or think!"

As we did after every concert, we met and talked with our guests. It was touching to see people with smiles on their faces holding tightly onto our CDs. Lauren Finalet, Dan Bird's 15-year-old granddaughter, sang with the choir on the tour and helped hand out CDs at the end of each program. After the tour, she sent me an email describing some of her impressions. What she had to say touched my heart. *"I recall one woman from Budapest who came up to me abruptly, appearing to be very flustered. I was passing out our CDs to the people leaving, and she stood in front of me, digging in her purse for something. She took out a wad of money and became frustrated trying to ask me, in her language, how much the CDs cost. I could understand by her gestures what she was trying to ask, so I handed a CD to her and said gently, 'It's free, no cost.' At first she stared at me, bewildered. Then with sudden comprehension that the CD was free, she placed her purse on the floor, took the CD from my hand, and wrapped her arms around me in a full embrace. Then she smiled at me, stroked my cheek, and left with joy. What a gift she gave me! I will never forget this experience with a woman I had never met before and who didn't speak the same language. It is amazing how a simple gift like a CD can be so big. I discovered that smiles are contagious in every language."*

Since the Mátyás Templom was not hosting a reception, Peter Wisst of Icontas Travel suggested that we meet at the Hilton Hotel, right next to the church, so we could have some time together to rejoice in what the Lord had done on the tour. Our gathering was held in the Dominican Church Courtyard, which contains the ruins of a church built there in the 13th century. It was the perfect place to end our tour. We could even see fireworks in the distance!

We used the time to say "thanks" to the many people who had made the tour such a success. These included our two bus drivers, Reinhard and Peter; our truck driver, Lothar; and our two tour escorts, Joe and Inge. Many times during the tour, choir members would ask Joe which song he liked best. He put off giving an answer until the last night. "You want to know which song is my favorite?" Joe inquired. "Of course, it is 'Give Me Jesus'!" Joe also told us he "got goose bumps" every time we sang and played. Finally, we gave special thanks to Ildikó Barbarics for arranging our Hungarian concerts. It was a blessed evening. Even though we did not get back to our hotel until close to midnight, everyone was rejoicing about all the Lord had accomplished during the tour.

Except for a few people in our group who had independent travel plans which allowed them to "sleep in," the rest of us rose early the next morning, July 14th, the last day of our ministry tour. We had been told to bring our large bags down to the lobby by 6:00 a.m. so they could be loaded onto the truck, along with our equipment, and taken to the airport by 6:15 a.m. When we exited our buses at the airport, Joe already had all of our large bags lined up ready for each person to pick up, and we then moved to one of three special check-in lines Joe had arranged. The process could not have gone more smoothly. Our luggage, handbell and audio equipment, and a few remaining boxes of CDs were checked through with no problems. Joe had done a masterful job from the beginning of the tour to the end!

We spent most of that day in the air. Our first flight was from Budapest to Frankfurt. Then we boarded a large airliner for our 11½-hour flight from Frankfurt to LAX. We arrived on time in Los Angeles in the early afternoon, got through immigration control, picked up our luggage and equipment, and cleared customs by 5:00 p.m. A bus was waiting to take us back to Solana Beach. The only problem was that we had to take a different route home because of a bad accident on the I-5 freeway. We did not reach the Solana Beach Presbyterian parking lot until almost 9:00 p.m., which was 6:00 on Tuesday morning European time. As we were getting off the bus, a choir member asked me, "When are we going on our next trip?" This was a question I did not want to even think about at that point!

The 2003 Eastern European Ministry Tour was a huge success in every way. We had overcome "impossible" hurdles to go on the tour. The ministry was not just a choir project; it had involved the entire church—from pastors to church leaders to parishioners. As a result, thousands of people were reached with the Good News of Jesus Christ, and many churches experienced renewal and revival. The choir returned home with a new sense of mission and ministry, as individuals and as a group.

The full impact of the 2003 Eastern European Ministry Tour will not be known until we are with Christ in heaven. However, we knew that the tour had changed our lives and the lives of many people in Europe. Now we needed to be on the alert for possible new ministry opportunities as God placed them in our path. The final verse from a song we sang on tour, "Greet the Dawning," says it all.

"You who love Him, come with singing,
Use your powers to give Him praise.
Join your voices in a chorus,
Make of this a day of days.
Alleluia, alleluia! Amen!"

CHAPTER EIGHT

Music With a Mission

> *"Instead, be filled with the Spirit, speaking to one another with psalms, hymns, and songs from the Spirit. Sing and make music from your heart to the Lord, always giving thanks to God the Father for everything, in the name of our Lord Jesus Christ."*
> *Ephesians 5:18b-20 (NIV)*

Upon returning from our 2003 Eastern European Ministry Tour, I had no idea what the future of the "Out of the Loft" ministry would be. Even when several choir people asked me, "Where are we going on our next ministry tour?" I had no answer. I simply replied, "Let's wrap up things from this trip first." And that is just what we did.

The choir returned to its usual ministry every Sunday morning and presented outstanding Christmas and spring concerts. Meanwhile, I was busy working on both audio and video projects from the 2003 tour. We came home with over eighty hours of video, plus audio recordings of all twelve concerts. My first priority was to produce a 20-minute video summary of the trip. Tony Bohlin and I accomplished this in August of 2003 and showed it to the choir in September.

We also produced a two-disc CD in the spring of 2004 entitled "Live From Europe." It contained all of the music we had sung on tour, selected from different concerts. Choir member Bill Fee worked with us to produce a 12-panel insert, which told the story of the ministry tour. By the end of March we were able to make the recording available to the congregation, as well as to friends around the country.

Producing the two-hour video documentary of the ministry was considerably more complicated. Such a project involved many steps. We first reviewed the 80+ hours of video, developed an overall outline for the story, and recorded reflections of the tour from various people in the choir. The process also included writing an introduction and conclusion for the video narrative, as well as writing narration to tie different sections together. Only then could we begin the actual editing and production of the video at the Bohlins. Tony and I worked on the video for several weeks in February of 2004 and again in August. The final product, "Dawn of a New Day," was shown to the choir in September of 2004. This video required a monumental effort by many people, but the final product was well worth it.

After we got home, the Choir Cabinet evaluated what had been accomplished and what we could do to make any future ministry tour even more effective. This evaluation resulted in a number of observations and conclusions about the 2003 Eastern European Ministry Tour. Perhaps the most significant of these was the positive feedback we received from the people to whom we had ministered. These reports indicated that the choir's message had invigorated and strengthened the people in Germany and Eastern Europe. For the people in German churches, who needed new life and vision, we had demonstrated the power and hope for the future which Christ provides. For the people in Hungary, whose daily lives often caused them to feel hopeless, our music and times of fellowship with them had given them a new sense of purpose. Obviously, there was still a need for this kind of ministry tour in Europe.

Another encouraging observation about the tour is that we had enthusiastic audiences at every concert. In Pohlheim, we knew the entire village was supporting us. In Leipzig, the pastor encouraged his congregation to come to the program. With Ildikó Barbarics's assistance, all of the Hungarian concerts were well-attended. However, other concert audiences had been small. On the two Lake Avenue tours, we had experienced nothing but "standing room only" concerts, while several concerts on the 2003 tour had only average attendance, and just a handful of people came to the concert in Prague.

The key to having a "full house" seemed to be how invested the local church leaders had been in the tour. The higher the level of their involvement, the more effective the ministry; if the leaders' involvement was minimal, the opposite was true. Thus, for any future ministry tour we needed to make sure that our local contacts took ownership of their part of the planning process and communicated with us regularly throughout the tour. Developing stronger contacts and a better "marketing plan" would not, however, negate the truth that the Lord brings to each concert whomever He chooses.

A great cause for rejoicing was that we had been able to meet all of the tour expenses and give substantial scholarship assistance to a number of choir members. The only area of the budget which cost substantially more than we had anticipated were the land arrangements, due to a weakening U.S. dollar and the fact that fewer people went on the tour than we had budgeted for. We were able to make up for those increased costs, however, because of the success of our fundraising projects. We concluded that in the future we should be more conservative in estimating the number of tour participants and should establish a larger "contingency fund" to cover possible changes in the value of the dollar.

Arrangements for the equipment on the tour had been both successful and problematic. On the positive side, the majority of our equipment was taken as personal luggage, which saved us a significant amount in shipping costs. Another positive is that we rented choir risers in Germany for use throughout the tour, eliminating the cost of shipping risers to Europe. However, we realized that we needed to make a few changes in handling our equipment. For example, in 2003 the handbell tables had to be shipped separately because of their size, which cost about $1,800. So we decided to find out if renting bell tables abroad would be cheaper than shipping them. Acquiring a Carnet for all of our handbell and audio-video equipment was a smart move, but it had been a mistake not to include the bell tables and rented risers on the Carnet, since this omission created problems at border crossings. Therefore, we planned to put all of our equipment on the Carnet in the future.

An especially significant outcome of the trip was the close relationships we had established with congregations and pastors in several of the places we sang. This was particularly true in Pohlheim, but it was also true to a lesser degree in the German cities of Leipzig, Halle, and Berlin. We also developed special relationships in Hungary at Budafok Baptist Church, the Baptist church in Kecskemét, and the Word of Life camp in Tóalmás. We felt strongly that our church and choirs should continue to build on these relationships. Thus, we needed to develop a strategy to strengthen our connections with the people we would minister to.

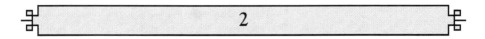

In April and May of 2004, our German friends Günter and Adelheid Wehrenfennig again came to California for a visit. This time they brought their son and daughter-in-law, Martin and Annette, who stayed with the Elliotts, the young couple they had hosted in Pohlheim in 2003. The days flew by as we showed our guests around the San Diego area. After the Wehrenfennigs left on April 15th, we had to change gears and prepare for moving to a house a couple of miles away. Earlier in the spring we had sold our large two-story house and had purchased a new, single-story home. Even though the new house was just a short distance away, we still had to pack boxes, throw out many things we didn't need, and make arrangements with the moving company. Moving is always such fun! Appropriately, Ildikó Barbarics from Hungary was one of the first visitors to stay with us in our new home.

During the first part of 2005, we began to think about the next place the Lord might call the choir to go "out of the loft." Dan decided to send an audition tape of the Chancel Choir to the American Choral Directors Association (ACDA). He believed that, with the 2003 ministry tour under our belts and the stellar concerts we had presented since then, the Chancel Choir had a good chance of being chosen to sing during the ACDA Western Region convention, which would be held March 1st through 5th in Salt Lake City, Utah. In July, the choir received an answer from the ACDA—and it was a big "yes"! Linda Smith and I began to make the flight and hotel arrangements for the trip, and the choir leaders challenged everyone in the choir to commit to the "mini-tour."

In preparation for the ACDA concert, the Chancel Choir learned and memorized seven pieces of music, which ranged from a classical piece, Tchaikovsky's "O Sing to God," to a new arrangement of the spiritual "Give Me Jesus," to a brand new composition by Dan Bird for choir, organ, and brass ensemble called "Pinnacle of Praise." Dan wrote the "Pinnacle" for the Centennial Celebration of La Jolla Presbyterian Church in October of 2005. Our ACDA program included three a cappella pieces, one piece with piano and flute, and three pieces with a brass ensemble. We were blessed to have the Westwind Brass join us for the ACDA program. They are an outstanding group of musicians from the San Diego area who give concerts all over the country.

It took extensive planning to get a group of 100 people—80 singers and 20 additional tour participants—to Salt Lake City, but we did it. The choir flew out of San Diego on Friday, March 4th. As soon as we arrived at the Salt Lake City airport, our buses took us to First Presbyterian Church to practice with the Westwind Brass, who had flown in from Michigan after a concert there the night before. At the end of our 90-minute rehearsal we went to a buffet restaurant, where we enjoyed food and fellowship. It was after 9:00 p.m. when we finally arrived at the Hilton Hotel.

Our choir was scheduled to sing for the ACDA at 8:40 a.m. on Saturday, March 5th, the final day of its convention. The thought of singing so early on a Saturday morning was a little daunting, but we were determined to give it all we had. We got up in time to have breakfast at the hotel at 6:00 and then walked to the Assembly Hall to begin our "warm-up" at 7:00. The weather had turned very cold the night before, so there was a light dusting of snow on the ground as we walked to the Assembly Hall. At 8:30 a.m. we were asked to take our places in the hall so we would be on the risers when the convention officially opened its morning session.

Perhaps because of the early hour and the fact that it was the last day of the conference, the Assembly Hall was only partially filled when we began our 25-minute program. By the end of the program, however, the hall was nearly filled. The choir presented perhaps the finest program we had ever sung. The president of the ACDA-Western Region told Dan afterwards, "We could not have had a finer conclusion to our conference than the performance by your choir." On Sunday morning we checked out of the hotel and returned to the First Presbyterian Church to sing in their 11:00 a.m. worship service. After lunch, we boarded our buses and traveled to the airport for our flight home. The entire weekend proved to be the "highlight of the year" for the Chancel Choir.

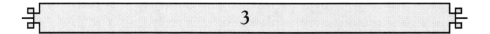

3

The catalyst for planning our three previous European ministry tours had been direct requests from contacts in Europe to consider ministry in their countries; the German pastors' visit in 1982 resulted in the 1984 tour, Ildikó Barbarics's plea in 1988 for us to minister in Hungary took the choir behind the Iron Curtain in 1989, and Erhard Jung's and Ildikó Barbarics's desire for the Solana Beach choir to ministry in Germany and Hungary culminated in our 2003 Eastern European Ministry Tour.

This time the person who challenged us to consider another ministry tour was Tom Theriault, the pastor for mission and outreach at Solana Beach Presbyterian. Ironically, this was the first time we had begun a tour exploration with a church missions pastor. We knew that organizing our next tour would be different from the way we had planned previous tours. Thus began the most extensive planning process we had ever been involved in—a process which would take four years.

Dan, Judy Enns, and I met with Pastor Tom in May of 2006 to discuss ministry tour ideas. Tom explained, "I believe that by focusing on missions, the choir can motivate the people of SBPC to be more involved in reaching the world for Christ. You as a choir are better equipped than ever to bring Christ's message to a larger audience." He then asked, "Is there a way for the choir to open a new missions link between SBPC and another needy area of the world?" Pastor Tom saw the music ministry as a "bridge builder" for future church missions work.

We now had to ask ourselves, "Where can we go to initiate a relationship between our church and the places we visit, while maximizing what the music ministry does best?" The idea emerged that we should consider going to fewer places and develop closer relationships with people by holding music and worship workshops in the places we gave concerts. We also felt we should explore how to connect with individuals, groups, churches, and other institutions on the tour.

Dan, Judy, and I scheduled a follow-up meeting with our senior pastor Mike McClenahan, Pastor Tom, and three other church leaders: Dan May, Jim Schoenick, and Carole Orness. Dan May challenged us to think "outside the box" and to consider ministering in China or Russia. Wow! The next step was to form a new Steering Committee to lead the planning process. In September, the committee held its first meeting and decided to focus on two tasks they felt should be completed as soon as possible.

The first task was for us to contact pastors and mission leaders in Europe about the possibility of a 2008 choir ministry tour. As we talked with these leaders, we would try to ascertain whether they had a passion for hosting the choir and whether they would work with us to bring about an effective ministry—not only in their church, but also in other churches in their area. We also would attempt to discern if the host organization had sufficient resources to provide outreach before and after the tour. The second major task the Steering Committee decided to focus on was preparing a Formal Proposal for Ministry, using Solana Beach Presbyterian's new "Ministry Effectiveness Profile."

The committee asked Dan Bird, Paul Smith, and me to write to pastors and leaders with whom we had developed a relationship: Erhard Jung in Pohlheim, Pastor Reinhardt Enders of the Paul Gerhardt Kirche in Leipzig, Dieter Wunderlich in Berlin, Ildikó Barbarics with Word of Life in Hungary, and Rich Hood with Czech Word of Life. Rick Jaynes, a member of our choir, was on the Board of Directors for Music Mission

Kiev, so he put us in contact with Roger and Diane McMurrin, who founded that ministry in 1993.

Doug Burleigh was recommended to us as an ideal contact for areas of the former Soviet Union. In addition, Paul Smith agreed to get in touch with a couple from our church who were then serving in southern France. Finally, Dan agreed to talk with Duane Funderburk from Lake Avenue Church regarding possible ministry opportunities in the Baltic republics, since Duane had ministered there.

The Steering Committee met two weeks later to begin putting together a Formal Proposal for Ministry. Committee members believed the tour should be a "congregation-to-congregation" ministry—one which could create long-lasting bonds between our church and other congregations. They also wanted to incorporate some of the young people in the church's Student Chorale to make the tour choir truly intergenerational.

The church proposal form asked us to formulate a mission statement for our ministry, so the Steering Committee tentatively came up with the following statement: "To present vital spiritual singing and playing to an international audience as our demonstration of God's love for us and the world and His saving grace for all." By October, the Steering Committee had completed the Formal Proposal for Ministry.

During this process, people sometimes asked us, "How does a choir mission tour compare with other mission trips?" We answered that the choir is a body with a pre-existing identity and set of talents. Choir members are already using their common gifts for music and worship, and they continue to serve together after the trip. A ministry trip deepens the relationships among the people in the choir, making them more effective in leading worship at home. Also, music is a unique way to share the gospel because it overcomes all language barriers.

In some ways, however, a choir ministry tour is much like any other mission trip in that it gives the participants an opportunity to experience missions first-hand and to return with a greater interest in reaching the world for Christ. The choir's preparation for a ministry tour is also just as rigorous as the preparation for any mission trip. Choir members must prepare for over a year as they learn and memorize many pieces of music and spend hundreds of hours in rehearsal.

In November Dan presented our four-page proposal to the Ministry Leadership Team (MLT), which includes all SBPC pastors and ministry directors. Since this was the first time the new ministry form was being used, we had no idea how the MLT would respond to our proposal. As a result of Dan's presentation, the Steering Committee held two additional meetings with Pastors Mike and Tom to further clarify what we wanted to accomplish through our next ministry tour. Pastor Mike then brought a one-page "Update on Choir Tour Proposal" to the MLT's February meeting. (A copy of this one-page proposal can be found in the appendix.) The MLT unanimously approved the proposal and sent it to the SBPC Session for their consideration.

By March of 2007 we had received letters from Ildikó Barbarics in Hungary, Roger and Diane McMurrin in Ukraine, and Doug Burleigh regarding Russia. Surprisingly, we had not heard from any of the other contacts, not even from Erhard Jung in Pohlheim. This was surprising, since we had developed such a strong relationship with Pohlheim dating back to 1984. However, we realized that God might be closing the door for us to minister in Germany on our next tour.

The initial planning and approval process for the ministry tour took much longer than the Steering Committee had expected when we began meeting in September of 2006. It was after Easter of 2007 before the church Session approved our proposal. We felt that we were finally on our way to a new ministry! (An "Executive Summary" of our proposed tour appears in the appendix.)

Once our tour was approved, the Steering Committee took two vitally important actions. First, we formed the Mission Trip Task Force committees, which are listed in the appendix. More significantly, we decided to move the date for the trip from 2008 to 2009. We believed we needed more time to nail down the places the Lord was calling us and to prepare for the tour. As we broke for the summer, the Steering Committee believed the choir was on the right track in discerning God's leading for our mission trip. We hoped the phone conferences we planned for September with our contacts in Hungary, Ukraine, and Russia would lead us to the places God wanted us to go.

4

By the time the Chancel Choir returned in September, the purpose and shape of our missions trip was coming into better focus. On Wednesday, September 5th, Dan Bird and I, along with Pastor Tom Theriault, met in the SBPC conference room for phone conferences with our contacts in Europe. Our first phone conversation was with the McMurrins. Dan had known Roger for many years, and Solana Beach Presbyterian had hosted the Kyiv Symphony Orchestra and Chorus in the fall of 2003. Roger and Diane were currently in the States for several meetings and were joined in the phone conference by their son, Mark, who then headed up the U.S. headquarters for Music Mission Kiev.

The McMurrins began the Kyiv Symphony Orchestra and Chorus in 1993 to reach out to musicians in Ukraine. In January of 1994, when Roger gave Bibles to his choir (most of the musicians had never seen one), they asked, "When are we going to start a church so we can learn to read this Book?" A month later during a worship service led by the McMurrins, ninety musicians stood, indicating their desire to receive Christ as their Savior.

Since then, the Kyiv Symphony Orchestra and Chorus has toured the United States eleven times, including several appearances at Carnegie Hall, and has performed in many other countries, including Muslim nations. The broad range of their ministry includes outreach, church planting, a prison ministry, Christian children's clubs, and a ministry to widows and orphans. All three McMurrins were passionate about the possibility of forming a partnership between Music Mission Kiev and our church. They noted that their ministry in Ukraine and our proposed mission trip both used music as the means to reach people for Christ. The Ukrainian people's love of music provided a path to their hearts.

Roger proposed a joint Fourth of July concert with the Kyiv Symphony Orchestra and Chorus in a major hall in the city. Roger told us that Ukrainians take inspiration from the freedom in the United States and hold their own "borrowed" July 4th celebrations. Roger felt we could play a significant inspirational role in these celebrations. He also encouraged us to hold one or more concerts on our own in Kiev. Diane indicated that she would love for us meet with their widows ministry; Roger added that we should count on participating in the Sunday worship service of St. Paul's Evangelical Church, the second church they had founded in Kiev. Dan and I were encouraged by our phone conference with the McMurrins and by the variety of ministry opportunities for the choir in Kiev.

During our second phone conference, we talked with Ildikó Barbarics and Alex Konya of Word of Life Hungary and Pastor Tibor Kulscar of the Budafok Baptist Church. Pastor Tibor told us that his congregation would love to have our choir return to their church. He envisioned having us participate in their Sunday morning worship service and giving a concert in their sanctuary on Sunday evening. He also suggested we look at the possibility of an additional concert in the Budafok community, perhaps in the new concert hall. Such a concert would provide an outreach to people in the community who did not have any connection with the church. Alex Konya from Word of Life added that having the choir return to their camp would help establish an ongoing partnership between WOL and SBPC. He urged us to present a concert in the village of Tóalmás, in which the camp is located, which would enhance Word of Life's relationship with the villagers and local leaders.

The last person we talked with on the phone was Doug Burleigh, our contact for Russia. Doug is an ordained Presbyterian minister and had spent 26 years in ministry with Young Life, much of it in the former Soviet Union. He told us about the special relationship he had formed with Father Alexander (Boris) Borisov, an Orthodox priest who had become a popular "renegade priest" in Moscow. Doug hoped we would have the rare opportunity as a Protestant choir to sing in a Russian Orthodox church.

In addition, Doug indicated that our choir could have a significant ministry in St. Petersburg. He gave us the contact information for Mark Bazalev, who had been involved in ministry in St. Petersburg and was currently ministering in the United States. Doug said Mark had numerous contacts in St. Petersburg, where many in his family still lived. They were members of the Central Baptist Church there, so it was likely that their church would be open to having our choir minister in their worship services. Doug explained that there are basically just three Christian church entities in Russia: the Russian Orthodox Church, the Baptist Church, and the Pentecostal Church. "The sad thing about the 'Church' in Russia," he said, "is that each denomination will have nothing to do with the others. I hope your coming to Russia will open up communication among the different churches."

Once we had determined that our mission trip would involve three countries (Hungary, Ukraine, and Russia) and four cities (Budapest, Kiev, Moscow, and St. Petersburg), we needed to get a bid to find out how much the trip would cost. I also talked with Joe Leonards about how to find tour providers who concentrated on Eastern Europe. Joe believed we would be best served by a tour provider located in a country we planned to visit. This precluded our using Icontas Service, our tour provider for the last two trips.

I then contacted Ildikó Barbarics Dobos (Ildikó married Béla Dobos in November of 2005) to see if she could recommend a tour provider. She told me that her cousin, Peter Barbarics, was in the travel business and suggested that we contact him. She added that a mutual friend of ours, Julia Winterberg Hamilton, had gone on a trip to Hungary and Romania with her church in Arizona, and they had used Peter's company, Melba Tours. Ildikó encouraged me to call Julia, which I did. I found out that Julia had been pleased with the way Peter handled their group. I then wrote to Peter, asking him if he would be interested in bidding on our mission trip. He expressed a great interest in doing so once we had solidified the details of our proposal. When we sent out the bidding documents in the spring of 2008, only Peter's company in Hungary responded with a bid. We were happy to accept it!

Dan and I also needed to take a planning trip in the summer. Fortunately, Peter Barbarics was able to work closely with me on the land arrangements for the planning trip. I also worked with Ildikó to schedule our time in Hungary and with Roger and Diane McMurrin to set up meetings in Kiev. We had a harder time finding the right contacts in Moscow and St. Petersburg, but Doug Burleigh was working on that. We decided to follow the same itinerary on the planning trip that the choir would follow the next summer.

This planning trip turned out to be completely different from the three previous trips. The most significant difference was that Dan was not able to go with me as we had planned. Dan had undergone successful surgery for prostate cancer at the end of April. He initially believed he would be able to go on the planning trip because it would not begin until June 26th, over eight weeks after his surgery. However, as time went on, he realized that the most important thing he could do during the summer was to rest and fully regain his strength and energy. Therefore, he regretfully made the decision to withdraw from the trip.

This meant I had to find a replacement for Dan. I approached a member of the Steering Committee, Paul Smith, about possibly accompanying me. Paul was a member of both the Chancel Choir and the Bells of Praise and had been a part of the 2003 ministry tour. At first, Paul did not think he could go because of work and family obligations. However, he worked out a plan: he could not participate in the first part of the planning trip in Hungary, but he would join me in Kiev for the remaining two-thirds of the trip. Therefore, I would have to conduct the Hungarian portion of the planning trip by myself.

I was already concerned about not having Dan with me, so the thought of being alone for the first six days of the planning trip was rather overwhelming. Fortunately, I already had been to Hungary several times and had developed close relationships with people there over the past twenty years. The most daunting aspect of the planning trip for me was being the official spokesman for our church and its mission. Dan had always taken the lead in meetings with potential contacts on previous planning trips; now this responsibility would fall entirely on me. To be honest, I was not sure how well I would fulfill that role. As I look back on that trip, I say to myself, "O ye of little faith." Never before have I felt the presence of the Lord as strongly as I did during that trip. In fact, it turned out to be the most productive planning trip we had ever taken.

5

I departed for Budapest on Thursday, June 26, 2009. My first meeting in Hungary was with Alex Konya, the director of Word of Life Hungary.

Alex, Ildikó, and I talked about a possible schedule for our time in Hungary. Alex was especially happy that our choir wanted to spend an entire day at the camp in Tóalmás. He then asked, "Will you bring some of your young people with you?" I told him we were still working on that. Alex also explained that he wanted to show the choir the kind of small group teaching sessions, such as English classes, which they hold for the campers, as well as some of their sports activities. We also talked about the possibility of holding a handbell workshop for interested campers.

Alex was especially intrigued by the possibility of working out some kind of long-term partnership between Word of Life Hungary and Solana Beach Presbyterian. When he asked whether one of our pastors would come with us to Hungary, I told him we hoped that would be the case. Ildikó and Béla also urged us to bring one of Solana Beach's pastors with us, perhaps Tom Theriault, our pastor of mission and outreach.

Later that afternoon the Tóalmás mayor, Magdolna Kovács, arrived at the camp. She was a gracious lady who liked Word of Life and wanted to improve the relationship between the village and the camp. She was thrilled that "such a quality choir" would want to sing in her village of only 3,000 people. Mayor Kovács said that the villagers loved music, but they did not have much opportunity to hear outstanding musical performances except in Budapest. She was also surprised and impressed that our concert would be free. We talked about where to hold the village concert, perhaps outside or in their newly-renovated cultural hall. The mayor said they might even put up a large tent for a reception after the concert. Alex promised that Word of Life would try to have several of their camp staff available at the reception to help translate. The mayor appreciated this offer, since she wanted us to communicate well with the villagers.

My time at the camp proved to be very successful. Then, since Ildikó and Béla were returning to Budafok, Ildikó suggested that Béla ride with me back to Budapest; she would then pick up Béla later at the hotel. I was glad to have Béla's company, especially since he knew how to get there! Later I was able to enjoy dinner with Béla and Ildikó at the hotel before they left for their home in Budafok. My first full day in Hungary had not been the disaster I had originally feared. Being with good friends had made all the difference!

On Sunday morning I made my way to Budafok Baptist Church and was greeted by Pastor Tibor and his family. Once the worship service began, the pastor also welcomed a visiting congregation from the town of Erd. That church had begun when five or six families from Budafok planted a new church in Erd. At first, they met in their homes. Then, as their church began to grow, they met in a small hall they rented from the local government. When that hall was rented to another business, they felt led to buy a house, even though it was rundown. The congregation raised over half of the money needed to buy the house and took out a loan for the rest. Since then, God had continued to grow their congregation in number, but more importantly, in faith. One of their founders was Zoltan Kovács, the second son of Pastor Géza Kovács.

When the church choir moved into the loft later in the service, the choir director motioned for me to join them and handed me a printed copy of some music in Hungarian. I looked at it and shook my head; I didn't think I would be able to sing with them. But Ildikó whispered to me that the piece was "Name of All Majesty," which the Solana Beach choir had sung many times. So there I was next to Pastor Tibor, a tenor, using my own form of Hungarian to sing music I had learned at Solana Beach several years before. That was a novel experience!

The pastor from the church in Erd gave the morning message based on I Timothy 1:12 (NIV): *"I thank Christ Jesus our Lord, who has given me strength, that He considered me trustworthy, appointing me to His service."* His message reminded me that even though I was there without Dan and had to represent the whole choir, God would give me strength for the journey. At the end of the service, Pastor Tibor introduced me to the congregation and told them that the church was looking forward to having our group from Solana Beach with them the following summer.

After the church service, I drove to the home of Ildikó's mother, Olga, for dinner. (Ildikó's father had passed away.) The food was delectable and the conversation was enlightening. Gabor Hellinger, the church choir director, his wife Kati, and their son Andres joined us. We talked all afternoon. Gabor said that the Protestant churches in Hungary were so conservative that their choirs could sing only Hungarian anthems or pieces by classical composers. He mentioned that he was constantly looking for new music which would speak to the hearts of their people, so he had greatly appreciated getting music from Dan over the years, which Pastor Tibor translated into Hungarian.

Gabor went on to say, "Most worship in Hungarian churches is very dull! This is a great contrast to the vitality and variety of the music of your choirs music which brought life to our worship in 2003." Ildikó added that the Spirit had gone out of many churches in Hungary. Their churches, she said, were so inwardly focused that they did not have a heart for their neighbors, their community, or the world. In short, they desperately needed a revival! I thought about our goal to be "Inwardly Strong" and "Outwardly Focused" on our mission trip. Evidently, this was the very message needed in Hungary's churches.

On Monday morning, Ildikó and I met with Pastor Tibor. He made several suggestions for our Music With a Mission trip. One idea was giving a music and worship workshop for pastors and ministry leaders from his church and other churches in the Budapest area. Pastor Tibor also told me that Budafok Church was beginning a handbell choir in the fall, so he thought it would be terrific if our Bells of Praise could give a workshop for Budafok's new bell choir.

After our visit with Pastor Tibor, we drove to the community of Erd to visit the church that had participated in Sunday's morning service at Budafok Baptist. It was intriguing to talk with the wife of Zoltan Kovács, who was a vocalist in the church's worship team and worked with the children and young people. At that time, the church was hosting a week-long day camp for their children and the children in the community as a major outreach to families in the area. The camp's theme for the day Ildikó and I visited was "King and Queen for the Day." When the children heard that my name was "King," they thought I should put on a crown and sit on the throne. I did just that while a number of parents took my picture!

Our last visit that day was with Géza and Ildikó Kovács. Géza (Jr.) has a deep understanding of the spiritual needs of the churches in Hungary. He has a PhD in biology and was a research scientist for many years. When he had turned sixty that February, he was able to "retire" and give his full time to his church. Géza told us, "What is most lacking in the church and in the lives of the Hungarian people is the hope for a better future. Your choir brings a message of hope and stimulates the faith of Hungary's Christians."

Géza thought it was amazing that our choir had been able to sing in the Mass and present a concert at the Mátyás Templom in 2003. He said that this kind of cross-denominational activity was needed in his country. For that reason, he encouraged us to set up concerts in non-traditional settings. Because the Mátyás Church would not be available the next summer due to renovation, he suggested that we work with a large new Baptist church in Vác, a city located north of Budapest on the east bank of the Duna River. Géza believed that we would enjoy visiting Vác, an historic city of over 35,000 people.

Géza and Ildikó both knew Attila Meláth, the pastor of the Vác Baptist Church, and thought he would be willing to work out something with us, either in his church or in the town's cathedral. Either way, a concert there could be used as a cross-denominational event. When Ildikó called Pastor Meláth, he sounded excited about the possibility of having our choir and bells there the next summer. So I took my rental car out of the hotel garage and Ildikó and I set off for Vác.

The Baptist Church of Vác is located in the hills overlooking the town below. Its beautiful new buildings include a sanctuary that seats 300-400 people and has a piano and organ. It seemed a perfect place for us to give a concert. After our visit to the Vác Baptist Church, Ildikó and I drove into the town to see the Vác Cathedral, a large building with an impressive Great Organ at the back. Pastor Meláth said he would talk with his contacts at the cathedral to see if they were open to the idea of our presenting a concert there.

After touring the cathedral, Ildikó and I went to the Old District of town. The central square of Vác is built in the Baroque architectural style and is both beautiful and charming. The Duna River is just a couple of blocks below the town square, so we walked down to the river and found a restaurant with shaded outdoor seating. Ildikó thought it would be a wonderful place for the choir to have a meal when they were in Vác.

Later that day I made my way back to my hotel in Budapest, where I spent a quiet evening by myself. For the past week, I had been on my own and the responsibility for making decisions had rested completely on my shoulders. At times during that week I had felt all alone, but in those times I reminded myself that I had an entire choir praying for me back home and that God was always with me. My last day in Hungary I met with Peter Barbarics in Szentendre and we went over all of our plans for the mission trip.

Having completed everything I had hoped to accomplish in Hungary, I now looked forward to flying from Budapest to Kiev the next day. I had never been to Ukraine, a republic of the former Soviet Union which is now an independent state. I was thankful that Paul

Smith would join me in Kiev and that we would be able to share our experiences in Ukraine and Russia.

6

Paul and I met up with each other at Kiev's Boryspil International Airport on Thursday afternoon, July 3rd. Paul had flown in from San Diego, and I from Budapest. We arrived within 2½ hours of each other. Paul was waiting for me in the baggage claim area just beyond the passport control booths. After we had gotten through customs with no problem, we saw Helen of Music Mission Kiev waiting with a sign that said, "Don King and Paul Smith." I had corresponded with Helen many times the previous year, but this was my first time to meet her personally. She had obtained a car and driver to take us to our hotel, the Hotel Dnipro. We discovered that we had a phenomenal view of Kiev from our room.

Helen then took us to the MMK offices, where Diane and Roger McMurrin greeted us. Roger had thrown his back out several days before and had just gotten out of bed for the first time since then. In fact, he had missed directing the Kyiv Symphony Orchestra and Chorus in their Independence Day concert the day before. Roger told us that it was the first time he had ever missed directing a concert.

After having dinner with the McMurrins in a small restaurant near MMK's offices, we returned to their apartment and had a good time just getting to know each other better. The next day we walked from our hotel to the Music Mission Kiev office; there we met the MMK staff: their two assistant conductors, the associate pastor of St. Paul's

Evangelical Church, and Natasha, who headed up the widows and food ministry under Diane McMurrin.

We then were driven to the headquarters of "CBN (Christian Broadcasting Network) in the CIS," (the Commonwealth of Independent States, a group of former Soviet republics). There we had a heartwarming visit with Vitali, an assistant to the regional director. CBN in the CIS broadcasts via radio and TV throughout the former Soviet republics.

Vitali shared his personal testimony with us. When he met Christ he was 21 years old, had just returned from the Red Army, and had never heard about Jesus. Then he found out about CBN in the CIS and wrote them a letter asking for information about becoming a Christian. Through the literature he received, Vitali began to understand that Jesus loved him and could change his life. Following the instructions in the material from CBN, he prayed to receive Christ and felt the presence of God so strongly that he began to cry. In the weeks that followed, he prayed regularly; he said that his most frequent prayer was "Help me!" As he grew spiritually, Vitali felt a growing desire to serve the Lord, so he joined the staff of CBN in CIS, the organization that had led him to Christ!

Vitali explained what CBN was doing to reach people in the former Soviet Union. CBN in the CIS receives thousands of letters each year from people who want to know Christ. They also get many phone calls, which are answered by staff members who respond to the callers' questions and connect them with Christians in their area. In addition, CBN has a far-reaching ministry with orphans. Vitali told us that they were anticipating our visit to Kiev the next year and that they would assist us in publicizing our concerts.

After our visit to CBN, we returned to the MMK office and joined the morning Bible study that Diane McMurrin led for approximately forty-five widows each week. As soon as we walked in, all of the widows stood up and applauded. They then started singing, "Happy Birthday America! Happy Birthday America!" We had completely forgotten that it was the Fourth of July. Obviously, they were looking at us not just as representatives of our church in California, but also as representatives of America, which serves as a beacon of freedom to the people of Ukraine. The widows then presented Paul and me with a bouquet of roses. It was a humbling experience.

After the lesson, the widows came over and gave each of us a big hug. Through MMK translators, many of them expressed their thanks for what Americans had done for them, saying things like "Thank you, America, for special medical help"; "Thank you, America, for food"; "Thank you, America, for sending us Roger and Diane McMurrin." Neither of us had ever experienced anything like it before and we were deeply moved.

Following the Bible study, the MMK staff served tea and muffins to the widows and then gave each of them a food package for the coming week. Approximately 350 widows receive food weekly from Music Mission Kiev. Government pensions for widows in Ukraine are minimal, from $80 to $100 a month, while their food prices rival those of the United States. Therefore, food and medicine are their primary concerns. The widows told us stories about World War II and their days under the Soviets, but they also shared their stories of faith—how they came to know about Jesus Christ and accept Him as Savior.

Ludmila's story is typical of the many stories we heard that day: *"My friend Katerina invited me to Diane's Bible classes, and from the first prayer at the lesson, I knew that I wanted to be in this spiritual family and that God had brought me here for a reason. I came to church the next day, and I told Katerina, 'This is a holy place to meet with God.' For years I had been alone with my diseases. I have only 40% vision in one of my eyes, so I always wear dark glasses because I am sensitive to light due to my eye disease. I also had pain in my spinal column, so it was hard to live.*

But during the Bible lessons and prayer group, my heart was full of joy and happiness. I prayed to the Lord and asked him to forgive my sin and come to my heart. Now I know that I am not alone. I am so grateful for His love and peace, and I talk with Jesus in prayer as my dear friend. Today I have a big Christian family and many friends. My legs don't move very well, but I am healthy in my spirit and grateful for the weekly food packets that I receive, for the visits to Gorenichi [the village where Roger and Diane now live] to attend meetings designed for aged people, for the church and Christian friendship, and for the McMurrins, who were sent by God to help us aged people. Jesus has changed my heart because of faith to Him. My life is absolutely new."

Paul and I were invited to have lunch with the MMK staff before we watched a recording session of the Kyiv Symphony Orchestra and Chorus at a special hall they used as a recording studio. They were completing another CD, which they planned to bring with them when they came to America the following September. Roger McMurrin made sure that Paul and I had plush seats up on the stage near the orchestra. Of course there was no audience—just Paul and me. We loved watching Roger work with the choir in rehearsal and during recording sessions. In our minds, we could hear Dan yelling at us in the same way. "Intonation! Intonation!" "Sopranos, don't screech at me like that!"

It was amazing that the choir recorded five pieces and the orchestra recorded an additional piece between 2:30 and 6:00 that afternoon. Paul and I enjoyed their music and were impressed by how well they worked together. When the recording session was over, Roger suggested that we have dinner with Sergei, their young assistant conductor, at a small restaurant near the MMK offices. It turned out to be the same place the McMurrins had taken us the night before. Thus ended our first full day in Kiev. What a day it had been!

The next morning, Helen met us at the hotel at 10:00. She had arranged for a car and driver to take us around Kiev so we could look at five venues in which our choir might sing. Finding the right venue in Kiev was more involved than we had first thought. One site was a well-known concert hall, the Philharmonia, located near our hotel. It seated 650 people and had a fine organ, an excellent piano, its own risers, and very good acoustics. The next place we visited was the 900-seat Central Baptist Church in the Podil District of Kiev, which was another excellent venue for the choir. Then we traveled to a Catholic cathedral which had no risers and no piano; we decided that the cathedral was better suited for chamber music.

The last place we saw was St. Nicholas Catholic Church, known as "Dome Organi Musiki," or the "National House of Organ and Chamber Music." It can seat 800 people and has a grand piano, two harpsichords, and one of the finest organs I heard on any of our trips. However, this site had some drawbacks. There was a $2,500 charge for its use, we would have to schedule our concert there at least six months in advance, and the church would not be available on either Saturday or Sunday.

Paul and I spent the afternoon checking out five different hotels that might be suitable places for the choir to stay—in addition to our hotel, the Dnipro. The hotels we saw left much to be desired, so we decided that the choir would need to stay in the Dnipro Hotel. Helen dropped us off around 4:00 that afternoon, and we collapsed in our hotel room for 1½ hours. We were exhausted from all our venue and hotel explorations.

That evening we had dinner in the McMurrins' apartment. It was prepared by one of the "Grace Gang" whom the McMurrins use as their cooks. The Grace Gang is a group of orphans, ages 17-25, who had been put out on the street. Ukraine keeps young people in orphanages only until the age of 17, after which they have to fend for themselves. Roger began the Grace Gang to teach the orphans job skills, help find them work, and, of course, share the love of Jesus Christ. As we talked in the living room after dinner, Diane urged us, "Tell this to the people in the Solana Beach choir who are undecided about taking the trip: 'We go to the mission field so God can show us something that He can't show us at home.'" That simple statement is profound.

The next day Helen took us and another couple to explore some of Kiev's famous sites. We stopped to see the Golden Gate, which is all that is left of the ancient city wall that once enclosed the old city. This is the "Great Gate of Kiev" that is portrayed in Mussorgsky's composition, "Pictures at an Exhibition." From there we went to see St. Sophia's Cathedral, built in the 11th century. For many years St. Sophia served as a burial place for Kiev's princes. Today it is protected as an architectural and historical landmark and is among the most popular attractions in Kiev. From there, we walked over to St. Mikhail's Monastery of the Golden Domes. The monastery was originally built in the 12th century, but was destroyed by the Communist government. It was rebuilt in 2001. Paul and I were impressed by the beauty of Kiev's many historic sites.

On Sunday we attended a worship service at the "Bieli Dom," as the MMK's rehearsal and worship facility is known. It is a fairly large hall on the fourth floor of the building. The choir and orchestra filled about one-third of the hall and the congregation filled the other two-thirds. We were seated in the first row next to Natasha. She spoke excellent English and translated for us. The theme of the service was "The Truth Shall Make You Free," a topic that tied in with the idea of independence which both the Ukrainian and American people had been celebrating that week. Roger concluded his message with the truth of the Gospel: "It is only as we rely totally on the atonement of Jesus Christ for our sins that we truly experience freedom."

That night we enjoyed a relaxed evening with the McMurrins and some of their friends. Roger asked if we would like to play "Mexican Train," one of his favorite games, which was unfamiliar to Paul and me. Nevertheless, we gave it the "old college try." We sat around their dining room table playing the game and eating popcorn until we realized that it was after 10:00 p.m. As we walked back to our hotel, Paul and I commented on the gracious hospitality Roger and Diane had shown us throughout our stay in Kiev.

Paul and I spent our last day in Ukraine seeing the great monastery, Kievo-Pechersky Lavra, and the National Opera House. The tourist information we picked up at the Lavra informed us, *"The 'Caves Monastery' is Kiev's number one tourist attraction both for Ukrainians and foreigners. The enormous ensemble of white church halls with green and gold rooftops has come to represent the spiritual heart of the country and symbolizes Kiev's survival throughout a millennium of adversity."* The National Opera House, built in 1901, is also a magnificent structure. While we were there we listened to a rehearsal for an upcoming opera. The singers were glorious; the sound, fantastic. After our tour of the Opera House, Helen arranged transportation for us to the Kiev train station and made sure we found the correct train, car, and compartment. Paul and I were about to embark on a long train ride to Moscow.

7

As Paul and I sat in our train compartment, we could not help but think back on our memories of the Cold War and the Soviet Union. We had visions of thousands of troops marching through Red Square on May Day with the Communist leaders looking down from a platform on Lenin's Tomb. We remembered watching movies involving the infamous KGB and reading books such as Tom Clancy's *The Hunt for Red October.* In all of these settings, the evil Communists were a constant threat to our freedom. We wondered if we would run into any problems with the Russian customs and border agents when we crossed the border into Russia.

Our train compartment was comfortable enough; it had two padded benches across from each other with a table between them. Our sleep that night was fitful, however, because of the stiff bed and paper-thin mattress. When the train pulled into the last town in Ukraine, it stopped so the Ukrainian border officials could board to check and stamp our passports. Then, about an hour later, the train stopped again, this time to let the Russian border officials check our passports and visas. Thankfully, that did not take long and the rest of the night was uneventful.

We arrived at the train station in Moscow at 6:40 a.m. and lugged our bags off the train. As we looked around for someone to meet us, we saw Anatoli Sokolov, who pastors the Baptist church in the town of Klin (pronounced "Kleen"), but lives in Moscow. He had arranged for a member of his church to bring a car from Klin and drive us to our hotel. The lobby of our hotel, the Hotel Cosmos, was a madhouse—jammed with travelers arriving, departing, and just standing around. It took a while before we, with Anatoli's assistance, could get properly checked in. The Cosmos is a huge, 25-story hotel that was built for the 1980 Olympics. Accommodations in Moscow are some of the most expensive in all of Europe, but the Cosmos is a major "tour group" hotel and therefore costs less. Some areas of the hotel were showing their age, but we were told that the rooms were being renovated.

Paul and I appreciated being able to get cleaned up at the hotel before we joined Anatoli Sokolov and began our drive to Klin, about fifty miles northwest of Moscow. It took us a long time, as traffic in Moscow is horrendous. I cannot think of any place in the world that has worse traffic. When we finally arrived in Klin, Anatoli took us to see the Tchaikovsky Home and Museum. He had arranged for an

English-speaking guide to take us through the house and grounds, which gave us a deeper appreciation of the great composer.

We then drove to Pastor Sokolov's church. He showed us around and told us about his ministry. Then he suggested that we get something to eat before we took the train back to Moscow. We were surprised and pleased to discover that two women from the congregation had prepared a homecooked Russian meal for us right there at the church. As we talked and got acquainted, Anatoli Sokolov expressed his strong desire for our choir to sing in Klin and for Solana Beach Church to establish a long-term relationship with his church.

When we arrived at the Moscow station, we took the Metro to a stop right across the street from our hotel. Anatoli insisted on paying for our train and Metro tickets; he could not seem to do enough for us. When we finally got back to our hotel room about 6:00 p.m., each of us took a shower and then relaxed for an hour. It had been a long day after a night of interrupted sleep on the train. Paul and I confessed the apprehension we had felt upon arriving in Russia; however, as a result of the generous assistance Pastor Sokolov had given us, we were looking forward to our time in Moscow.

Dr. Alex Kozynko, the former president of the Moscow Baptist Theological Seminary, met us at our hotel the next morning. We immediately bonded with Alex and felt free to talk openly with him. Alex is a man of deep faith who is one of the most respected leaders within the Russian Evangelical churches, of which the Baptists are a part. Because he is familiar with the many needs of the Russian church, he is often called upon to minister and speak all over the world. Alex founded the Moscow seminary and served as its president for a number of years, but he left that position to devote more time to his worldwide outreach.

Alex said he was looking forward to having our choir present a full program at Moscow Central Baptist Church, one of the largest Protestant churches in the city. The senior pastor of the church was

Sergey Zolotarevski and Alex was one of the "teaching pastors." We learned that the church had just begun a handbell choir with a three-octave handbell set given to them by a church in America. As a result, we discussed the possibility of not only presenting a concert, but also holding a handbell workshop at the church. Alex and Pastor Sergey also urged us to consider a second Moscow concert, possibly at a Lutheran or Catholic church. They felt that an additional concert in a different kind of church would allow us to reach beyond their congregation and their Baptist denomination into the greater community.

Alex asked us what we would like to see in Moscow, so I suggested Red Square and the Kremlin. We took off for the center of the city and, after Alex found a place to park, we started out on our 25-mile hike. (It really wasn't that long, but it felt like it.) During our walking tour of Red Square and the Kremlin, we felt overwhelmed by the vastness of Moscow and its many centuries of history. Since I majored in history in college and taught world history for many years, I was fascinated by everything we saw. Naturally, I had my video and digital cameras going the entire time!

We also took a long walk to a major shopping street in Moscow, the "Stari (or Old) Arbat." While there, we happened to meet Central Baptist's music director, Irina. We told her that we hoped to see her the next day when we met with the senior pastor of the church and attended their Thursday evening prayer service. Both Paul and I had a good feeling about a possible relationship between Central Baptist and Solana Beach Presbyterian. We told Alex that we hoped our senior pastor, Mike McClenahan, would be able to come with us to Moscow.

One of the many shops in the Stari Arbat sold fine china. I knew that I needed to get something for June on the trip, so I bought a lovely, deep blue teapot which now sits majestically in June's teapot collection. I am not sure how far we walked during the three hours we trudged through central Moscow, but our feet were so sore afterward that we could not wait to get back to the hotel and put our feet up. Paul told me later, "I never expected to be standing in the middle of Red Square," and I agreed.

The next day, we met with Pastor Sergey Zolotarevski at the Moscow Central Baptist Church and attended their Thursday night prayer service. At our meeting before the service, Pastor Zolotarevski told us that he would love to have our choir present a concert in his church. He also broached the idea of setting up a possible handbell workshop for both the Bells of Praise and their church's handbell choir. Then Alex and the senior pastor showed us around their church. We found out that Central Baptist Church is the only church in Moscow which was able to hold continuous worship services throughout the Soviet era. Even though they had to deal with the anti-church policies of the Soviet government, they remained faithful to their calling.

Alex told us stories about the anti-Christian policies of the Communist regime. One story was about the Cathedral of Christ Our Savior, the seat of the patriarch of the Russian Orthodox Church. In December of 1931, Stalin had the cathedral dynamited into rubble so he could build a huge monument to socialism called the "Palace of the Soviets." It was to be topped with a gigantic statue of Lenin. The structure was never completed, however, because the site could not sustain that amount of weight and Soviet leaders were preoccupied with the German invasion of Russia in 1941. All that remained of the once-grand cathedral was a huge hole in the ground, which was turned into a swimming pool. Alex said that he swam there as a child.

The second story Alex told us was more personal. He remembered that his grandmother had taken him to church as a young boy. When they got to the front door, they were turned away because the government under Khrushchev had decreed that children were not allowed to attend church. This was Khrushchev's attempt to end Christianity in Russia. When Alex and his grandmother returned home, she taught him from her personal Bible. Because of his grandmother's faithfulness, Alex accepted Christ as his Savior at the age of 13.

Just before the prayer service, Alex asked me if I would be willing to read a psalm during the service. He told me to choose any psalm I wanted. I therefore selected Psalm 119. (Just kidding!) Actually, I decided to read Psalm 100 because it expresses the reason we were there—to sing and worship. It was also my honor to bring official greetings from Solana Beach Presbyterian Church and to lead the congregation in prayer. I read the following words from Psalm 100 (NIV):

> *"Shout for joy to the Lord, all the earth.*
> *Worship the Lord with gladness;*
> *Come before Him with joyful songs.*
> *Know that the Lord is God.*
> *It is He who made us, and we are His;*
> *We are His people, the sheep of His pasture.*
> *Enter His gates with thanksgiving*
> *and His courts with praise;*
> *Give thanks to Him and praise His name.*
> *For the Lord is good*
> *and His love endures forever;*
> *His faithfulness continues through*
> *all generations."*

After the service, Alex took us to the Leningradsky Train Station and we boarded the "Red Arrow" train to St. Petersburg. This compartment was much nicer than the one in the train to Kiev: the beds were softer and no one woke us up to examine our passports. We were relieved that we could get a good night's sleep.

8

The train did not pull out of the Moscow station until 11:55 p.m., but we arrived in St. Petersburg promptly at 7:55 the next morning and took a taxi to the Ambassador Hotel. We had not been able to make contact with anyone from the Baptist church in St. Petersburg whom Mark Bazalev had recommended, so St. Petersburg was the only city on our planning trip where no one was there to meet us. Since we could not seem to reach anyone, Paul and I decided to take our own "walking tour" of the city. We knew the choir would want to do some sightseeing in St. Petersburg, so we figured we might as well check it out. St. Petersburg is known as one of the most beautiful cities in Europe. Built on the Gulf of Finland by Czar Peter the Great in the early 18th century, St. Petersburg is filled with magnificent Baroque buildings and is crisscrossed by a multitude of canals. No wonder it is called "The Venice of the North."

After five hours of walking and sightseeing, we were glad to get back to the hotel. When we entered our room, we found a message from Tatyana, a person Mark had said might be able to serve as our interpreter. We tried to call her for the rest of the day and into the next afternoon, but we always heard either a "beep, beep, beep" or a recorded message. By the time we returned to our room after dinner, Paul and I realized that we might not be able to contact the Baptist church.

Then we received another message from Tatyana giving us a different phone number. We tried that number and, behold, Tatyana actually answered! She asked how she could help us. We told her that we wanted to meet with people at the Central Baptist Church, but we had been unable to reach anyone who spoke English. She promised to make some phone calls and get back to us. A few hours later, she called to say that the church was expecting us on Sunday. She apologized for not being able to interpret for us because she had to teach English at a young people's camp that Sunday, but she assured us that she would send her husband, Anton, as a "substitute."

Anton met us in the hotel lobby on Sunday morning and we took the Metro to Central Baptist Church. Years before, the Communist government had forced the church to give up its central location in the historic center of the city and move north to a place we might call "out in the boonies." The congregation took over an abandoned Orthodox church building there and expanded it. In the years since their move, the neighborhood had grown rapidly. Thus, God used the Soviets to place Central Baptist in a vital new part of the city.

We met with Pastor Victor Sipko in his office and told him about SBPC and our proposed Music With a Mission. He was thrilled that our church was so interested in missions. He then invited us to attend their 11:00 worship service. While we were in Pastor Sipko's office, we heard the choir warming up and practicing their music for the service. It sounded just like our choir's "warm-ups" on Sunday morning. Some things are the same the world over! The church had a huge choir loft that could seat over one hundred people, so we and other guests were asked to sit in the loft with the good-sized choir. There was plenty of room for all of us!

In America, we get fidgety if a service lasts longer than an hour, but this congregation sat patiently through three different sermons, two offerings, four hymns, four choir anthems, and numerous prayers! The service, which had begun at 11:00 a.m., ended "promptly" at 1:15 p.m. After the service Paul, Anton, and I met with Vladimir, the director of music. He wanted our choirs to present a full concert at their church on a Saturday evening the following summer and then to sing in their Sunday morning worship service the following day. He mentioned that we also might be able to sing in a large Lutheran church at the center of town on Nevsky Prospect.

When we got back to the hotel, Paul and I began to prepare for our flight home. Since the plane was scheduled to leave at 6:15 the next morning, we had to leave the hotel no later than 3:30 a.m.! Then it would be a long trip back to the United States and home.

Paul and I learned an important lesson from our time in Russia. Just when the two of us thought we would not be able to meet with anyone at the Baptist church in St. Petersburg, God had provided a way for us to talk with the pastor and share a worship service with the congregation. Even though it was difficult to make personal contacts in Russia, God had allowed us to share our vision for ministry with the leaders of two large churches—one in Moscow and one in St. Petersburg. Also, we had been given the privilege of meeting a prominent Christian leader in Russia, Dr. Alexander Kozynko. It was clear that God was calling our choirs and our church to mission and ministry in Russia.

As we left Russia, Paul and I replayed in our minds the refrain of a hymn we had sung that Sunday morning at Central Baptist Church in St. Petersburg:

"Praise the Lord, praise the Lord! Let the earth hear His voice!
Praise the Lord, Praise the Lord, Let the people rejoice!
O come to the Father through Jesus the Son,
And give Him the glory – Great things He has done!"
(Words by Fannie Crosby - 1875)

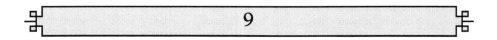

9

Paul and I were excited about everything we had learned on the planning trip, and we could not wait to share our experiences with the Solana

Beach choir. The choir's major task after we got home was preparing for three large fundraising projects. Again, there was no question in my mind about who should head up the Fundraising Committee—Marguerite Walker—but this time we added a co-chair.

As Marguerite recounted, "*We were challenged by having only sixteen months to complete our fundraising. This time I co-chaired the Fundraising Committee with Nick Stahl. Based on experience, we decided to streamline our efforts and select fewer fundraising projects with potentially larger financial impact. Nick chaired the golf tournament in August, and I was in charge of the gala dinner/auction in October. On February 20th and 21st, the choir presented another musical revue, "Passport to the World," to enthusiastic audiences. This program included popular numbers by the choir, fun songs by various ensembles such as a barbershop quartet, and solos by our special guest artists, Soprano Barbara Tobler and Tenor Leonard Tucker. We also sold SCRIP for individuals going on the trip.*

God's timing and provision were evident. We solicited donations for the golf tournament and the dinner/auction and held both events before the beginning of the recession in November, 2008. All three events were successful. Interestingly, despite working with a consultant and having celebrities attend the gala in 2008, we made about the same amount as we did in 2002. We fell short of our total goal, but what we raised was exactly what the choir needed to cover its expenses. Both times, God led us and provided what was needed, and we were very thankful."

However, people in the choir were slow to commit to the trip. Beginning in 2008 and continuing into 2009, many of them were feeling the fallout from the recession. Several people found themselves out of work, and others were concerned about whether they could keep the jobs they had. The economic picture was bleak, discouraging many in the choir from committing to the tour. The Steering Committee decided that in order for the tour to take place in 2009, we needed to have at least 50 singers registered to participate in the mission trip. Knowing that a decision could not be put off indefinitely, we set the first of March as the deadline for people to turn in these commitments. When we failed to meet that goal, the trip was officially postponed until the summer of 2010.

At the same time that we postponed the tour, we reassessed the proposed itinerary. When Paul and I came home from the planning trip, we were sure that the choir was being called to minister in Budapest, Kiev, Moscow, and St. Petersburg. This itinerary required a 19-day trip with a projected cost of over $6,000 per person. Considering the current economic situation, we realized that $6,000 would be too much for many choir members to pay. So in March we developed a simple, open-response survey for every choir member to complete. It asked just one question: "Whether or not you previously committed to go on the Music With a Mission trip to Eastern Europe in the summer of 2009, what would it take for you to go on the Music With a Mission trip in the summer of 2010?"

By the end of April we had received responses from seventy-five choir members, over 80% of the choir. The Steering Committee met to go over these responses and to discern what the choir was telling us. Two themes dominated the surveys: the length of the trip should be shortened to two weeks and the cost of the trip should be reduced. After extensive discussion and prayer, the Steering Committee decided we would drop the three-day St. Petersburg segment of the trip and limit our itinerary to Budapest, Kiev, and Moscow. We noted that our contacts in these three cities had communicated with us regularly, while we had not heard much from the people in St. Petersburg.

We then proposed a 16-day trip beginning on Friday, June 25, 2010, and ending on Saturday, July 10th. This schedule would involve only ten working days, since the Independence Day holiday fell during that time period. The total cost per person for all transportation, food, and lodging would now cost $5,000—$1,000 less per person. The choirs' response to the Steering Committee's new plan was very positive. A number of choir members who had previously said they would be unable to go on the trip now indicated that they would like to participate.

We decided that all proceeds from our fundraising projects would go to "general ministry expenses." Since we had raised over $100,000, we were able to absorb the costs for the 2008 planning trip, the translation and printing of our tour programs, the printing of the prayer calendars and information packets, piano rentals, Russian visas, group insurance, the Carnet, and other miscellaneous expenses. Those costs totaled approximately $97,000. We included a "contingency fund" in the budget, which represented 5% of the total trip cost. By the time we came home from the trip and all expenses had been paid, we ended up with a surplus of approximately $15,000!

All choir members were strongly encouraged to send out "support letters" to family and friends asking for donations to help with the tour costs. Unlike the 2003 ministry tour, when only a few people had sent out support letters, over half of those who went on the 2010 MWAM trip received financial support through these support letters. In fact, some raised over sixty percent of their entire cost this way! In addition, many in the choir participated in the SCRIP program to raise additional money for the tour.

Final preparation for Music With a Mission went into full throttle at the beginning of 2010. Registrations for the mission trip showed that we were approaching our minimum of 50 choir participants, and the choir was working hard to learn and memorize all of the music for our tour concerts. The choir leaders planned four workshops to prepare those going on the trip. The first workshop included a talk by a special guest, Doug Burleigh. Doug shared what he had experienced while ministering in Russia and told the choirs what to expect there. He also answered our questions about travel in Russia and gave us insight into Russian culture.

Another important part of the first workshop was a presentation which explained how to complete the application for obtaining a Russian visa. Linda Smith went over the application line-by line, telling us what to put in each blank. Obtaining visas for everyone would be a major project and had to be done quickly. The seminar continued with a presentation by Dr. Henderson and Linda J. Smith, a physician's assistant, about medical information everyone would need to know, and Cecily Jaynes finished off the seminar by reviewing travel logistics such as luggage weight and necessary clothing.

The next workshop was designed to give our choirs a greater understanding of the culture, history, religion, and customs in the three countries we would be visiting: Hungary, Ukraine, and Russia. A former FBI agent shared information about safety issues and other travel concerns in Eastern Europe. I had been asked to present the last part of the workshop about general travel logistics, so I talked about passports, hotel accommodations, the American consulate, and even what kind of weather to expect. I put much of this information in a handout so choir members could tell their families how to contact them in each city.

Mission preparation was the main topic of the third workshop. Tom Theriault spoke about how to spiritually prepare for the trip. He also announced that he would be joining us during our week in Hungary. Carol Orness, a Steering Committee member, then reviewed the various mission activities we might be involved in. The workshop concluded with a presentation by Dr. Henderson and Linda J. Smith about how to do CPR. They scheduled a fourth workshop for people who wanted to actually practice CPR. Naturally, we hoped that we would not have to use this information, but we felt it was prudent to be prepared.

We were now coming down the home stretch in our preparations for Music With a Mission. After we collected the final payment from each tour participant and made our last payments to Peter Barbarics at Melba Tours and to Delta Airlines, the two major items that still had to be finalized were obtaining our Russian visas and obtaining a Carnet. Linda D. Smith was the primary player in our acquisition of visas. After we returned from the trip, Linda told the story of how that process went. *"In preparation for the MWAM trip, I learned that, ultimately, God is in control! Dianne and I worked diligently to make sure all 61 Russian visa applications were completed correctly. This was not an easy task, as the applications were complicated and intimidating. We submitted the applications, along with everyone's passports, to the visa service as instructed, 90 days before we would enter Russia. We thought that our job was done, but we soon found out that there was one more important step—prayer.*

The visa service had great difficulty getting the applications processed. Both the San Francisco Russian Consulate and the New York Consulate refused to process applications until 45 days prior to entry. The clock was 'clicking' as our applications were shipped around the country while we looked for a consulate that would take them. The applications finally landed in Washington D.C., where the visa service worked with the Russian Embassy. Even so, the process was very slow. The embassy accepted a few applications at a time, with no promise of when the visas would be granted. We were told that due to the laid-back attitude of embassy workers, there was an outside chance that some visas would not be issued in time! In desperation, we forwarded some applications to a consulate in Seattle. Throughout this process, prayer was our only hope. The passports with visas attached dribbled in slowly. Three weeks before departure, we received the last passport and approved visa. God was in control!"

The "Carnet" was another matter. As I explained earlier, a Carnet is an official customs and immigration document that allows equipment and materials to clear customs in each country on a group's itinerary.

I first become acquainted with Carnets in 1989 when the Lake Avenue choir ministered in Western Europe and behind the Iron Curtain. We used a Carnet again for Solana Beach's 2003 tour to Germany, the Czech Republic, Austria, and Hungary. As you may remember, we ran into problems on that trip because we had not listed our handbell choir tables and foam on the Carnet.

For the 2010 tour, we asked Jenny Post to oversee the acquisition and control of the Carnet. Jenny was a member of the Bells of Praise who had taken a fall in our church choir loft and had broken her wrist. Since she could not play the bells, she was asked to direct the Bells of Praise. Jenny taught music in the public schools and was a perfect choice to lead the bell choir. Her leadership also allowed Dan to concentrate on the Chancel Choir and to rest during concerts while the bells played. Since much of our equipment was for the handbell choir, Jenny seemed the natural person to take charge of the Carnet.

When Jenny agreed to be responsible for the Carnet, she had no idea of the problems that were to come. After we returned from the trip, she shared her experiences. *"When the Chancel Choir traveled to Europe last summer, I was in charge of the Carnet. The Carnet listed all of the equipment we took to Europe which we wanted to bring back to the United States—namely, the handbells and handbell equipment and the audio-video equipment. Each time we either left or entered a country, I showed officials the paperwork that needed to be inspected and the forms that needed to be filled out and stamped by customs officials in each country. Upon our return, that paperwork was returned to U.S. Customs.*

Our pastors had done a great job of teaching us about words that strengthen our faith—words such as 'hope,' 'love,' 'peace,' 'blessing,' and 'prayer.' When Don King asked if I would write about my experiences with the Carnet, I must admit that the words which came to my mind were not positive words! We had anticipated that questions would arise about our Carnet, but we did not expect to have the level of difficulty we actually encountered. I met with customs officials eight times over the course of the two weeks we were overseas, and six of those times we encountered some kind of difficulty.

One problem was out of our control: a box was left in New York and didn't make it to Budapest with us. Luckily, Hungary's Customs office let us take the rest of the equipment to our hotel on the day we arrived in Hungary. Karen and I then returned to the airport the next day to collect the last box and get the paperwork signed. However, U.S. Customs had an issue with our numbering system. Every box and case had a number, but our numbering system mixed Carnet and non-Carnet items, something the U.S. Customs officials did not appreciate. We will need to correct this problem on any future tour.

In Ukraine and Russia, customs officials wanted the paperwork in their native languages. I had to spend two extra hours in the Kiev airport with Lee and Chuck Hawley while our Carnet was translated into Ukrainian. When we got to the Russian border, the customs officials refused to sign the Carnet because it was not in Russian. However, the train engineer told the officials that our train had to depart immediately to stay on schedule, so the Russian officials waved us on. Our Carnet was never translated into Russian.

Upon our return to the United States, I made an error in communication. This caused some of our passengers to check their luggage through to San Diego from New York instead of waiting for the other passengers to disembark. This meant that I could not show the entire Carnet to U.S. Customs. Because Russia had refused to sign anything, there were blank pages in our paperwork. I had to talk to seven different customs officials in New York City before one was willing to sign the papers.

Through all of these challenges, God was with us—sometimes in obvious ways, at other times behind the scenes. We all made it to each city. No one lost luggage. Even though traffic was bad at times, we made it to our destinations and managed to keep smiling. Most importantly, we were able to do God's work. The joy on the faces of the people who attended the concerts and spent time with us confirmed that our work had produced fruit. With God's help, we were able to get past the challenges and to focus on the reason we were there—to share God's Word and God's love.

Now I can look back on that amazing experience and thank God for the work He did in my life, as well as in the lives of the people we met in Europe. Going on the mission trip changed me; it gave me the ability to approach the difficult times in my life with a new outlook because I know that He is there with me, even when I'm not aware of it. When I reflect upon the frustration I felt and reread what I wrote in the daily journal I kept on the trip, I realize how much I have grown in patience and in understanding of what I can expect from God. In this time of immediate gratification, we can get caught up in the need to see results right now, but God doesn't work on our timetable. Appreciating what He can do also helps us understand that we need to step back, take a breath, and let God show us—in His time—the path we need to take.

I still shudder when I think of the word 'Carnet,' but I can also look back with a new appreciation for how God works in all our lives. The words which now come to mind when I reflect back on the responsibilities I had in Europe? 'Patience,' 'confidence,' 'understanding' — not just about the tour, but also about the bigger picture, the role God plays in our lives every day."

By the time we were ready to leave on our Music With a Mission trip, 48 singers were committed to go, plus Dan and Susie. The choir was exceptionally well-balanced with 15 sopranos, 15 altos, 7 tenors, and 11 basses. In fact, the ratio of men to women was the best of all our tour choirs. Fourteen "choir associates" also joined the group, including spouses, one son, one grandson, Pastor Tom, and Pastor Mike and his wife, Amy. Pastor Tom Theriault would be with the choir in Hungary, and Senior Pastor Mike McClenahan and his wife would join the choir for the last week of the trip in Kiev and Moscow. Our group also included Solana Beach Presbyterian members, Dan and Radona May, who joined the choir during our time in Kiev.

As our departure date approached, we were confident that we had done everything possible to prepare our people for the trip, including giving every MWAM tour participant an extensive "information packet." If that information did not get them prepared for the upcoming trip, nothing would! The participants told us later how much they enjoyed reading the information in the packet and how much it helped them throughout the trip. A list of the items in the packet appears in the appendix.

Thirty-seven people took our "group flight" from San Diego to Budapest on Friday, June 26th, with a stop at New York's JFK Airport. The rest of the tour participants took other flights or flew to Budapest early, one to three days before the main group arrived on Saturday, June 27th. I was among those flying to Budapest early so I could meet with Peter Barbarics to review all of the logistics for the trip before the choir arrived.

I was excited about the trip, but I would miss the company of my wife, June. Her health and her stamina were not up for such a long trip. This was the only choir ministry tour that she would not be a part of. It was a great disappointment that June and I could not share the experience. However, I would not be alone. Over sixty people were accompanying me (!) and I knew that God would be with me. I relied on God's promise in Deuteronomy 31:6 (NIV), *"Be strong and courageous . . . for the* LORD *your God goes with you; He will never leave you nor forsake you."* This verse gave great assurance to us all.

CHAPTER NINE

Seeing God at Work
(A Tale of Three Cities)

> *"We are not alone, we are not alone*
> *We are not alone, God is with us.*
> *We are never alone, for God is with us.*
> *Now, through all our days, always.*
> *For ever and ever, we are never alone.*
> *And God will make us strong, for God is with us.*
> *We will press on, for God is with us.*
> *Our God is with us now."*
> *From "We Are Not Alone"*
> *Words and Music by Pepper Choplin*

The 2010 Music With a Mission trip involved the most extensive planning we had ever done for a ministry tour. It was also the last major "Out of the Loft" trip I helped organize, so I was determined to do everything I could to make this trip the best ever!

Each ministry tour has its own unique challenges. My challenge was going on the trip without my dear wife, June. I was, of course, excited about the trip and all that we believed the Lord would do in and through the choir, yet I felt very much alone. One of the songs the choir sang on the trip is called "We Are Not Alone." This piece ministered to us, as well as to our audiences. As I look back on the MWAM trip, I realize how much this song gave me strength throughout my time in Budapest, Kiev, and Moscow.

Unlike on previous tours, I planned to fly to Europe before the rest of the choir to work out logistics with Peter Barbarics of Melba Tours. My e-ticket said that I would be flying from San Diego to Chicago. There I would catch a flight to Frankfurt and then another flight from Frankfurt to Budapest. I checked in online for my flight to Chicago the next afternoon, June 22nd, and I was all ready to go to the San Diego airport the next morning. Later, for some reason, I decided that I should check to see if my 1:33 p.m. flight to Chicago would be leaving on time. To my dismay, I learned that my flight would not be late—it had been canceled! I began to panic.

The person who answered when I called United Airlines Reservations must have been from some far-away country, as I could barely understand what he said because of his accent. I gave him my sob story: I needed to get to Budapest immediately because I was in charge of a group of 60 people who would arrive there in two days. My pleading had no effect on him. After putting me on hold for a half-hour, he said that he could not get me on any flight to Budapest, either that day or the next. In fact, all he could offer me was to refund my money. That was crazy, since I was using frequent flier miles!

When I continued to plead on the phone, he relented and asked if I wanted to talk with his supervisor. Thankfully, I could understand what the supervisor said. I again related my sad story and the supervisor said he would see what he could do. When he finally came back on the line, he gave me the great news that I could take a flight to San

Francisco and fly from there to Frankfurt. This would allow me to make the connection I already had from Frankfurt to Budapest. He then informed me that he could only make the change by having all my flights bumped up to business class. Is there really a God in heaven? You bet! Thus, I had to suffer for Christ in my business class seat, which allowed me to actually get some sleep that night.

Our tour provider, Peter Barbarics, met me at the Budapest airport when I arrived on Thursday afternoon. Ildikó Barbarics Dobos joined Peter and me for dinner that night at my hotel. We went over the entire Hungarian itinerary and made only one small modification in the schedule. We also had to make several trips to the airport that day to pick up choir members who had taken individual flights and had arrived in Budapest before the main group was scheduled to get there on Saturday.

As I went to my hotel room that night, I thought back on my trip to Budapest. The Lord had opened the way for me to get there—even when it looked like I might be the one who was "left behind." This gave me the assurance that the Lord would continue to keep His hand on our travel arrangements. When the United Airlines supervisor I talked to had been able to solve my problem, I told him that he was an answer to prayer. I don't know what he thought of that, but I didn't care. He was God's answer to my prayers. Praise the Lord!

Friday was a good day; I had time to rest and to greet those who arrived. Some of them got to Budapest without their luggage, but eventually all of the "early birds" were reunited with their bags. That evening some of the other early arrivals invited me to join them for dinner at the hotel. Their fellowship lifted my spirits after I had spent most of the day by myself. That night I thought of the phrase, "We are never alone, for God is with us," and these words kept coming back to me throughout the trip.

2

After 3½ years of planning for our Music With a Mission trip, we officially began our tour when the "main group" arrived in Budapest on Saturday morning. Their travel had not been without problems—various choir members had dealt with canceled flights, delayed flights, missed connections, and connections made without luggage. But, except for one couple, everyone was there. Our long-awaited mission trip had begun!

Unfortunately, we were missing two people, Bill and Sylvia Fee. Bill was then 88 years old, but he was determined to go on the trip. He and Sylvia flew out of San Diego with the main group, but soon Bill began having serious medical problems on the plane. Here is Sylvia's account of what took place: *"Half an hour into our flight from San Diego, Bill turned to me and said he was feeling really bad. My heart sank. Thoughts whirled in my head, 'Oh, no, not now—not after the years of planning and fundraising, not after the morning's chaos at the airport, not when we had just gotten going!' Bill was turning pale and faint before my eyes, and a cold fear gripped me. Help soon arrived: flight attendants, two doctors and two nurses from our group, and (God wasn't stingy) an emergency room doctor who had almost finished his residency. Several choir members came by to let me know they were praying for Bill.*

Bill was taken to the rear of the plane and laid on the floor of the galley, where choir member Katherine Dingle hooked him up to an I.V. The next few hours were a blur. The doctors asked me for details about Bill's symptoms. A passenger behind me offered the use of his computer, which accepted the thumb drive containing the choir medical history forms that everyone had filled out 'just in case.' When I wasn't answering questions, I was praying silently for every person aboard the plane.

Another 'God thing' was that Pastor Tom was on our flight. He exchanged his seat for the galley floor, sitting for hours with his back against the airplane wall, cradling Bill's head in his lap. What an intercessor he was, praying for Bill and encouraging him! At one point, a flight attendant asked her colleague, who had been in the back on the plane, how things were going. She replied, 'They're singing back there!'" Eventually, Bill improved enough that it was decided the flight did not need to divert to Pittsburgh and could land in New York as planned. But Bill and I still had to leave the plane in New York and go by ambulance to the nearest hospital. Bill had the presence of mind to arrange for the items we were carrying for the tour to be transferred to other choir members.

After the Jamaica Hospital medical staff had conducted several tests, reviewed Bill's medications, and made a couple of adjustments, they were satisfied that we could leave. Now all we had to do was catch up with the choir. However, since it was the height of the tourist season, we had to cool our heels for a few days before we could take an Air France flight to Paris and from there to Budapest."

On Saturday night, the choir was treated to a superb welcome banquet prepared by our hotel. The tables were set to perfection, and each course was a culinary treat. It was good for the choir to have that time together to share trip adventures and look forward to our ministry. At the end of dinner Peter Barbarics, our tour provider, made a few remarks which set a positive tone for the next two weeks. After Peter spoke, Ildikó told us how much the Hungarian people were looking forward to our ministry over the next five days. Dan then shared his heart with us about our upcoming ministry, followed by Pastor Tom Theriault, who gave us a final thought.

Pastor Tom said that on the previous Wednesday he had run into a SBPC missionary, who asked about the choir mission trip. She then prayed with Tom for our choir and for unity among everyone involved in MWAM. Tom said that the missionary had prayed for the one thing we needed most to preserve—our spiritual unity. He reminded us that Satan loves to divide people, especially when they are engaged in ministry. "When we get stressed and tired," Tom reminded us, "it is easy to say or do things that cause dissent." Tom ended our time together by praying for our spiritual unity. After all of the excitement of our travel and arrival, a fine dinner, and encouraging words from our leaders, we were ready for a good night's rest before we began our first intensive day of ministry.

I was responsible for sending the official MWAM blog to the church every day; my blog was then posted on the church's official website. Each evening I found my way down to the hotel lobby or "business center" to use a computer with Internet access. When I could not write the official blog at night, I would get up early and try to do it before breakfast. Upon our return from the trip, many people in the congregation told me how much they had appreciated being able to read about what we were doing each day. They concluded, "It felt like we were right there with you!"

That Sunday we were just getting into the swing of loading and unloading our equipment. We took it out of the locked storage room in the hotel and put everything on the bus. After the buses were filled with people and equipment, we headed out on our first full day of ministry. For some of us, returning to Budafok Church was a reunion. Dan Bird and I had worshiped with that congregation several times since 1988, and a number of people in the choir had participated in our 2003 ministry tour. But, for others in the choir, it was a new experience.

As the Budafok Church's morning worship service began, Pastor Tibor Kulscar enthusiastically welcomed us. Our good friend, Ildikó, translated Pastor Tibor's comments and his opening prayer. We then sang "Amazing Grace" together with the congregation—they in Hungarian and we in English. Our Bells of Praise had already decided to play

"Amazing Grace" during the service, so the congregation got their fill of God's grace that day! Our choir also sang two numbers before Pastor Tom Theriault was introduced to bring the morning's sermon.

Tom presented a challenging message from the Book of Jonah. As Ildikó translated Tom's sermon, she switched easily back and forth between English and Hungarian, which is not an easy task. Yet it went so smoothly that one would have thought Ildikó had received an advance copy of what Tom would say. They made an amazing team. Toward the end of the service, which ran almost two hours, their choir joined us in singing the anthem, "Name of All Majesty," each choir in its own language. If this had been the Day of Pentecost, as portrayed in the Book of Acts, people might have believed that we were speaking and singing in tongues. They also may have wondered, as did the people in Jerusalem, if we had had too much to drink!

Following the service, our people were divided up into groups of two, three, or four and were taken to the homes of different Budafok families for Sunday dinner. Even though there were some language difficulties, all of us had a wonderful time getting to know these special people, hearing their stories, and sharing their generous food and hospitality. When the choir returned to the church at 4:00 p.m. to prepare for the evening's concert, we all talked about how much we had enjoyed our Budafok families.

The concert went exceedingly well, the audience was enthusiastic and appreciative, and at the end they kept asking us to sing more. However, we were so exhausted from jet lag and the rigors of travel that I do not think we could have sung one more song. I should mention a Spirit-filled moment during the concert. After the handbells had played their second set of music, Pastor Tom shared a short personal testimony. We could see that the congregation was glued to every word Tom was saying, and we felt the powerful impact that his testimony was having on them. He ended his brief remarks by saying that if anyone there did not know Jesus as Lord and Savior, it was our hope that they would accept Him.

Having a pastoral dimension to our ministry that year added a powerful dynamic to the mission. It was a gift from God that we were able to have Pastor Tom join us for our five days in Hungary and later to have Pastor Mike and Amy with us in Kiev and Moscow. After the Budafok concert we were treated to an upbeat reception; the tables were piled high with wonderful food and we loved talking with the people. When the choir finally made it back to our hotel after 9:30 p.m., we were exhilarated—even though we were exhausted. Our full day of music, fellowship, and worship with the Budafok congregation had energized and inspired us as we began our two-week trip in Central and Eastern Europe.

3

Following a full day at Budafok Church on Sunday, the choir had some free time the next morning. We had several activities to choose from. One choice was to take a city tour of Budapest, which was ideal for the people who had not been to Budapest before. For those of us who had been part of the choir's 2003 trip to Eastern Europe, a tour was also offered to the town of Szentendre, about an hour's drive from our hotel. Those who were too tired to take either group tour could hang out in the hotel, sleep, or shop—whatever they desired. The day was perfect for sightseeing. During the weekend the skies had been overcast, with a few showers, but Monday dawned with a beautiful blue sky dotted by floating white clouds.

Since I had taken several Budapest city tours over the years, I chose the Szentendre tour. The town dates from Roman times, although most of the historic section was built in the 18th and 19th centuries. When we arrived there, the women went shopping, while the guys explored the town, took pictures, and ended up at a street café for a cold drink or a cup of coffee. Sure enough, when everyone got back on the bus, the gals held a "show and tell" of the items they had purchased, while the guys shared the photos they had taken. It was therapeutic for us to have a complete change of pace.

Our mission for the day, however, was to present a concert on the opening night of the Baptist Union's Church Music Convention. Church musicians from all over Hungary attend this gathering every year. That year the convention was held at the Ujpest Baptist Church, located in the northern section of Budapest. (We found out that "Ujpest" means "New Pest." Quite a name for a church!)

Each concert venue has its own set-up challenges: how the choir should be arranged, where and how the handbell choir would be set up, and where to place the microphones and other audio recording equipment. Ernie headed up our audio recording team, along with two others. The video team was overseen by Jay, a choir spouse, who was assisted by the two teenagers on our trip, Luke and Glen. Before each concert they had to find a place in the sanctuary, usually in the balcony, where they could set up their video camera and tripod without blocking the view of the audience.

Before the program began, Pastor Tom offered us some words of encouragement. He said that our choirs had sung and played "beyond themselves" the previous evening in Budafok. Many of us still did not know all of the words and some of us were not yet totally confident about the music, but Tom told us not to worry about that. He said, "The Lord has taken your sacrifice of learning and memorizing the music, as well as your total commitment to the ministry, and He has empowered you to reach a new level of spiritual singing and playing." We deeply appreciated his words.

It was great that the church had a choir loft so our choir members could sit whenever we were not singing. After we all squeezed into the loft, the area was a bit crowded, but it worked. Susie Shick, our organist/pianist, always did an outstanding job of working with the many different pianos and organs she encountered on the tour. That day she arrived at the church a half-hour before the choir in order to become familiar with the pipe organ. Unfortunately, the organ was being tuned when she arrived, so she had very little time to try out the organ before the concert. I thought the organ sounded fine, but Susie told me the next morning that she was not happy with the way she had played. The audience, however, loved her playing. She is an amazing musician—and, like most musicians, a bit of a perfectionist.

I had expected the audience that night to be on the older side, but many young people were also in attendance. Most of them went up into the balcony, while the adults chose to sit on the main floor. This evening's program was different from the program we had presented the night before in Budafok. First, after the choir sang our usual "Praise to the Lord" in the round and moved up into the loft to sing "Greet the Dawning," a pastor preached a 15-minute sermon on "singing" from the Book of Revelation. We therefore had to shorten our program by cutting out the first set of handbell numbers. The ushers gave us hymnals so we could sing with the congregation, and we did our best to correctly pronounce the Hungarian words. But I am quite sure that no one paid any attention to our Hungarian. Everyone in the church was focused on praise and worship, singing the hymns in parts and filling the auditorium with gorgeous harmony. It was obvious that this group of church musicians loved to sing!

Those of you who have taken a musical tour know that there is often a letdown after the first concert. Adrenalin usually gets people through the first program, but then as they begin to relax after a long journey and a full day of ministry, they find it difficult to recharge their batteries. In spite of this, the Lord used our gift of song and praise to His glory. This audience insisted that we sing another piece after we had finished the concert with "When I Survey the Wondrous Cross." Dan finally agreed to repeat our opening number, "Praise to the Lord," as an encore. They loved it!

The next day the choir took off in a dozen different directions during our morning off. Our activities ranged from taking the Thermal Baths at the Gellert Hotel, to visiting the Franz Liszt Museum, to walking through the Grand Market in downtown Budapest. However, Dan Bird and Pastor Tom Theriault did not have the morning off. The two of them were scheduled to lead a seminar on music and worship for people attending the Baptist Union Music Convention, the same group we had sung for the previous evening.

Pastor Tom shared what happened that morning: *"The best-laid plans of mice, musicians, and mission pastors often go astray. I long ago learned the truth of Proverbs 19:21: 'Many are the plans of a man's mind, but it is the Lord's purposes that prevail.' Only God knows how meticulously each event on the 2010 musical mission trip had been planned. Don King, Dan Bird, Linda Smith, and so many others labored intensely for several years to put together an itinerary that was as exciting as it was detailed. I fit into the first leg, the Hungary portion of the mission trip.*

I was told well in advance what my role would be during each performance. I was to give a verbal witness to the gospel to complement the choir's musical witness. I knew exactly where I would speak each day and to whom I would be speaking, so I planned my talks accordingly, tailoring my message to the people in each location. Having preached with interpreters on many occasions, I knew to brief my translator ahead of time so he/she could take my alliterations, rhymes, etc. and come up with local equivalents. Ildikó, our translator in Hungary, was superb. She was able to translate not just the content, but also the flavor, style, and fervor of my speaking.

Our first concerts in Hungary in two lively Baptist churches went off without a hitch. Our musicians were Spirit-filled and my messages seemed to really connect. Dan and I were especially excited about our third 'performance,' giving a workshop for interested people at the Hungarian Baptist Music Conference. We envisioned a room full of church choir directors, experienced musicians, and spiritual leaders. Both Dan and I had prayed long and deep about what we might offer these dedicated servants of Christ. Ildikó and I had gone over my notes the day before, so we were ready to roar as we were taken to a large room in the church and eagerly awaited the arrival of our Hungarian colleagues.

As they filed in, Dan and I looked at each other with alarm. With a couple of exceptions, the Hungarian church musicians facing us were all teenagers!!! They were NOT the current generation of music leaders; they were the NEXT generation of Christian worship leaders! Dan and I looked at each other and laughed nervously as we agreed that our prepared talks were out the window. We shot up a quick prayer: "O.K., Lord, what do You want us to say?" I leaned over to Ildikó and told her to forget the notes I had shown her the day before. We were going to wing it in the Spirit.

Because Dan was the senior of the two of us and because I was a coward and needed more time to think of something to say, I deferred to him: "Dan, you go first!" Dan took a deep breath, stood up, and let it flow. It was far from the professional talk he had prepared, but it was even better. Dan was warmly and humorously personal about his own walk with the Lord as a young musician and how his music and his faith had melded together into a rewarding life. I was touched, as were the teenagers in front of us. When it was my turn, I followed suit. Rather than giving the talk I'd prepared on theological/biblical aspects of worship leadership, I simply shared how I had been led to Jesus through music. . . .

I was sixteen and had never set foot in a church or read the Bible. My family was troubled, but very musical. When my best friend invited me to sing in his church's youth choir, I agreed. At first I felt a little out of place, but I loved to sing and soon found common ground with the other young singers. Eventually, I found Jesus Christ. I told my teenage audience that it was Jesus who had made my life sing for over forty years. I challenged them to develop their musical gifts and to use music as a bridge to lead others into God's kingdom. I've seldom felt more carried along on the wings of the Spirit as I felt in front of that group of young musicians, an audience I had not expected to address on the trip. The moral of the story: We make our plans, but God's plans are always so much better. Our job is to be prepared and to trust the Lord for whatever HE has prepared. We must leave room for surprises! What an exciting way to live!"

At 1:00 that afternoon, we boarded our two buses and headed to the city of Vác, an hour's drive north of Budapest. It is an ancient city, originally settled by the Romans, which suffered major destruction during attacks by the Turks during the Middle Ages. The city was rebuilt in the 1800s in the Baroque style, and its old town center is sensational. The group enjoyed surveying the large square and the various shops around it.

One shop in particular attracted quite a number of our people. It was a special china shop which had a reputation for selling fine china at reasonable prices. The only drawback was that this shop did not take credit cards or U.S. currency—only Hungarian forints. In spite of the need to exchange money, several people came away with treasured purchases. I must admit that I was one of them. I needed to find something to take home to June, and I knew she would love another teapot to add to her collection. What I found, however, was a complete teapot set—a teapot, two cups and saucers, and a cream and sugar set, all on an elegant tray. I decided that I just <u>had</u> to have it!

Later that afternoon, all of us had dinner at the Halászkert Restaurant right on the Duna (Danube) River. We ate outside at tables sheltered by a permanent awning and watched the river flow by. It was great to relax in such a charming setting. Ildikó had done an outstanding job of interpreting for the local pastors, for Dan, and especially for Pastor Tom, and we were indebted to her for all of her help. We expressed our appreciation by presenting her with a piece of Hungary's finest china at our dinner that afternoon. Obviously, someone had been in the china shop I mentioned earlier. Ildikó was surprised and moved by that token of our love.

The Baptist Church of Vác was only a couple of miles from our restaurant, so we made it to the church in plenty of time for our 6:30 p.m. concert. The church was pastored by Attila Melath, a young man who had a vibrant ministry in Vác. An interesting fact about Pastor Melath is that his uncle was pastor of the Baptist church in the city of Pécs when the Lake Avenue Sanctuary Choir ministered there in 1989.

It was quite warm that night and the church, like most churches in Hungary, did not have air conditioning. The chancel and choir loft, therefore, were not the most pleasant places to be. However, the choir and bells presented another exhilarating program, and Pastor Tom shared a touching message. You could see tears in the eyes of many in the audience and in the eyes of some choir members as they listened. Pastor Tom has an unusual gift for sharing the love of Jesus Christ with any group of people. The fact that God had chosen Tom to be there with us was confirmed over and over again that week.

Two occurrences made that evening especially poignant. I shared earlier how Bill and Sylvia Fee were delayed in New York due to Bill's medical problems and had difficulty arranging a flight to Hungary. The last information we had received from them was that they were supposed to arrive in Budapest on Wednesday morning, the day we would spend at the World of Life camp in the village of Tóalmás.

Rob, one of our choir members, wrote about a pleasant surprise at the Vác church that night: *"Halfway through the concert, we were enthusiastically singing 'Worthy to be Praised,' a lively gospel song that includes tambourines and clapping. Just then, Bill Fee walked into the narthex of the church with a walker and moved down the aisle to the front row—while we were singing! You could feel a sudden surge of renewed energy throughout the choir as we clapped and sang praises all the more! All of us were ecstatic. The words of the song seemed all the more apropos: 'Join all and sing Hosanna. Oh praise ye the Lord. Oh, let every voice sing out that He's worthy to be praised. Our grateful voices raise; Praise His holy name! I will sing, I will shout, He's worthy to be praised!'"*

After Bill had been nursed back to health in New York, he and Sylvia boarded a flight to Hungary on Day 5 of the 16-day trip. When they arrived at the airport, they knew we would be singing in a remote town that evening, so they arranged for a taxi to drive them all the way to Vác! Bill seemed to feel refreshed and renewed, and he stayed in good health for the rest of the trip. He was especially effective in ministering to the many seniors we met during the trip. His recovery illustrates Isaiah 40:29-31 (NASB): *'He gives strength to the weary, And to him who lacks might He increases power. Though youths grow weary and tired, and vigorous young men stumble badly, Yet those who wait for the Lord will gain new strength. They will mount up with wings like eagles, They will run and not get tired, They will walk and not become weary."*

The second poignant event that evening took place throughout the concert. Don, a choir member who shares my first name, was one of those particularly moved by this situation. In his "Seeing God at Work" story, he wrote the following: *"My most memorable and impacting stop came at the Vác Baptist Church in Hungary. The church was filled with people of all ages and I could feel the anticipation of the congregation.*

One of the last to be seated was a mother and her wheelchair-bound son, who was severely disabled and limited in speech. They came up the center aisle and his mother 'parked' his wheelchair in the aisle next to the pew where she was sitting. The young man was very animated, but I couldn't tell from his mother's actions if his rapid movements were triggered by his disability or were caused by his excitement at being there.

Once we began to sing, he quieted dramatically. When the Bells of Praise began playing, a hush fell over the congregation—and peace came over the face of the young man in the wheelchair. He later attempted to clap with his mother's assistance and spoke joyfully after every song. Pastor Tom's message that night dealt with the challenges Tom and his wife had faced as a result of their daughter's pregnancy and the joy that followed. The relevance of his message could be seen in the faces of many in the congregation. As the choir came down from the chancel and surrounded the congregation for our last song, Dan made his way down the center aisle to direct us. As Dan neared the wheelchair, the young man reached up and touched Dan. I saw such joy, tenderness, and peace in his face. The Holy Spirit surely had touched him, as I know I had been touched."

Pastor Meláth was very gracious to us and had a wonderful sense of humor. After the concert, the church provided a reception of crisp salads, cold meats, and fresh fruit. Pastor Meláth vowed, "When I'm able to visit Los Angeles, I will be sure to come down to San Diego and visit you." Dan retorted, "San Diego is much more beautiful than Los Angeles!" The pastor also said, "When I come to America, I'd like to sing a duet in your church with Mike Rosensteel [our tenor soloist]." Pastor Meláth then insisted that he and Mike practice right there. He went over to Mike and the two of them began to sing, "A...men, A...men, A...men, Amen, Amen." We all had a great time fellowshipping with the people at the church in Vác.

We spent our last full day in Hungary in Tóalmás, a village of approximately 3,000 people that is located about 1½ hours east of Budapest. Word of Life Hungary is located in this village. As I mentioned earlier, it occupies the former estate of the Andrassy family, who were among Hungary's elite. The main building, which Word of Life calls "the castle," is a national historic building, and the grounds cover approximately 75 acres of land, much of it wooded. It is truly a picturesque site.

Our choir arrived at Word of Life a little after ten that Wednesday morning, the last day of June. This was the first week of Word of Life's seven week-long summer camps. The first two camps each summer are for children ages 8 to 12; the last five camps are for teenagers. About ninety campers were at Word of Life that week. When we arrived, we had a chance to wander around the grounds and through the castle before we had to get ready for the abbreviated concert we were presenting to the kids at 11:30 a.m.

We sang the lighter music in our repertoire for the campers, including spirituals and gospel songs. The children especially enjoyed the Bells of Praise. When Pastor Tom gave a short message, he related so well with the kids! At the end of our brief concert, the campers were invited to come up and see how the handbells and hand chimes were played. You should have seen their expressions as they rang and listened to the sounds of the bells!

After the program, we joined the campers for lunch in their dining hall. Listening to them took many of us back to the days when we attended church camp. The campers came up with a game before they left for their afternoon activities: they had two kids hold an empty glass behind their backs and had two others stand a little distance behind them with loaded water guns. The object of the activity was to see which team was able to get more water into the glass. I don't know how much water ended up in the glasses, but much of it soaked the boys who were holding them. The kids ate it up! Once these shenanigans were over, we presented each camper with a gift—one of our CDs, a baggie filled with school supplies, and, of course, candy.

That afternoon Alex Konya, the director of Word of Life Hungary, showed us a video which celebrated the twenty years Word of Life had ministered in Hungary. Then we mingled with the campers. Glen, a young person on the trip, joined the campers in playing soccer. Barbara Tobler, our soprano soloist, got together with a small group of campers working on their English. They had loved her singing in the concert and were excited to talk with her.

After a dinner cookout of hot dogs and salad, we changed into concert dress and left for the cultural hall in the village to present a concert. Our choir had been invited to sing there two years before when I first met the mayor of Tóalmás, Magdolna Kovács. At that time she told me that the people of Tóalmás seldom get to see good cultural events in the village and would love for us to come. Thus, we were there that day to share the love of Jesus Christ through music. The town council had printed up fliers advertising the concert and had hand-delivered them to every home in the village. Even so, we had no idea how many people would come, especially since Hungarians are predominately Catholic. Yet, according to Ildikó, they are nominal Catholics who attend Mass only at Christmas and Easter.

We set up for the program and waited for the villagers to arrive. We had been advised that Hungarians are often late getting to programs such as ours, but only a few people had arrived as the concert time moved closer. Then, shortly before the concert was to begin, the skies opened up in one of the worst thunderstorms that Alex Konya could remember. At one point, I thought we might lose our electrical power. We found out after the concert that the mayor and most of her City

Council were there, but the drenching rain, thunder, and lightning had kept many people away. I believe it was the smallest audience we had sung for in all our trips up to that point.

Small in number though they were, the people of Tóalmás were most enthusiastic. While we were disappointed by the size of the audience, we were encouraged by the way the people received the music and the message from Pastor Tom. Mayor Kovács told us after the concert that this was the finest cultural event they had seen in Tóalmás for decades and that it would probably be another ten years before they had another event of such high quality. The mayor's remarks may have been somewhat exaggerated, but she was sincerely grateful.

After we got home, Ursula, a choir member, shared her story about the Tóalmás concert: *"The concert was sparsely attended due to a violent thunderstorm. I was discouraged at first, but God had plans. After the concert we were greeting the attendees. A man came up to me and profusely thanked me for the fire engine we had donated to his nearby community. I was befuddled! Through a translator, I told him that we were here to worship and sing and had nothing to do with the donation of the fire engine. This man had braved the storm and had walked several kilometers to come and thank us. I don't think he would have come just to hear us sing. He again thanked me, his face shining with joy. 'I am glad I came,' he said, 'Thank you. You all are angels.' He then kissed me on the cheek."*

The five days we spent in Hungary were filled with God's presence and power as we met many dear people and ministered to them in worship services, seminars, conventions, and a camp meeting. As we prepared to fly out of Hungary to Kiev, Ukraine, the next day, we were full of gratitude to God for giving us the privilege of ministering in Hungary.

4

Thursday, July 1st, was the first day since our arrival in Hungary the previous Saturday that we did not have a concert scheduled. Our first task that morning was to put our luggage out in the hallway before 8:00 a.m. The luggage then had to be loaded onto the bus, along with nearly forty boxes and several cases of handbell and audio equipment, plus boxes of CDs, programs, and several other disposable items. All of our people and equipment made it onto the buses, and we left for the Budapest airport shortly after 9:00 a.m.

Our arrival at the airport was more chaotic that we would have liked. We first had to identify all of the Carnet items so the Hungarian customs agents could officially stamp them out of Hungary. Unfortunately, the officials could not decide which check-in line we should go to, since forty of the choir members were checking in their own suitcases as well as a second checked bag containing equipment. Malev Airlines finally opened up several lines so we could check in our luggage, get the Carnet stamped, and run to the gate before the plane was scheduled to take off at 12:50 p.m. We accomplished all of this, but with little time to spare.

The 1½-hour flight from Budapest to Kiev was smooth, the plane had comfortable seats, and the flight attendants actually served us a sandwich and a drink. Arrival at the Kiev Airport was another matter. The easiest part was going through passport control. We then had to get all of our luggage and equipment off the conveyor belt, divide the Carnet items from the non-Carnet items, and group all Carnet items together to take to Ukrainian Customs. This arrangement was required before they would stamp the Carnet and allow our equipment into the country.

Unfortunately, Ukrainian Customs did not like the way the items on the Carnet had been listed and approved by U.S. Customs. So they insisted on typing up the document the way they wanted it, which they said would take at least another hour. Jenny Post, who was in charge of the Carnet on the tour, had to remain at the airport until the document was re-typed and stamped. Chuck and Lee Hawley graciously offered to stay with Jenny so she would not have to wait there by herself. Peter Barbarics also arranged for a shuttle to pick up the three of them when they were ready to leave the airport and take them to our hotel in Kiev.

When we reached our hotel, the Kiev Radisson SAS, we were grateful that the hotel was modern and had unusually well-appointed rooms. The Radisson was exceptional compared to the Best Western Hungaria, our hotel in Budapest, and was far superior to the Dnieper Hotel in Kiev where Paul Smith and I had stayed in 2008. When we had planned the 2010 trip, we had tried to book another hotel in Kiev, but that hotel did not have enough room for our group. Therefore, we ended up at the Radisson, a better hotel which was actually less expensive! We were even more enthusiastic about the hotel when we discovered that it was located only a few blocks from the Music Mission Kiev (MMK) headquarters. It could not have been more ideally situated!

Because of the problems we had had getting our equipment out of the airport and traveling through the unbelievable Kiev traffic, we did not reach our hotel until 5:45 p.m. We had been scheduled to have dinner at the MMK building at 5:00, but obviously that was not going to happen. When we entered the hotel, however, we found Matt McMurrin waiting for us in the lobby. Matt assisted his dad, Roger McMurrin, in leading the MMK ministry. Sometime that afternoon Matt had realized that we would not get there in time to eat the dinner at MMK headquarters, so he asked the staff to prepare sandwiches and drinks for us, which he brought to our hotel.

Time was still a problem, however, since we were scheduled to attend the ballet at the Kiev Opera House at 7:00 p.m. We quickly checked into our rooms, came down to pick up food, went back up to change clothes, and finally gathered in the lobby so we could walk to the ballet together. I was especially pleased that Jenny Post and the Hawleys got back from the airport in time to enjoy all of the ballet performance except the first act.

The Taras Shevchenko National Opera House of Ukraine, better known as the Kiev Opera House, is an architectural marvel. A devastating fire demolished the building in 1896, but it was rebuilt in 1901. A well-known architect, Victor Schröter, designed the new building. The exterior of the building was built in a refined neo-Renaissance style, and the opera house's interior is lavishly decorated in "Viennese Modern"—large Venetian mirrors adorn the foyer, porcelain lamps brighten the marble stairs, and carvings in bronze, marble, and gold cover the walls. The huge opera house, which can hold over 1500 guests, is known for its stage—one of the largest in Europe—which was designed to meet the needs of both the performers and the audience. Thus, people can hear and see well no matter where they sit. The scenery was gorgeous, the dancers superb, and the music delightful. After the stress of traveling from Budapest to Kiev, we agreed that watching a ballet was the perfect way to end the day. I heard nothing but raves from everyone who attended.

Friday was our first day of ministry with Music Mission Kiev, or MMK. At 9:00 a.m. we took the ten-minute walk from our hotel to the MMK headquarters to meet their staff and to share morning devotions with them. Then, since the next activity was not scheduled to begin until 11:00, Sergei, a young MMK staff member and assistant conductor, took us to St. Vladimir's Cathedral, one of Kiev's many beautiful Orthodox churches. The cathedral was built in 1822 to commemorate the 900th anniversary of the baptism of Prince Volodymyr the Great, also known as St. Vladimir; his baptism was the official beginning of Christianity as the state religion of Ukraine.

St. Vladimir's Cathedral marks the place of Vladimir's baptism. Built in neo-Byzantine style, the cathedral has six piers (raised structures supported by pillars), three apses (semicircular vaulted recesses which overlook the chancel), and seven cupolas, or domes, which soar as high as 151 feet. Mosaics, frescoes, and relief bronze sculptures decorate the interior. As one visitor put it, "The interior is magnificent, the lighting is spectacular, and the atmosphere is full of grace."

When we returned to the MMK offices, we joined a group of about 15 ladies—members of MMK's pensioners choir and knitting group. Once all of us had squeezed into the room, it was so crowded that we wondered whether a few of us might have to hang from the ceiling! Natasha, who was in charge of MMK's widows and orphans ministry, introduced us to the widows and encouraged them to share their stories with us. Several of them sang special songs for us, and the entire group sang "Happy Birthday to America," since they knew that Sunday, July 4th, was Independence Day. Ukrainians look upon Americans as representatives of freedom.

After the widows meeting, we walked up the street to the Golden Gate, the main gate into the city of Kiev in the 1100s. After a lunch of hearty beef and vegetable soup, we walked back to our hotel and soon departed for the Bieli Dom, the building in which the Kyiv Symphony Orchestra and Chorus hold its rehearsals. We climbed the many flights of stairs to the rehearsal room on the fourth floor (the building has no elevators), where the orchestra was rehearsing under Roger McMurrin's direction. He then asked us to join their chorus so we could rehearse the music we would sing in a joint patriotic concert on Monday evening.

Some of the pieces were conducted by Roger and others by his son, Matt McMurrin. It was great to see Matt, then thirty-two years old, preparing to possibly take over the ministry from his father. Matt told us that he wanted our choir to sing out strongly on the American numbers such as "America the Beautiful" and "God Bless America" to help the Ukrainians with their English. We, in turn, were able to learn the Russian words by listening to the Ukrainians as we sang the choral part of Tchaikovsky's "1812 Overture." I was thrilled to hear the Ukrainian basses sing those deep, rich notes—much lower than our basses could go.

Saturday, July 3rd, was our third day in Kiev. It seemed that each day of the tour had its surprises. This day was no exception. The first surprise came when our group entered the Bieli Dom to join a meeting of the widows of St. Paul's Church, which was started by Music Mission Kiev. We had met with about fifteen widow musicians on Friday at the MMK facilities, but on Saturday we encountered over 150 widows and pensioners who were attending Diane McMurrin's weekly Bible study and Steven Ministry.

By the time we arrived, the women had completed the Bible study and were ready to begin a time of prayer. However, they stopped as we walked into the room and gave us a standing ovation. The widows greeted us in English, saying "Hello, America" and "Hello, Solana Beach." Diane then asked Dan to tell the widows more about the choir and the reason we were there. Eventually the group started praying, and Natasha translated their prayers into English for us. The widows' prayers were touching; they thanked God for bringing us to them, for the food that was provided weekly by MMK, for God's love and provision, for the joy of music, and for many other things. Their prayers truly came from their hearts.

While the widows were collecting their food sacks, Natasha divided us into fifteen groups— about four to a group—and assigned each group a particular widow to visit. Someone from MMK then accompanied each group to translate for them and to guide them to and from the widow's home. Some groups traveled by bus, others by Metro, a few by foot, and some by a combination of two or more methods of transportation. When we heard from the groups later that day, it sounded like the widows lived all over the city.

Five people were in our group: Sally and Ernie, Marguerite and Keith, and I. We were accompanied by our guide/translator, Natasha, and one of the widows. Our mode of transportation to the widow's home was on foot, which really was not so bad since by then we were used to walking. We soon arrived at the home of Alla, the 88-year-old widow we were visiting. Alla was homebound, as she did not have the strength to get out, so people brought her food and supplies from MMK. Her small apartment consisted of only two main rooms: a living room/bedroom combination and a kitchen, plus a small bathroom and one tiny closet.

In her younger years, Alla had served as the concert master of the most important orchestra in Ukraine; she was also the premier concert master at the Kiev Opera for many years. She shared her story with us. As a young girl, Alla had survived the Time of Starvation which was instigated by Stalin in the early 1930s. She then told us about fleeing from Kiev when the German army overran Ukraine. We in America cannot begin to imagine the horrors so many Ukrainians experienced at the hands of the German army and the Russian Communists. One wonders how any of them survived.

While Alla was sharing her story, two widowed sisters joined us. Margarita had been a ballet dancer, and her sister Tamara was a former professional singer. Tamara was supported financially on a regular basis by Charlotte, a Chancel Choir member. Charlotte had really wanted to meet "her widow" but was unable to go on the trip because of health issues. In her place, Sally presented Tamara with a special communication from Charlotte. Tamara was so excited!

The three ladies then royally entertained us. Alla played a couple of pieces on her piano and then accompanied the other two as they sang a duet. She also passed around a plate with slices of an apple on it and insisted that we each take a slice to eat and enjoy. Talk about generosity! Her sacrifice reminded us of the "widow's mite." We then gave each widow a large cloth bag with the words "Solana Beach Presbyterian Church" written on it. Each bag contained a CD of our choir and some packages of dried California fruit. The women were overjoyed to receive those gifts. When it came time for us to depart, the widows give each of us a hug.

When our people got back to MMK after visiting "their" widows, we heard all kinds of stories. I asked choir members to write down their experiences with the widows. A couple of their stories will have to serve as examples of what we all experienced. Dr. Richard Henderson wrote the following: *"My wife and I wish to share with you a unique experience of God's love and power during our 'Music With A Mission' in Eastern Europe. After meeting with the widows at the MMK offices in Kiev, we waited at the bus stop so we could travel to our widow's home. The weather was quite hot and humid. I noticed a frail lady, unsmiling and pale, probably in her late 80s. I saw her stumble toward a bus bench already full of people. No one seemed to notice. Being 30 feet away, I hurried over just in time to help catch her and make room for her on the bench. She was clammy, with increased heart rate and respiration, and appeared to me to be dehydrated. Our guide said she knew where the lady lived, which was on the same route we were taking by bus and subway. Our guide shouldered most of the work of helping the lady into the subway.*

I sat next to the elderly lady on the subway, wedging her between me and the metal door to keep her from falling. My worries continued. She stayed pale and cyanotic with cold hands. I can't describe the fear and loneliness in her face. 'What can I do?' I muttered, 'I'm a physician. I need IV fluids, electrolytes, oxygen, and monitor.' Quickly I realized that the strongest medicine was still available to us. In a short prayer, I asked God to ease her fears and give her strength. I then reached down and took her hand in mine. Her transformation was remarkable over the next few minutes. Pink color and warmth returned to her hands and face, she relaxed, and a smile spread over her face. When I helped her off the subway at her stop, she turned with a grin, kissed my cheek, and said, 'God bless!'"

Carole Orness also wrote her recollections of our time in Kiev and that day with the MMK widows: *"On our choir's mission trip in Kiev, we were struck by many things. Our foremost impression was that Kiev was a city of contrasts: skyscrapers shared land with 11th century buildings; Mercedes and BMWs drove down the streets alongside little yellow buses; high-powered wheeler-dealers in expensive clothes and women in high heels walked next to widows & orphans. We saw the 'haves' and the 'have-nots,' and there was not much in between.*

On the morning of July 3rd we met with 150 widows at their prayer group, and they prayed for us! Their affirming prayers for our travels, health, concerts, and families touched us. We were then escorted by a widow and a translator to visit a housebound widow. [My] husband George and I, together with Rob and Linda, went by "little yellow bus"—the typical form of transport for the average Kiev resident—to a location quite far from the center of the city. When we arrived, it was evident that this woman had cats, so George could not enter the apartment because of his severe allergy. After we struggled through our introductions, our 80-year-old hostess suggested that we go outside so we would have room to sit together during our visit. We had gone to see this woman in order to be a blessing to her, but she ended up blessing us by her interest in us, our families, and America."

After we got home from the tour, I received an e-mail from Natasha. *"It was a great and blessed visit to our homebound widows and widowers who are in bed and disabled, sick and alone, but have great hope and joy in Jesus. After prayer time in Bieli Dom, Kiev, where our aged people get every week food packages, 60 American Christian friends divided into 15 groups with interpreters and left to visit our homebound sisters and brothers in Christ. Here are a few of the stories our widows shared with me."*

Maya: *"I remember time when I was coming to MMK office for food and during many years I got this food in Roger's home and I painted for them beautiful picture of roses. Today I am ready to give all roses of the world for Diane and Roger and for you, dear American friends. Thank you for friendship. Thank you for visit!"*

Mikhail, an 82-year-old widower: *"I am happy that I became a part of big American family! How wonderful family came to me to visit me! We made friends very easy without translation. Both languages were understandable; it was a language of Christian love and friendship! Thank you, dear friends that you came to me and my son, who is disabled in bed. Thank you to Diane and Roger, who have such great friends! America is great! God bless America!"*

Zsdan, 83: *"How nice it was to know that guests would come soon! When they came—I decided— they are not guests, they are my family! They showed me beautiful family pictures and shared the thoughts. I only came from the hospital and was in bed at home, but when friends came I understood. I am strong and full of energy because I have such beautiful Christian friends! America the beautiful! Visit me again! My love to you all in Jesus!"*

Following a quick lunch at MMK, we returned to our hotel and got dressed for our concert at the Kiev Central Baptist Church. This concert had been widely publicized. The church had been asked to invite its congregation, MMK had promoted the concert to its staff and widows, and even the Christian Broadcasting Network (CBN in the CIS) in Kiev had advertised our concert on TV and radio. The church held more than 900 people, the largest church so far on our tour.

About 4:45 p.m. Pastor Mike and Amy McClenahan arrived at the church. When their flight from Rome had landed in Kiev at 3:30 p.m., Matt McMurrin met them and brought them directly to the church. When they walked into the narthex, our entire group broke out in loud applause. We had not seen the McClenahans for two months, so we were overjoyed when they arrived, especially since we had not expected them to get to the church in time for our concert.

Roger and Diane McMurrin were at the concert, along with Matt and Trish McMurrin and their three small children. Several of the MMK staff also joined us. However, in spite of all of the publicity, we ended up with the smallest audience we had ever sung for. At the time, no one seemed to know why so few people had turned out. In spite of the small audience, we were buoyed by the warm response from those who did attend and by the chance to speak with most of them after the concert. The next morning, Pastor Mike and Dan went with Roger McMurrin to meet with the pastor of the Central Baptist Church. He told them that there had been a misunderstanding about which night the concert was to take place, so their congregation did not know about the previous evening's program. Both Roger and the pastor were very apologetic.

Carole Orness best summarized our feelings that night: *"Our concert that evening was in the Kiev Central Baptist Church. This was a huge, beautiful sanctuary. When we arrived, our programs had been placed on every seat and we thought the place would be filled. As it turned out, there was some miscommunication that I am still unclear about, but only about 30 people came to hear our concert. We sang our hearts out anyway. Mike and Amy arrived just before the concert to join us for the remainder of the tour. Although it was wonderful to reunite with the McClenahans, God had something else to teach us that evening about our expectations and about whom we sing to and for. It was an exhausting day, a day of contrasting experiences and expectations,* but God blessed every experience and showed us that we can never assume or underestimate what He has planned. Often great blessing comes out of discouraging situations. I will close with a statement made by the Anglican priest at our last concert in Moscow: 'Wherever we make music, alleluia ... the angels are there ...'"

The angels were certainly around Karen that evening. At the end of the concert, Karen, who is a member of the Chancel Choir and Bells of Praise, experienced the first major medical problem of the tour, not counting Bill Fee's ordeal on the flight to New York. She was on the trip along with her young son, Glen. Karen had been under an ophthalmologist's care in San Diego for a potential detached retina and had been told to watch for certain symptoms. Unfortunately, she experienced those symptoms that afternoon.

I asked Karen if she would write her story about that episode: *"Right before our sixth concert, I lost the vision in my left eye. Even so, God helped me sing, play the bells, and keep calm. After the concert I was instructed to lie flat, keep my eyes closed, and get to an ophthalmologist immediately. My wonderful choir family rallied around me and took me to see a specialist in Kiev at 10:00 on that Saturday night. It was a miracle that the ophthalmologist was available and that he spoke English! He found that I had a detached retina, but said he would not be able to get a retina specialist to perform the surgery to reattach my retina until Monday or Tuesday. I gave him a program from our concert and he seemed interested in the message we were bringing through music.*

Even though there was a risk that I would permanently lose the vision in my eye if I traveled, I decided to fly home to have the surgery. My amazing choir family looked after Glen so he could stay on the tour. They also helped me make the flight arrangements, pay for the flight, and get to the airport. Even though I traveled by myself with my eyes closed for 26 hours, I never felt alone. The words to a song we had memorized kept running through my head: 'We are never alone, God is with us.' That was so true for me. I felt God's presence with me throughout the long trip home and through the two surgeries I underwent after I got back to San Diego. God and my retina surgeon restored my vision.

I am also thankful for what my son Glen learned from being on the mission trip. Since we returned home, he has donated money to the Word of Life Camp and hopes to be a counselor there. In addition, Glen loved his experience with MWAM so much that he became part of the Afar Team and went to Ethiopia to teach English. He has already raised the money to educate an Ethiopian girl for one year, and his next goal is to raise enough money for ten Ethiopian girls to attend school.

I met so many people while I traveled, and I told all of them about our trip—about Pastor Tom's message to the kids at the Word of Life Camp that they are smart and talented and that Jesus loves them—and the widows at Music Mission Kiev, former opera singers and ballerinas, who had suffered torture, abandonment, and starvation, but found Christ through the support of Music Mission Kyiv. The people I talked to were moved by what we were doing to bring joy and music to Eastern Europe. Through this whole experience, God taught me to 'walk by faith and not by sight.'"

Isn't it interesting how many people were helped by a piece we all had learned and memorized, "We Are Not Alone"?

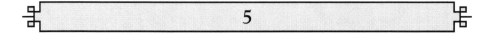

5

After the disappointment of the poorly-attended concert the previous evening, on Sunday we were surrounded by the loving people of St. Paul's Evangelical Church and Music Mission Kiev. That afternoon we met with the Kiev group for worship at St. Paul's, which was started by

MMK in 2008. During the hymns, "Joyful, Joyful We Adore Thee" and "Great is Thy Faithfulness," the congregation sang in Ukrainian while we sang lustily in English. Together we made great harmony. The congregation also sang two responses, the Nicene Creed and a Ukrainian prayer, in beautiful Eastern Orthodox musical style.

After Pastor Mike McClenahan's message on Psalm 145, we gave the offertory, singing the ethereal Mozart "Laudate Dominum" with Barbara Tobler as soloist, accompanied by the Kyiv Symphony Orchestra strings. (In Ukrainian churches, the offertory comes after the sermon, not before.) The climax of the service was singing the "Hallelujah Chorus" with the MMK musicians, as others in the congregation joined in. It was truly a moment of resounding praise.

After we changed into more casual clothes, we were bused out to the home of Roger and Diane McMurrin, who live in the village of Gorenichi about 17 miles outside of Kiev. Three of the McMurrins' "grad orphans," who cook and help out with special events, started setting up tables on the different patios in the large yard. We saw that they had an outdoor fire going, with wood coals cooking skewers of marinated pork. Since it was the 4th of July, after dinner we sang "God Bless America" and "The Star Spangled Banner." The McMurrins were such gracious hosts! We realized that we had spent the entire day with family—God's family, the Body of Christ. Whether American or Ukrainian, we were indeed one body that day.

Marguerite Walker has written about that day from another perspective: *"On the fourth of July, we attended an afternoon worship service at St. Paul's Evangelical Church. The choir sang with the orchestra, and Pastor Mike preached. Afterwards we were invited to a picnic at the McMurrins' home. The rain had stopped, so we explored the spacious backyard surrounded by woods. Roger and Diane gave tours of their newly-built home, pointing out the brick fireplace that some of the young Music Mission Kiev staff members had helped to build.*

We had a barbecue dinner outside while relaxing and enjoying the beautiful setting. Maria, one of our Ukrainian tour guides, sat at our table. When we asked her if she would like to visit the United States, she said 'no.' We discovered that her knowledge of our country was based on unrealistic movies and television shows, so we explained that most Americans are just like Ukrainians—they go to work, raise children, and spend time with family and friends. Later in the evening Maria said that she had changed her mind and that she might like to visit America someday.

During our conversation, we asked Maria about an advertisement we had seen for tours to the Chernobyl Nuclear Power Plant, a two-hour ride from Kiev. We questioned the accuracy of the ad, which—after it acknowledged that visitors would be exposed to above-average doses of radiation—insisted that this radiation was 'harmless.' Maria said the tours were real; since times were hard, people did whatever they could to make money. Maria had difficulty speaking about Chernobyl because, at the time of the nuclear accident there, she was a young child living in the area with her family. They were exposed to high levels of radiation for four days before being told of the danger. Then the government ordered everyone to leave the area immediately, taking only what they could carry.

For several years, Maria and her family lived with relatives in western Ukraine where the people mainly spoke Polish. She felt like a foreigner in her own country. Maria admitted that this experience had been so painful for her that she hadn't shared it before. We were grateful for the opportunity to hear her story and to share with each other openly and honestly. As the sun began to set, we all gathered for group pictures. We were thankful to God for a lovely evening of fellowship and for the blessings of the mission trip."

On Monday, July 5th, we had free time until 3:00 that afternoon, so many of us went on a walking tour of Kiev. The Ukrainian guide from our "blue bus" took us first to see the St. Sophia Cathedral, which dates back to the 11th century. Today it is a museum protected by UNESCO. It was spectacular to see the golden domes of the church gleaming in the sunlight. Looking out from the entrance to the St. Sophia Bell Tower, we could see down the broad street to St. Michael's Cathedral. Its golden domes contrasted with the beautiful blue outer walls of the church. Stalin destroyed the original church in the 1930s in order to construct large government buildings on the site, but most were never built. In 1991, after Ukraine gained its independence from Russia, the city decided to rebuild St. Michael's. Because many pictures and sketches of St. Michael's existed, this church is probably the most accurately restored building in Kiev.

That evening was a highlight of our trip, a joint freedom concert with the Kyiv Symphony Orchestra and Chorus at the Dom Organi Musiki, or the National House of Organ and Chamber Music of Ukraine. The building is actually the St. Nicholas Church, an impressive Polish Catholic church, but it is obvious from its new name that the church is now used primarily for concerts. The church holds 800 people, and our joint concert was sold out. The concert was officially called "Happy Birthday, America." It was an exhilarating program featuring American songs and music by American composers.

The program began with the Ukrainian National Anthem and "The Star-Spangled Banner." Then our combined choir sang stirring arrangements of "America the Beautiful" and "Give Me Jesus." Our choir then had a chance to sit down while the Kyiv Symphony Orchestra and Chorus sang a gorgeous Mack Wilberg arrangement of "Shenandoah." The orchestra and a truly superb pianist performed George Gershwin's "Rhapsody in Blue," followed by an upbeat performance of "Camptown Races" and "New York, New York" by the orchestra and chorus. The first part of the program concluded with Ovid Young's arrangement of "God Bless America," sung by both choirs. The audience responded with tumultuous applause.

The second half of the program got off to a great start with the KSOC orchestra playing the "Fanfare for the Common Man" by Aaron Copland. Our joint choir then sang the John Rutter arrangement of the "Battle Hymn of the Republic" and the spiritual "Steal Away." At this point, the KSOC chorus was able to sit down as we sang two numbers by ourselves: "My Soul's Been Anchored" and "Didn't My Lord Deliver Daniel." The applause following "My Soul's Been Anchored" seemed to be the most enthusiastic applause of the evening. When Dan sat back down next to Roger McMurrin, Roger leaned over to Dan and said, "You really nailed it!" Wow! The KSOC then took over, performing "Buckaroo Holiday" from Aaron Copland's "Rodeo," followed by Jester Hairston's spiritual, "Hold On." They also sang "Yankee Doodle" and "You're a Grand Old Flag." The finale was a performance of Tchaikovsky's "1812 Overture" by the orchestra and combined choir. What a night!

By the end of the concert we were all exhausted. It was extremely hot in the church and we were literally dripping by the end of the program. MMK provided food and drinks for the concert participants in a building next to the church. It was pouring rain as we ran for our buses, many of us without umbrellas, which was a "splashy" way to end a fantastic evening together. The freedom concert and our time with the Kyiv Symphony Orchestra and Chorus exceeded what we had hoped and prayed for.

Pastor Mike McClenahan had an interesting perspective on that night's concert: *"The highlight of the trip for me was hearing the choir sing in the 'Fourth of July' concert in Kiev. (The concert actually took place on July 5th.) The Solana Beach choir sang along with a large orchestra and a bigger choir of younger singers, so we assumed that the other choir would be louder. But when our choir sang, both in the combined choir and on their own, their voices soared over the Kyiv choir and orchestra. Here is why I think that was so. In spite of all the* circumstances that were out of our choir's comfort zone—from inadequate time for rehearsal, to no sleep on an overnight train, to hot sanctuaries—they sang from their hearts. That is the real value of our choir. They are a 'called choir,' not a paid choir. They sing from their hearts because of their faith. Their testimony came out strongly in the Fourth of July concert."

After we got home from the ministry tour, we received a letter from Diane McMurrin telling us how much our time at Music Mission Kiev had meant to them: *"I remember that wonderful concert with you for the 4th of July. Your group was such a blessing to us. We still display at our house the certificate from your church signed by Dan Bird. The picnic at Gorenichi was such a joyful event and spearheaded many more picnics with the Ukrainians after you left. The widows still remember and talk about your home visits. It was the first time we had such a large group of Americans minister to our widows. Though you helped us in many practical ways, perhaps what we value most is the encouragement you gave us as missionaries in a foreign land. Truly, this was a gift from the Lord: to share our common effort to bring the Gospel of Christ to Ukraine."*

The next day we were able to relax after our hectic schedule with Music Mission Kiev, so 47 people from our group signed up to take an optional guided tour of the great Kiev-Pechersk Lavra. We had originally scheduled the tour for 9:00 that morning, but we had not realized how tired choir members would be after the joint concert. The program had lasted until 10:00 p.m. and was followed by a reception, so we did not get back to the hotel until after 11:00. Choir members soon began to ask if we could start the tour later so they could sleep in, so we changed the time to 10:00 a.m. Then when the choir came down for breakfast the next morning, they pleaded with us to postpone the tour until the afternoon. We finally compromised; the tour would begin at 12:00 noon so everyone could be back to the hotel by 4:00 p.m.. Just before we boarded the bus for a trip to the Lavra, the skies opened up in a hard, steady rain and we could not board the bus without getting drenched, so we had to wait about 15 minutes until the rain let up before we could set out for the Lavra.

The Kiev-Pechersk Lavra has an interesting history. Some monks started the Lavra in the 11th century, living in caves along the banks of the Dnieper River. They stayed in these caves for the rest of their lives, in complete solitude. Food would be taken out to each cave every day. If the food was still there the next day, it was assumed that the monk had died. When the monks passed away, their bodies were placed in little niches in the caves—and later in catacombs. Orthodox churches, as well as a monastery, then began to be built over these catacombs. Today the Lavra is divided into two main sections: the upper Lavra, which contains various churches, museums, and monastic buildings, and the lower Lavra, the location of the caves and catacombs. Visitors are given candles to hold as they enter these narrow underground passageways and then descend to see several of the mummified remains.

After dinner we once again loaded our luggage and equipment onto the two buses and departed for the Kiev train station. Peter Barbarics had worked out a great plan; we would place all of the Carnet items (handbell and audiovisual equipment) in one compartment, guarded by Jenny. Peter and I were then placed on one side of her and TJ and Kim on the other. That's protection! The train compartments were roomy; since only two people were assigned to each compartment, they even had enough space to put all of their luggage in the compartment.

As we pulled out of the Kiev station at 9:30 p.m., everyone got settled in. Then around midnight the train made our first stop at the last town in Ukraine. The Ukrainian officials came on board, checked all of our passports, and collected the exit papers we had filled out when we entered the country. All of that went smoothly, but we were more concerned about how the officials would view our Carnet items. The

Ukrainian officials discussed this at length with Jenny, Peter, and Oksana, our Ukrainian guide. At last, they decided to stamp our Carnet and we were once again headed for Russia.

Jay, a choir spouse, later told us about his concerns as we crossed from Ukraine into Russia: *"As we were on the train leaving Ukraine, the border guard had a problem with me because my appearance no longer matched the picture on my passport. I was afraid that I would have trouble again when we were examined by the Russian border guards, but they barely looked at me. 'We are not alone, God is with us.'"*

6

Three hours after we left Ukrainian border control, the train again came to a stop, this time to let on the Russian officials. They took our passports and the entry/departure papers we had filled out for our time in Russia, and then left the train with our passports. That was a scary feeling! While the border officials looked over our paperwork, the customs people debated what to do with our Carnet and all of our Carnet equipment. This time, they decided <u>not</u> to stamp the Carnet, saying that they could not stamp it because it was written in English and they could not read it. However, they told us that since the Ukrainian officials had stamped us out of Ukraine, we should have no problem getting the Russian officials to stamp us out of Russia at the airport when we flew out the next Saturday. We surely hoped they were correct. After the delays at the Ukrainian and Russian borders, we finally were able to get some sleep.

We arrived in Moscow at 10:50 a.m., unloaded our luggage and equipment from the train, and once more loaded everything onto the two buses we would use during the three days we were in Moscow. The bus drivers drove to a place just outside Red Square and let us off. We ate lunch at a nearby restaurant called the Boris Godunov. It was originally a monastery, but it now served physical food instead of spiritual food. We were treated to some "traditional" Russian dishes: shredded cabbage salad, borscht, and dumplings.

We had hoped to tour Red Square that day, but we had to get back for the 2:00 handbell workshop that afternoon at the Central Baptist Church. Alex Kozynko was waiting for us, along with Sergey Zolotarevski, the senior pastor. Members of the Bells of Praise joined a group of young people from the church who were interested in bell ringing. The workshop went well and lasted about an hour. Meanwhile, we kept an eye on the clock, since we had to leave in time to make the last tour of the day at the Kremlin, between 4:00 and 5:00 that afternoon.

When Paul Smith and I were in Moscow on the planning trip, we did not have time to tour the Kremlin, so I was looking forward to taking lots of video on the Kremlin tour. Unfortunately, we were informed that "professional grade" cameras could not be taken inside, which meant that I had to leave my video camera on the bus. Fortunately, I was able to take my small digital camera with me. I was disappointed that I could not use my video camera, but I was not disappointed in the tour itself. I had read so much about the Kremlin that I was interested in everything about the tour.

Our group was told to stay together and not to "wander off" on our own. Early in the tour, we were all gathered in one place when we noticed that Dan Bird was "wandering" across the street toward the Kremlin Armory. Two Russian guards were pointing at Dan and telling him to return to the group. Dan, whose right ear was plugged up, could not hear what they were saying. He just waved to them in a friendly manner and continued on toward the Armory. Dan's grandson, Luke, tried to get Dan's attention before Dan got himself arrested. Fortunately,

Dan finally heard all the yelling and returned to the group. That was a close call!

We had scheduled a tour of Moscow the next day which would include Red Square, a place we had not been able to see earlier. Some people wanted to tour only Red Square and then return to the hotel. Others wanted to take the entire city tour, including the special lunch we had planned for that afternoon. The rest wanted to cancel the tour altogether. It was clear that people were beginning to reach the limit of their endurance. We decided to divide into two groups: the "Grand Tour Group" who wanted to take the entire tour and the "Short Tour Group" (or, as they liked to call themselves, "the Smart Group") who wanted a shorter tour so they could return to the hotel by noon. Most of our people ended up in one of the two tour groups, since they realized that this was probably the only time they would ever be in Moscow.

Red Square is bordered on one side by the Kremlin and by Russia's Gum department store on the opposite side. At the northwest end of the square stands Russia's Military Museum, while St. Basil's Cathedral is situated at the opposite end. Olga, the Moscow guide on our "blue bus," was the guide for the "Grand Tour Group." She turned out to be one of the best guides we had on the trip. She was knowledgeable about Moscow and Russian history and was able to articulate it in excellent, understandable English.

While Olga was telling us about the history of Red Square, a group of Cossacks walked into the square, accompanied by their priest. As soon as our people heard that the Cossacks were there, they pulled out their cameras and frantically took as many pictures as they could. Cossacks are famous for their distinctive loose-fitting garb and dark fur hats. It was fun to see them behaving like any other group of tourists; they took pictures of each other and were delighted when some of our people took pictures of them.

The Cossacks belong to independent communities drawn from various ethnic groups that formed in Ukraine and other parts of Russia around 1400. They were fierce horsemen who once protected the Russian frontier. In recent years, Russian leaders have given the Cossacks an increasing role in law enforcement to crack down on illegal migration and to fight in regional conflicts such as the war in Chechnya. Most Cossacks are traditional Christians who are respected for their high standards of conduct. It is interesting that they also have a tradition of choral singing.

Walking through the Gum department store was like strolling down Rodeo Drive in Beverly Hills. Unless you had loads of money, all you could do was window shop. Since we had taken the tour of the Kremlin the day before, we moved on to St. Basil's Cathedral. Everyone assembled there for a group picture with the church in the background. That picture became one of our favorite tour photos.

From Red Square we took the bus along the Moscow River to the Cathedral of Christ the Savior, the country's premier cathedral. It is the home church of the Patriarch of the Russian Orthodox Church. In 1992 when the Soviet Union collapsed, the people decided to restore the cathedral to its original design. The present church was completed and was consecrated on August 19, 2000. It is not only a magnificent place to see, but also an active, worshiping congregation—not just a museum. We were not allowed to take pictures of any kind inside the church and were not even allowed to talk in the sanctuary. Of course, there were no such restrictions inside the gift shop!

Our last sightseeing destination was the Novodevichy Cemetery and Convent. The cemetery is covered with trees and shrubs, and imposing headstones and statues of those buried are found throughout the cemetery. Many prominent government figures are buried there. The grave of Boris Yeltsin is in the shape of a flag. We also saw the burial place of Mikhail Gorbachev's wife. Perhaps the most famous grave was that of Nikita Khrushchev. We did not have time to go inside the convent, but we had an enchanting view of it across a nearby lake. Olga told us that the Russian composer, Tchaikovsky, was inspired to compose his most famous ballet, "Swan Lake," after watching the swans swimming on this lake.

Following our excursion, we had dinner at a local restaurant which served traditional Russian food. As is customary, the meal started with a cabbage salad. Then we were served a flavorful mushroom mixture inside a small roll that was crisp on the outside and soft on the inside. After eating a Russian soup, we were served the main course of broiled chicken on skewers and mashed potatoes. For dessert, we had ice cream with tea or coffee. It is a good thing we were spending only three days in Moscow; if we had stayed much longer, we would have gone home several pounds heavier!

The concert that evening at the Central Baptist Church was like a family affair. The church has a prayer service every Thursday night and we had the privilege of being part of it. Before the service, a young man came up to us speaking good English. He asked about our choir and what we had been doing. He then walked over to the tenor section and introduced himself, hugging each of the tenors in turn. We discovered that he was a musician himself and had a fine tenor voice. At the end of the concert when we surrounded the congregation to sing "When I Survey the Wondrous Cross," he sang right along with us. Many older women in the congregation came up afterward and insisted on giving us hugs to thank us for coming.

After the service we went upstairs for a reception in a large fellowship room. Pastor Sergey told us that Central Baptist was the only church which had remained open throughout the Soviet era. In fact, he said that for a number of years it was the only worshiping congregation in Moscow. Dr. Alexander Kozynko then described what it was like growing up in Russia during the Communist years. The Russian

Christians suffered much for their faith; several people at the reception told us about relatives who had been imprisoned for years because of their Christian testimony. Yet, in spite of the persecution, they continued to worship the living God. We have much to learn from them.

Shortly after we returned home from the tour, Pastor Mike expressed what it meant to him to preach at Central Baptist that day: *"The highlight for me in Moscow was preaching at the Baptist church. Pastor Alex was a tremendous host. As we were talking before the service, he told me about the history of the church and how he had been kept from attending church when he was six years old. Alex also explained that Central Baptist was the only church that had stayed open in Moscow during the 70+ years of Soviet rule.*

Then I remembered that in 1984 Amy and I had attended the Urbana Mission Conference in Champagne-Urbana, Illinois. There we heard Billy Graham speak about his recent time in Russia and describe how he had preached at a Baptist church. At the end of his remarks, the 20,000 students at the conference stopped and prayed for the people of that church and for all of those in the Soviet Union. It didn't occur to me until I stepped into Central Baptist's pulpit that evening that I was preaching at the same pulpit Billy Graham had used! I was amazed that God had given me the opportunity to bring the Word of God to people I had prayed for in 1984. That was a significant personal connection for me on the trip."

We were a tired, but uplifted group of people as we returned to our hotel. The next day, our last full day in Moscow, we were on our own until we had to leave for St. Andrew's Anglican Church later that afternoon. Dan, Pastor Mike, Amy, and I met at 1:00 p.m. with Father Alexander Borisov, the Orthodox priest that Doug Burleigh had told us about. Father Borisov had an amazing ministry in Moscow. However, when he had asked permission from his superiors for our choir to sing in his church, he was turned down. You may remember that Father

Alexander was considered a "black sheep" in the Russian Orthodox Church.

Yessa, Doug Burleigh's administrative assistant in Moscow, who spoke excellent English, met the four of us in the hotel lobby and escorted us to the church. Father Alexander was a gracious, soft-spoken man in his early sixties with sparkling, intelligent eyes. After we introduced ourselves, he described the ministries they offered the congregation and the problems they experienced. One reason he was "under a cloud" with his church leaders was his belief that belonging to a denomination does not make one a Christian and that salvation comes only from a personal relationship with Jesus Christ. Father Alexander also said that it was hard to teach his congregation how to meet the needs of the poor because, under the Communists, it was the state that took care of the poor. Now, he told his congregation, if the poor are to be helped, the church will have to do it by ministering in "the Jesus way."

After the meeting, the four of us from Solana Beach had lunch with Yessa and her friend. We asked the two young women about their religious background. Yessa's friend replied that she had grown up in a Baptist family; Yessa said that her background was atheist. When Pastor Mike asked Yessa how she had become a Christian, she said that she had accepted Christ at a Young Life camp. Doug Burleigh had ministered with Young Life throughout the former Soviet states for years, so Yessa is just one example of the many people who have come to Christ because of Doug's ministry.

The choir was scheduled to arrive at St. Andrew's Anglican Church at 5:30 that afternoon for a 7:30 concert. There is always heavy traffic on the Moscow streets, but on Fridays it gets even worse as many Muscovites leave Moscow for their dachas outside of the city. The traffic was terrible, and our bus driver had trouble finding the narrow street on which St. Andrew's is located. He evidently missed the turn the first time and had to circle back through the traffic to the correct street. The bus had to let us off some distance from the church, so we had to carry all of the handbell and audio equipment, English-language programs, and CDs, which was exhausting work. By the time we had trudged several blocks to the church, we were a half-hour late.

St. Andrew's was the only concert venue I had not previously visited. Alex Kozynko got the idea of having us sing at this church after Paul Smith and I had returned from our planning trip. Alex then gave me the name of the canon at St. Andrew's, but it was not until after we arrived in Moscow that I had the chance to talk with him by phone. I must confess that I was apprehensive about our whole arrangement with St. Andrew's, since I had not been there before or met those in charge. The fact that we had arrived late made me even more nervous.

Simon Stevens, the canon of St. Andrew's, met us at the gate and led us into the sanctuary. Our natural inclination was to get busy setting up for the Bells of Praise and figuring out how to arrange the choir on the chancel. But when we started to do this, Simon insisted that we sit down and relax. He then shared some of the history of St. Andrew's. English traders originally founded the church in Moscow 400 years ago during the reign of Czar Ivan the Terrible. It has ministered to the English-speaking community in Moscow ever since then, except during the Communist era. The Communist government took over the church buildings and used them for its own purposes. After the collapse of the Soviet Union, the buildings were returned to the church and the congregation was again allowed to hold worship services.

The church sanctuary provided us with one of the finest acoustical environments on the tour. The Soviets occasionally used the sanctuary as a music recording studio, so it was a dream setting for a concert. We were finally able to get set up, but without much of a warm-up or rehearsal. Like every place we sang, it was hot and sticky in the church. Eastern Europe was suffering through an unusually hot spell while we were there, and the only buildings that had air-conditioning were some of the hotels.

Before the concert Pastor Mike asked all of us to meet in an adjoining room. Since this would be our final concert and the last night of our tour, he asked us to share how we had seen God at work during our Music With a Mission trip. Choir members shared many touching stories, and we ended with a time of prayer. We definitely needed that time together before the concert, since everyone felt frazzled after the difficulties we had encountered getting there. The concert itself went very well; the audience became more and more responsive as the concert progressed. Our concert at St. Andrew's was probably our finest performance of the trip. Pastor Mike was thankful that he could speak there without a translator, since St. Andrew's draws primarily from the English-speaking community. We left the church knowing that we had ministered to them.

Following the program, we said our good-byes to Pastor Mike and Amy, who were on their way to England, and to ten people in our group who were leaving for the train station to begin a two-day tour of St. Petersburg. The rest of us had an informal "farewell dinner" at a restaurant. We had a wonderful time as we shared stories and toasted the many people who had made the mission trip a success. We closed our time together by having each bus group sing its "bus song." Our bus, the "blue bus," sang our song to the tune of "Blue Moon." Wasn't that clever?! Our song was definitely superior to the one the people in the "yellow bus" came up with.

On Saturday morning, the main group left for the Sheremetyevo International Airport to catch a Delta flight to New York's JFK Airport and then to San Diego. I was not going on that flight, so I met the group in the hotel lobby to see them off. When the buses drove away, I suddenly felt lonely and realized how much I missed June. I was scheduled to take a United Airlines flight from Moscow's Domodedovo International Airport, located about an hour southeast of our hotel, so I took a taxi to the airport. When I arrived at the terminal, I tried to find a place to check in. I felt lost; the place was full of people, and I could not see my 12:45 flight listed on the board. I finally found a woman at an information counter who spoke English. She politely pointed me to the United Airlines check-in counter.

I flew on a Boeing 767-300 from Moscow to Washington Dulles International Airport. After clearing U.S. Customs, I found the gate for the next leg of my journey, which would take me on a Boeing 777 to Denver. During my two-hour layover in Denver, I called my wife, using the phone card I had bought for the trip. When June answered, I was so choked up that I could hardly speak. I had not realized how very much I had missed her during my three weeks in Europe. June told me that Ed, our neighbor and good friend, would bring her to the airport to meet me when my flight arrived at 10:53 p.m. She told me to call Ed on his cell phone when I had gotten my luggage, and he would then drive from the cell phone parking lot to pick me up.

For some reason, when I arrived in San Diego I was unable to get my phone card to work and I did not have any U.S. coins. Since it was very late, the airport was clearing out quickly and I could not find anyone to assist me. I began to panic. How would I let Ed and June know I was there? I walked outside to see if they might have decided to come to the baggage claim area, but there was no sign of them. I then worried that I might not be able to get back inside the airport, so I was relieved when the doors opened normally. I again tried to get my phone card to work, to no avail. Just then I saw June walking down the hall toward me. I was so relieved that I hugged her with all of my strength and just sobbed. I felt completely drained, physically and emotionally. I had never experienced anything quite like that before.

Even though the Music With a Mission Trip had been a great success, it felt good to be home. As we all tried to get back on Pacific Daylight Time after the 11-hour time difference from Moscow, we recognized that God's hand had been on our ministry throughout the trip. As on every mission trip, there had been problems and schedule changes. Some of the concerts were, from our perspective, poorly attended. We had encountered medical issues that could have disrupted our ministry. Yet, in spite of all this, we had felt God's presence everywhere we went. That, if nothing else, gave us the desire to magnify the Lord. Music With a Mission was more than a three-year process; it was a vital learning and growing experience for each of us.

King David expressed similar thoughts when he wrote Psalm 138. As I look back on the 2010 trip four years later, I want to join David in saying:

> *"I will praise you, Lord, with all my heart;*
> *before the 'gods' I will sing Your praise.*
> *I will bow down toward Your holy temple*
> *and will praise Your name*
> *for Your unfailing love and Your faithfulness,*
> *for You have so exalted Your solemn decree*
> *that it surpasses Your fame.*
> *When I (we) called, You answered me (us);*
> *You greatly emboldened me (us).*
> *May all the kings of the earth praise You, Lord,*
> *when they hear what You have decreed.*
> *May they sing of the ways of the Lord,*
> *for the glory of the Lord is great."*
> Psalm 138:1-5 (NIV)

Note: The city of Kiev can be spelled either as "Kiev," the recognized transliteration of the city's name in Russian, which is most familiar to Americans, or as "Kyiv," the transliteration of the city's modern Ukrainian name, which is its official spelling. I have chosen to use the spelling "Kiev" when referring to the city in general and have used the spelling "Kyiv" when referring to the McMurrins' musical groups. The two spellings are used interchangeably.

CHAPTER TEN

The Song Goes On

> *"I can tell the world, I can tell the world,*
> *I can tell the world about this, about this.*
> *I can tell the nations I'm blessed,*
> *Tell 'em what my Lord has done,*
> *Tell 'em that the Comforter has come,*
> *And he brought Joy, Joy, Joy to my soul."*
> *From "I Can Tell the World" by Jester Hairston*

The spiritual, "I Can Tell the World," was a signature piece on the Lake Avenue Church Sanctuary Choir's two European ministry tours. Although the Solana Beach Chancel Choir did not sing this piece, it encapsulates what we have been trying to accomplish through all of our tours: to tell the world through music and personal interaction about the joy the Lord has brought into our lives.

The focus of the Music With a Mission trip was not only to share the love of Jesus Christ through vital spiritual singing and ringing; it was also to explore the possibilities for a new long-term mission partnership for our church. As a result, Dan and I had an exciting meeting with

Pastor Tom in the fall of 2010. After reviewing what we had learned from our time in Hungary, Kiev, and Moscow, we believed that the Lord was leading us to establish an ongoing partnership with Ildikó and Béla Dobos and Word of Life Hungary. Pastor Tom and I decided to bring this possibility to the Choir Cabinet and the MWAM Steering Committee, as well as to those in our church's "Next Generation and Youth Ministries." It was thrilling to see how God brought this about.

In January of 2011 we held a joint meeting of the Choir Cabinet and the MWAM Steering Committee. At this meeting, Pastor Tom Theriault proposed that we pursue a long-term partnership with Word of Life Hungary. After a positive discussion, the Choir Cabinet formed a committee to explore that possibility. We also decided that any partnership should involve our Student Ministries department. Over the next few months, the choirs and those in Student Ministries agreed to move ahead with the partnership and began plans to send a team to minister at the Word of Life Hungary camp during the summer of 2012. The Steering Committee decided that the $14,000 refund we had received from Peter Barbarics would be designated for our partnership with Word of Life Hungary.

Solana Beach Church sent its first team to Hungary in late July, 2012, to assist in one of the week-long high school camps. The 15-member team included several teenagers. They taught English, coached soccer and baseball, and helped with maintenance. Our "Pastor for the Next Generation," Josh Kirkhoff, led the team that summer. In the team's report to the congregation after they returned, several young people said that the mission trip had been a "life-changing" experience for them. Then, in the summer of 2013 a second team of 16 youth and adults ministered at another high school camp for Word of Life Hungary—this time led by our pastor for mission and outreach, Tom Theriault.

Glen, a teenager who went on the 2010 MWAM trip, shared his thoughts about ministering at the Word of Life camp in Hungary in 2012 and 2013: *"The Word of Life camp was the first place I ever visited on a mission trip. As a thirteen-year-old, I formed a deep spiritual attachment to the people and to the grounds of the camp. Since my first trip there in 2010, I have grown to see the camp as a fragment of heaven on earth which reminds me of God's tireless actions across Hungary. Each time I go the camp, I get the chance to rejuvenate my relationship with God and meet new people who offer me a different perspective on life. I've had the privilege of serving twice as an American sports counselor with the SBPC Word of Life Hungary Team. Through this I have formed long-lasting relationships with many Hungarian teenagers. I find that sports can act as a universal language and is a bridge between cultures which allows relationships to form, even without any conversation.*

As an American, I am inclined to think that I always need something newer and better just to be happy. However, after spending time with kids who have far less material wealth than I do, I have learned that I can find simple joy in spending time with others. I came to Word of Life Hungary thinking that I could teach Hungarian kids about sports and spirituality, but I discovered that there was so much more they could teach me."

Joan, a Chancel Choir member, was part of the 2013 team that went to Hungary to help in a Word of Life camp. She explained her experience this way: *"Upon joining the choir at Solana Beach Presbyterian Church, I began to hear stories about the mission trip the choir had taken in 2003 and about Ildikó Barbarics, who everyone said had been so helpful to the choir. Then I met Ildikó and her husband Béla when they came to visit our church. I first saw the Word Of Life Camp in Tóalmás, Hungary, on the choir mission trip in the summer of 2010. Walking around the camp and experiencing the love and caring of Ildikó, Béla, and Ildikó's cousin Peter was quite heartwarming to me. I felt that this was a place I could share my gift of teaching with the young Hungarian campers at some point in the future.*

The first mission team from the church headed to Word of Life while I was still temporarily living in China, but I heard wonderful things about the outcome upon my permanent move back to San Diego. After attending a meeting in which Ildikó and Béla presented their ministry with Word of Life to the Solana Beach congregation, I was moved by God that this would be a wonderful opportunity to go on a multigenerational mission trip the following year with my grown daughter, Laura. I could share my gift of teaching and she could share her gift of dance.

As is always the case when doing God's work, things were not as I had expected. It turned out that I worked with teenagers and Laura was needed for another sport, but we both accepted these changes as God's leading. We certainly had challenges with the record heat wave and some physical limitations, but God also opened the door to untold blessings! I was amazed by the teenagers in my English class. They were extremely smart, loving, sharing, curious, and desirous of hearing our experiences with God. They ended up teaching me. I was extremely blessed by them and have missed them so much since we left!! Laura was placed with some talented and generous adult baseball coaches and some teen assistant coaches. (Some of them were Americans, some Hungarians.) They became very close and worked together to support, teach, and witness to these kids.

The way the mission team worked together was such a surprise. Most of the teens and young adults were willing to help no matter what the task, and they rarely complained. Their insight into what God was doing that summer was so amazing. I learned a lot about myself and I gained a new appreciation for how God uses the gifts and abilities of His children, no matter what their age. I also gained a new global perspective of our God. It is such a blessing to see Him at work in people's lives around the world. We may speak different languages, but we have the same needs that only our Heavenly Father can fulfill."

Pastor Tom Theriault has also given his perspective about our partnership with Word of Life Hungary: *"It was off the beaten track from the beginning. In all my years as a mission pastor and in all my conversations with other mission pastors across the country, I've never heard of a church choir initiating a new mission partnership. One insight I picked up from my study of mission history is that God loves to 'work from the periphery.' Some of God's best ideas in advancing the gospel have not come from the inside circle of mission leaders and experts. Rather, those excellent ideas percolated up at the periphery and were then embraced by the center circle.*

When our awesome Chancel Choir grabbed a hold of Dan Bird's "Out of the Loft and into the World" vision for music ministry and set it as the guiding star for a possible tour in Europe, I opened my mind to possibilities. Our church already had three long-standing global partnerships, one of which appeared to be closing. Was God working in our choir to raise up a new place of ministry for our whole church to embrace? Dan and company planned their Summer 2010 journey as not just a ministry venture, blessing people with Spirit-filled music; they also approached it as a 'Joshua-Caleb searching out the land' for a possible mission partnership for our church. I was privileged to accompany them on the first leg of that unusual mission adventure.

As Providence would have it, this first leg took us to the Word of Life Camp in Hungary. We spent just one day there, plopping down in the camp during a week when the place was teeming with grade schoolers. I was overwhelmed by the laser-sharp vision of the camp for evangelism and discipleship. I was also taken by the top-quality young people the camp had raised up over the years who were now its leaders. Not only was the setting beautiful, but also the way the idyllic location was being used to advance the Kingdom was truly inspiring. Because the camp is of a quality similar to Forest Home, which is well-known to our church people, young and old, and because the camp depends on teams of Americans each summer to provide the sports and English instruction that attracts Hungarian kids, it seemed to me that it could be a superb extension of our church's growing commitment to intergenerational ministry. We have something vital to offer the camp—sports enthusiasts and English speakers, and the camp has something vital to offer us—bold evangelism outreach and a setting for intergenerational mission teams.

After returning from their 'mission discernment' tour, the choir leaders met with the leaders of our mission ministry. It was our unanimous conviction that the Word of Life Camp was a perfect fit for us and us for them. Since then, we've sent two teams of teens and adults to serve at their summer camping program. Everyone involved has confirmed our belief that this missional leading is from the Lord. Our challenge now is to spread the vision for this newest global partnership into our music and student ministries and from there to the entire church body. To God be the glory!" (See Hungary Partnership Proposal in the appendix)

Dan Bird was the visionary who first brought the idea of our Out of the Loft ministry to the choir. Returning from our MWAM trip, Dan explained how he viewed our new Hungarian partnership as the fulfillment of his dreams for the ministry. In his sharing about our Hungarian partnership in the "Seeing God at Work" video we produced in 2011, Dan said: *"Looking back on the trip, the thing that gives me the greatest joy is the fact that the choir and the church are in the process of developing an ongoing partnership with Word of Life Hungary. It was in 1988 and 1989 that I had my first contact with ministry in Hungary. Little did I realize then that my choirs would be called to continued ministry among the Hungarian people and with Word of Life Hungary in particular. As we at Solana Beach have made the enhancement of intergenerational worship and ministry our primary goal, God has given us the opportunity to partner with Word of Life Hungary in reaching young people for Christ. To see that the choir's ministry has resulted in future partnership with them has been the fulfillment of everything I have ever hoped for from our Out of the Loft ministry. Praise the Lord!"*

Epilogue

> *"Fight the good fight for the true faith.*
> *Hold tightly to the eternal life to which God has called you,*
> *which you have declared so well before many witnesses."*
> *I Timothy 6:12 (NIV)*

Returning from the choir's 2010 Music With a Mission trip seemed different to me than coming home from any of the previous ministry tours. For one thing, I was totally exhausted, both physically and emotionally, and it took me much longer to get back to my "normal" self. (Of course, I realize that I am also a lot older than when we began the "Out of the Loft" ministry in 1982!) Many in the choir wondered how we could build on our MWAM trip. I had to acknowledge the fact that I might not be the one to lead future "Out of the Loft" trips. Instead, I needed to consider the possibility of "passing the torch" to the next generation—not only to those within our own choir and church, but hopefully to other churches, choirs, and worship leaders. Thus it is my hope that through my own journey and experiences, I can share the vision and plant the seed in other lives.

Whether it was through the many relationships we established over the years, the audio and video ministry, or the detailed planning that went into each of the choir trips, the Out of the Loft ministry has impacted literally thousands of lives in our two choirs and churches as well as in Europe. The past thirty years have also been an amazing journey for me personally. The "Out of the Loft" ministry has provided a focus and direction for my life and has enabled me to discover and utilize gifts I had not thought I possessed. Most importantly, this ministry has had a profound effect on my spiritual life. One of the most significant spiritual lessons I have learned over these years is to <u>trust</u> and <u>obey.</u> This is never an easy thing to do, but I keep working at it. As the old gospel hymn says,

> *When we walk with the Lord in the light of His Word,*
> *What a glory He sheds on our way!*
> *While we do His good will He abides with us still,*
> *And with all who will trust and obey.*
> *Trust and obey, for there's no other way*
> *To be happy in Jesus, But to trust and obey.*
> Words by John H. Sammis (1887)

Also, from the very beginning of this ministry I have experienced God's faithfulness, even when I could not see it. I guess that is what Paul meant when he said that we "walk by faith and not by sight." When the choirs faced huge financial challenges and it looked as if we could never achieve them, God always came through. Every trip was fully funded and we never ended a tour in the red. In fact, our last mission trip ended with a $14,000 surplus. More and more, I have learned to see God as *Jehovah-jireh*, or "The Lord Will Provide."

In addition, I have seen God's faithfulness in His provision of an excellent, well-balanced choir for every tour. The choirs may not always have been the size we thought we wanted or needed, but every time the Lord provided just the choir He could use to share the love of Christ through spiritual singing. I have also witnessed how God has worked in the lives of individual choir members as they have responded to His call. Sometimes their needs were financial; other times they had needs for health, family, or work. In every case, the choir members' trust and obedience was met with God's faithfulness.

Probably the lesson I most needed to learn was to rely on God's strength and not my own. In I Peter 4:11 (NIV), we read: "*If anyone serves, they should do so with the strength God provides, so that in all things God may be praised through Jesus Christ.*" I have often struggled to let go of my limited strength so I can depend on God's infinite power. The Apostle Paul wrote in II Corinthians 12:9 (NIV), "*But He* [the Lord] *said to me, 'My grace is sufficient for you, for my power is made perfect in weakness.'*" Time and time again, I have seen how God's power is best displayed when we are weak.

For example, when we were powerless to find the required unleaded gasoline on our 1988 planning trip, God provided it through people in Czechoslovakia who could not even speak English. When I was feeling tired and alone during our Music With a Mission trip, God gave me the strength to keep going and brought people to help me. One of these people was our tour provider, Peter Barbarics. Peter became an invaluable tour leader and a true friend. He was God's gift to the choir and to me.

As a result of the ministry tours, I have also learned not only to depend more on God, but also to depend more on others. My natural tendency is to take charge of projects, so it is not easy for me to delegate tasks or share responsibility with other people. However, over the years of planning and organizing the ministry tours, God has helped me learn to utilize and rely on the skills and experience of others whom He has made available. The more I have relied on God's leading, the more He has provided the people needed to bring a project to fruition. Seeing choir members grow in skill and confidence as they have stepped out in faith to assist in the choir's ministry has been one of the most affirming results of my learning to share the load.

Where does all this leave us regarding future "Out of the Loft" ministry? Will the choir again be called to embark on a Music With a Mission trip to Europe? Will it involve Dan Bird and me, or will other people answer the call? Only God can answer these questions, so we must leave the future of the ministry up to the Lord. He is the One who calls; it is our job to be available.

Recently the Chancel Choir participated in one of the most beautiful Good Friday services I have ever experienced. One song we sang, "My Song is Love Unknown," spoke to my heart and helped me realize that God's purpose for me and every other Christian is that we spend our lives in "sweet praise" to Jesus Christ.

> *"Here might I stay and sing of him my soul adores;*
> *Never was love, dear King, never was grief like yours!*
> *This is my friend in whose sweet praise,*
> *This is my friend in whose sweet praise*
> *I all my days could gladly spend."*
> Words by Samuel Crossman (1664)

"When I Survey the Wondrous Cross" has been my favorite hymn for many years. I first became acquainted with this hymn when I sang in the choir at the First Presbyterian Church of Ann Arbor, Michigan, during my college days. The organist, Hugh Wallace, accompanied the hymn so magnificently that each verse took on a special meaning for me. On the 2003 and 2010 Solana Beach ministry tours, we ended every concert by surrounding the congregation and singing this hymn, which left the audience and all of us with a feeling of wonder, worship, and gratitude. The hymn and the anthem summarize what this ministry has been about. The final verse also states most majestically my own heart's desire.   It is my prayer that these words will continue to take root in many hearts as the torch is passed to the next generation.

> "When I survey the wondrous cross
> On which the Prince of glory died,
> My richest gain I count but loss,
> And pour contempt on all my pride.
> Forbid it, Lord that I should boast,
> Save in the death of Christ, my God!
> All the vain things that charm me most,
> I sacrifice them to His blood.
> See, from His head, His hands, His feet,
> Sorrow and love flow mingled down!
> Did e'er such love and sorrow meet,
> Or thorns compose so rich a crown?
> Were the whole realm of nature mine,
> That were a present far too small,
> Love so amazing, so divine,
> Demands my SOUL, my LIFE, my ALL! Amen!"
> Words by Isaac Watts - 1707

Don King
Escondido, CA
July, 2014

Song Lyrics Copyright License Permission

THE MAJESTY AND GLORY OF YOUR NAME
Tom Fettke/Linda Lee Johnson
© 1979 Wordspring Music, LLC, Word Music, LLC
All Rights Reserved. Used By Permission

HERE I AM LORD (84336) (c) 1981, 2000, OCP,
5536 NE Hassalo, Portland, OR 97213.
All rights reserved. Used with permission.

THE BOND OF LOVE
Otis Skillings Copyright: © 1971
Lillenas Publishing Company (admin. by Music Services) All Rights Reserved.
International Copyright Secured. Used by Permission. SESAC

GREET THE DAWNING
Words by Bryan Jeffery Leech; Music by Jan Sanborn
© 1987 Fred Bock Music Company.
All Rights Reserved. Used by Permission.

WE ARE NOT ALONE
Words and Music by Pepper Choplin
Copyright (c) 2005 by Harold Flammer, a division of Shawnee Press, Inc.
International Copyright Secured All Rights Reserved
Reprinted by Permission Reprinted with Permission by Hal Leonard Corporation

WORTHY TO BE PRAISED
By BYRON J. SMITH
© 1993 WB MUSIC CORP. (ASCAP)
All Rights Reserved. Used by permission.

I CAN TELL THE WORLD
by Jester Hairston
©Copyright 1959 by Bourne Inc., Assigned 1961 to Bourne Co., New York, NY
Copyright Renewed
All Rights Reserved International Copyright Secured
ASCAP

LORD, YOU ARE OUR LIFE
Words and Music by Stuart Dauermann
© 1989 Stuart Dauermann
Used by Permission
www.interfaithfulness.org

APPENDIX

Here is some helpful Information for those who wish to explore an "Out of the Loft" Ministry. Since it is my desire to "pass the torch" to other church choir directors, pastors, and Christian leaders, I have included several documents and other information below which I hope will be helpful to those who are considering their own "Out of the Loft" ministry.

UPDATE ON CHOIR PROPOSAL
Tom Theriault, Mike McClenahan and Dan Bird
February 20, 2007

<u>Background</u>

Dan presented to Mike in early fall 2006 the concept of the Chancel Choir planning a tour in the summer of 2008. Dan and the Out of the Loft team met to align the choir tour with our vision and strategic plan. Dan presented to the MLT in November 2006, and the MLT referred Dan and the team to meet with Tom and Mike to discern how the choir tour could be shaped to be missional.

Tom and Mike met with Dan and the Out of the Loft team twice to discuss the concept of doing a choir tour in the summer of 2008 with the Chancel Choir, Bells of Praise, and Student Chorale. The Out of the Loft team is supportive of the alignment process and open to modifying the trip to be in sync with where we are going as a church.

Missional Alignment

1. Inwardly Strong, Outwardly Focused. What if, as a result of this tour, 100 people from the choir and bells understood and experienced what it meant to be missional? *Key leaders would take Perspectives class this summer as part of their equipping (outwardly focused). Make sure the choir does what they do best (inwardly strong).*

2. Make A Friend. How can we design the trip to have fewer stops and more investment in relationships with the people? How can the choir become a catalyst for ongoing partnerships between our church and the people? *The team would screen potential locations based on their ability to pioneer lasting partnerships where there could be follow-up in subsequent years, potentially with other SBPC groups.*

3. Meet Real Needs. Can we choose organizations and locations that have a kingdom strategy beyond the concert? Is it an outreach to the community to meet spiritual needs, or is it encouragement of churches in their development of vital spiritual worship? *Money and time invested in another tour would have a benefit to the choir, benefit to the tour partners, and a benefit for the kingdom. The choir would limit their venues to places where there is preparation for and follow up to their event.*

4. Give God Credit. Where are the opportunities for sharing testimonies, inviting others to join the kingdom? *Build on past experiences where the choir was praying, sharing, part of outreach efforts.*

Next Steps
    1. MLT agrees to support concept and move forward.
    2. Session agree to support concept and move forward.
The Out of the Loft Team needs to develop specific plans for the trip in coordination with the Choir Cabinet.

MUSIC WITH A MISSION 2009
Executive Summary October 30, 2007

This summary provides an overview of what we propose as the purposes, partners, and activities of the SBPC European Music Mission Trip in Summer 2009. Please refer to other supporting documents for background and contextual information describing the principles, processes, and activities that have guided and defined our work to discern and articulate our sense of calling for this proposed mission trip.

OBJECTIVES: Why are we going on a music mission trip?
- To use and develop our primary gifts of music ministry as a choir to glorify God, evangelize nonbelievers, and encourage and equip believers as we join with our European friends to explore and expand the role of worship in our lives.
- To send a multi-role team of over 100 people from Solana Beach to demonstrate and expand the kingdom of God in Europe as we WORSHIP, CONNECT, GROW, SERVE, and IMPACT one another and our partners.
- To create intense short-term partnerships in which we build relationships, learn, and serve with our partners.
- To explore the potential for developing long-term partnerships in several locations.

- To return a changed people with a deeper sense of relationships and a heightened global missional perspective that will permeate not only the choir and the chancel but also the congregation and the campus.

DESTINATION: Where are we going? Why there? Who will we work with?

Where:
- Budapest, Hungary
- Kiev, Ukraine
- Moscow and St. Petersburg, Russia

Why: To meet real needs

Decades of oppression under communism and socialism may have officially ended, but the proud Hungarian, Russian, and Ukrainian people still suffer under a spirit of oppression. They face poverty, rapid societal change, instability, breakdown of the family, and corruption. Stress can drive them to despair, alcohol and drug abuse, and suicide. The church has also suffered from persecution, division, and decay. The need and the opportunities are great. The young people are open to many secular and spiritual influences and are hungry for meaningful activity. The people are hungry for life solutions that bring hope. The churches are hungry for renewal, revival, and restoration. This region has an historical tradition and cultural affinity for choral music and so music's use as a form of outreach provides opportunities to speak directly to the hearts of the people.

Who: We will work with those connected with local churches and Christian organizations.
- Hungary
    - Ildikó Barbarics Dobos of Word of Life Hungary
    - Pastor Tibor Kulscar of Budafok Baptist Church

- Russia
    - Russian American Christian University
    - Father Alexander Borisov, visionary priest of one of the largest Russian Orthodox churches in Moscow
- Ukraine
    - Roger and Diane McMurrin of Music Mission Kiev

ACTIVITIES: What will we do? How will our activities meet real needs?

"The Spirit of God, the Master, is on me because God anointed me. He sent me to preach good news to the poor, heal the heartbroken, announce freedom to all captives, pardon all prisoners. God sent me to announce the year of his grace—a celebration of God's destruction of our enemies—and to comfort all who mourn, to care for the needs of all who mourn in Zion, give them bouquets of roses instead of ashes, messages of joy instead of news of doom, a praising heart instead of a languid spirit. Rename them 'Oaks of Righteousness' planted by God to display his glory." Isaiah 61:1-3 (The Message)

WORSHIP
- Demonstrate the use of music and the arts to revitalize worship by participating in a series of concerts, services, and other events where we offer passionate, authentic Spirit-filled worship through diverse styles of music.
- Dialogue with local partners to study how music and arts can be used in worship and mission, both to evangelize and to disciple.

CONNECT
- Work with local partners to plan musical events in places and ways that will be most inviting for unreached people in the community.

- Assist local partners to connect with other Christian organizations in their area.

GROW
- Develop relationships and faith as we learn from team members and local partners through times of small group study, sharing, and prayer.

SERVE
- Bring our presence and musical gifts as offerings.
- Reach out to comfort and encourage the poor and discouraged, especially orphans and widows.

IMPACT
- Work with local organizations to plan for harvesting seeds planted during our visit.
- Work with SBPC to plan to use insights gained from trip in our congregation.

PARTICIPATION: Who will go?

The purpose of this trip is not for the choir to go on tour. It is for the people of SBPC to serve and learn from the people of Hungary, Russia, and Ukraine. The heart and soul of the trip will be the use of music and the arts in worship. Our arms will reach out in service to youth, orphans, widows, and next-generation leaders. Our minds will seek potential long-term partners. Our team must represent people with all those passions.

Members of musical ensembles:
- Chancel Choir
- Bells of Praise
- Student Chorale

Leadership:
- Music Leadership
- Steering and Planning Committee Members
- Pastoral Leadership
- Individuals with particular passion and gifts for:
    - Reaching out to Central and Eastern Europe
    - Exploring the use of music and arts in worship
    - Equipping authentic next-generation leaders
    - Reaching out to the poor, especially orphans, youth, and widows
    - Discerning potential for long-term partnerships

CONGREGATION: How might SBPC members be involved?
- By praying
- By preparing outreach materials
- By financial support
- By studying about the region and people
- By exploring the use of music and arts for worship and mission
- By becoming involved with future partnership activities

LONG-TERM IMPACT: What will we learn? What will develop?

- Participants will have an expanded heart for the world, a missional focus, and an informed concern for God's people in this region.
- Music ensembles will hone their musical and relational gifts through practice in a number and range of settings.
- The team will have studied and learned from the unique strength of each of our partners. Music Mission Kiev will greatly expand our understanding of how to use music for outreach. Word of Life will demonstrate ways to reach youth and equip next-generation leaders. An experience in the Russian Orthodox Church could be inspiring and transformational as we add to our repertoire of ways to worship

and as we experience the zeal and courage of a pioneering priest whose vision for Christ and his kingdom is unique and challenging among all Russian Orthodox churches.

- Seeds will be planted for various kinds of ongoing activity, including individual mission, short -term partnerships, and long-term partnerships with activities both here and in Europe.

2009 CHOIR MISSION TRIP
Mission Trip Task Force

Steering Committee

Charge: To coordinate the planning of the 2009 choir mission trip

Communication Committee

Charge: To coordinate all communication about the 2009 choir mission trip to the choir, congregation, and community.

Finance Committee

Charge: To oversee all of the receipt and expenditure of funds, keep records of each participant's personal account, monitor the mission trip budget, follow-up with donor "thank- you" letters.

Medical Planning Committee

Charge: To plan for all medical needs for the 2009 choir mission trip.

Fundraising Committee

Charge: To assist and encourage mission trip participants in raising individual mission support and planning possible group fundraising in conjunction with the mission trip Steering Committee and the SBPC Session.

Travel Planning Committee
    Charge: To plan all air and land arrangements for the 2009 choir mission trip. Tour

Documentation Committee
    Charge: To plan for documenting the 2009 choir mission trip through audio recordings, photographic documentation, and video productions.

Prayer Support Committee
    Charge: To plan for and coordinate the ongoing prayer for the mission trip within the choir, the congregation and beyond, and to prepare the prayer calendar for the mission trip.

Physical Fitness and Preparedness Committee
    Charge: To suggest various ways the trip participants can prepare themselves for the rigors of the mission trip

Concert Attire Committee
    Charge: To select the concert attire for the choirs and oversee the acquisition of the attire for the choir members

TOUR INFORMATION PACKET

Things To Know Before You Go
    Leave a Safe Home
    Other Things to Do Before You Go
    European Times
    Baggage Allowance
    Going Through Security
    What to Look for in a Suitcase
    Planning Your Travel Wardrobe
    Money
    Small Electrical Appliances
    Suggested Packing List
    Cell Phones
    U.S. Customs
    Valuables
    Insurance
    Summer Traveling Information
    Airline Stretches
    Hungarian Words and Phrases
    Ukrainian & Russian Words and Phrases

General Information and Suggestions
- Group Flight Instructions
- At San Diego Airport
- In-flight Considerations

BUDAPEST
- General Considerations Throughout the Trip
- Travel Considerations
- Touring Etiquette
- Photography
- Hotels
- U.S. Embassy Information
- Summer Weather Conditions
- Concert and Sunday Apparel Guidelines

While in Budafok
- Bus Assignments
- Summary
- Travel Highlights
- Group Flight Information
- Hotel Accommodations Information
- Concert Schedule
- Detailed Itinerary

Maps
- Travel Information Map of Europe
- Map of Budapest
- Map of Ukraine
- Map of Kiev
- Map of Commonwealth of Independent States
- Map of Central Moscow

HUNGARY
- Map of Hungary
- General Facts
- History
- Budapest Places of Interest

UKRAINE
- General Facts
- Kiev Introduction
- Kiev History
- Kiev Golden Gate
- Places of Interest

RUSSIA
- Introduction
- History
- Moscow
- Main Sights

Tour Participant Lists and Information
- List of Participants by Group
- List of Participants Alphabetically
- Rooming List
- MWAM Group Flight List
- Bus Assignment Lists
- MWAM Associates List

Envelope Packet
- Baggage Tags
- Group Insurance Policy Coverage
- Delta Group Flight E-ticket

WORD OF LIFE HUNGARY GLOBAL MISSION PROPOSAL

As a result of the Choir's 2010 Mission Trip to Eastern Europe, a new SBPC Global Mission Partnership was created in 2011. This is a joint vision of SBPC's Worship Ministry and Student/Family Ministry.

Through our church's focus on intergenerational relationships and the relationship building that takes shape between adults and students during KidsGames, it seemed natural to partner with the Word of Life Camp in Hungary. The Word of Life Camp depends on volunteer teams of Christians from the U.S. to support their staff in English instruction and coaching sports to 1000 kids from all over Hungary who come to spend a week at the camp. Many of the children and teens come from difficult backgrounds such as foster homes, orphanages, and abusive family situations. For many, it is their first time hearing the gospel. There have been many reasons for this new partnership:

- Our choir has visited this camp twice and has felt a warm connection with the amazing staff there. We have especially developed a longstanding relationship with Ildikó and Béla Dobos, missionaries at WOL for many years.
- Native speakers of English are a draw for the camp.
- Word of Life can teach us a lot about creative outreach strategies.
- Intergenerational teams are desired, making this an ideal mission experience for parents and students.

- All skills are needed, from sports to light construction to hospitality.

Some statistics:
- Hungary is #3 in alcoholism in the world
- Hungary is #1 in suicide in the world; the suicide rate for teens has doubled since 1998
- There is incredible peer pressure to smoke

In many ways, this is a lost generation, since the parents of these teens were raised under communism. It is the camp's mission to proclaim the message of hope to this lost generation, to disciple young Hungarian believers, and to teach them how to serve others, how to grow in their faith, and how to share the gospel. We go to encourage through our lives and through our love for the Hungarian people. Our aim is to join hearts as we reach the children and teens in Eastern Europe with the gospel of Jesus Christ. Over 200 campers make a decision to dedicate their lives to Christ every summer and many more indicate they want to follow Him. Many come from non-Christian homes.

SBPC sent the first mission team of 16 people ranging in age from 7 to 70 to serve in the summer of 2012 during a week of WOL's high school camp. Among our prayer requests before leaving were "that we would meet God in deeper ways than we could ever anticipate, for continued unity with the team, and that when we return, we would love God and others more than when we left." Without question we were blessed far more than we ever anticipated, God definitely answered that prayer!

Our intergenerational team served in various capacities to support the activities of the camp from teaching English to coaching volleyball, baseball, and basketball to helping repair camp facilities. Some even performed in the talent show! Relationship building came out of ordinary activities such as simple discussions and impromptu Frisbee games. All of our teens were absolutely fantastic in their ability to enter into relationships with campers, volunteers, counselors, and staff at the camp. The Frisbees that we brought for each camper, volunteer, and staff member created an immediate connection without any language barrier. All of our teens gave moving testimonies, several in front of the entire camp at the campfires. Our three-parent/child pairs were a wonderful example to the campers. To everyone—campers, camp staff and volunteers —it is a big deal that we come so far to spend time with them loving, playing, teaching and encouraging.

A few more important reasons for this partnership, quotes from the mission team:

"The teens in my English group were a gift from God. I thoroughly enjoyed every minute with them. Another highlight was the campfire. I felt as if I was with Jesus on the Jordan River as I watched the teens rush down to accept Jesus and learn from Jesus."

"I loved being able to work with kids my age, both the kids at camp and the other teenagers on the mission. I think it brought a feeling of energy to the team that most mission trips do not have."

"Having members of our group (adults and teenagers) playing ultimate Frisbee with about 20+ Hungarian counselors and campers was one of many moments when the language barrier was not a problem and brought everyone closer together."

"It was a rich experience for family members, youth, and different ages of adults."

"This trip helped teach lessons on sharing and interacting with people from another language and culture. I gained insight and knowledge on how to work as an ambassador of God in the world."

The Hungary Partnership Team would like to continue to develop the partnership, continue the work we have begun, and continue to respond to the call we feel God has placed on our church. Therefore, we hereby proposes the following:

1. That SBPC officially commit to a continued partnership with Word of Life Hungary for the next 5 years, to be reviewed in 2017.

2. That SBPC commit to sending an intergenerational mission team each summer to serve at the camp according to their needs.

3. That we commit to looking at additional ways to assist WOL Hungary in furthering their mission in Hungary such as camp improvements, the Bible Institute, Outreach Ministries, the Internship Program and church planting.

4. That we commit to adding Ildikó and Béla Dobos to our missionary support list as soon as our budget allows. Please see the attached for their information.

Respectfully and Prayerfully submitted,

Carole J. Orness, Hungary Partnership Team

For more information about Word of Life Hungary please refer to their website:

http://eletszava.org/en/

TOUR DOCUMENTATION

One way to extend the choir's influence is to share videos and CDs with others. The purpose for documenting our ministry tours over the years has been to give choir members a chance to see and hear what God accomplished through them in Europe and to share their experiences with the congregation, their friends and family, and people in the community. We hope these audiovisual documents have helped people in the U. S. to become more aware of the needs in Europe and have motivated them to participate by giving to various European ministries or even by going to Europe themselves. Even more importantly, we have been able to give free CDs to all of the people at our concerts over the past thirty years.

Perhaps the major reason we have had such success in the audio and video documentation of our Out of the Loft ministry is that we had such talented and committed people with a vision for the ministry. Tony Bohlin has assisted us in so many ways in our audio and video efforts from the very beginning, stretching 30-plus years. He personally oversaw that documentation on the two Lake Avenue trips, loaned us video equipment, and was a principal participant in the editing and production of the CDs and videos from our two Solana Beach trips. Mike Maduras has also been involved in the ministry from its inception and has been a major contributor to the audio recordings of our

Solana Beach ministry. Without these two people, we would never have produced so many high-quality CDs and videos.

By the end of the four "Out of the Loft" ministry/mission tours, we had amassed an amazing collection of audio and video documentation.

Audio Recordings:
    God is Our Song (1984)
    I Can Tell the World (1989)
    Ain'a That Good News (1989)
    Sing, and Be Not Silent (2003)
    God is Our Song 2003
    Live From Europe (2003, 2-disc)
    God is Our Song 2010
    Happy Birthday America (2010, 2-disc)
    Music With a Mission (2010, 2-disc)

Video Productions:
    God is Our Song 1984 (30-minute)
    Dawn of a Ministry 1984 (2 hours)
    Journey to Macedonia (1998 planning trip)
    1989 tour – short version
    Out of Despair HOPE 1989 (2 hours)
    1994 planning trip (50 minutes)
    2002 planning trip (40 minutes)
    Dawn of a New Day 2003 (2 hours)
    2008 Planning Trip (1 hour)
    2010 short video (20 minutes)
    Seeing God at Work 2010 (90 minutes)

How to Produce Tour Documentation

For the Solana Beach trips, we used two Canon GL2 video cameras that produced very high-quality video using Sony Mini DVC – 60 min. tapes. It is also imperative to have a sturdy tripod that can be used by the stationary camera. We used one of the cameras to video the entire program at every concert, while the other camera was used as a "roving" camera. Both cameras were also used to capture places we visited, historic and cultural sites, and choir activities. We also utilized the many digital photographs taken by various tour participants. The videographers should have some experience in using the cameras and should always be thinking of how the footage might be used in production, rather than just shooting everything they see.

We found that producing a 15-30 minute video of planning trips we took in preparation for the tour itself proved to be extremely effective—not only for the choir, but also for church leaders. These brief videos helped everyone visualize the many possibilities of the ministry. People who had been doubtful about the mission often became strong supporters of the ministry after viewing the video.

Each time Tony Bohlin and I started a new project, we put pressure on ourselves to improve the product and make it more meaningful. We were able to accomplish this in spite of the problems we inevitably encountered. When we ran into difficulties, Tony would say, "Satan apparently does not want to see this project produced." This thought always gave us the determination to persevere. The computer software we used for our video editing was Pinnacle Studio Ultima and Adobe Premiere Pro. Each of our videos developed a central theme that was carried throughout the production. You will find that producing a video takes a great deal more thought, preparation, and actual editing time than you had planned. In the end, though, it will be worth it.

For example, the greatest challenge in putting together the 90-minute video version of the 2010 trip was determining the theme for the production. In the fall of 2010, Pastor Mike preached a message about "seeing God at work" in our lives. That phrase struck a chord in my heart and made me realize that those who had gone on the trip needed to share how they had seen God at work through Music With a Mission. I therefore asked everyone who participated in the tour to write stories about the ways they had seen God move during the mission trip. By early spring, I had received approximately forty stories. In addition to using live video of choir members' testimonies, Tony and I decided to include the live performance of three pieces the choir had sung on tour.

Producing CDs of the music sung on the tour is also a challenge. It takes great patience to review all of the music recorded at the concerts and determine which rendition of each piece is the best. Preparing an informational insert for the CD that has excellent graphics is also effective in getting people excited about the ministry. The computer software program we used for editing our music CDs was Adobe Audition. Since 2010, we have used <u>CCI Solutions,</u> located in Olympia, WA to duplicate and prepare our CDs and videos for sale. We have been extremely satisfied with the quality of their work.

As I mentioned earlier, Mike Maduras has recorded all of our concerts since I came to Solana Beach.. He also loaned us the equipment to record the choir on our two Solana Beach ministry trips. At my request, Mike wrote out for use in this book the following information and suggestions for recording similar ministries.

AUDIO EQUIPMENT USED FOR MINISTRY TRAVELS TO EUROPE

PREMISE:

Travel light, minimize audio components, and maximize effectiveness of use.

IMPLEMENTATION:

The primary purpose of recording the choir on tour was to render a high-quality archival audio library suitable for later reproduction to CD. We therefore decided to use top-quality recording instruments that would support professional on-site recording techniques with minimum fuss and maximum capability to retrieve the usually good acoustics of European churches and cathedrals.

European churches and cathedrals are usually constructed with acoustic-enhancing materials such as stone and hard plaster, which combine to render a live sound space with good reverb times, enabling fine audio recording even for very modest-sized choral groups and soloists.

Since travelling choirs usually make use of in-place house organs and pianos rather than instrument ensembles, microphones may be limited to a pair of cardioids mounted on a single

15-foot stand in an ORTF configuration (a 114-degree angle between microphones).

Placement of the microphones should be a maximum of perhaps 15 feet in front of the choir, with closer spacing when soloists (vocal and/or instrumental) are being utilized. (As an alternative arrangement, individual solo microphones could be added if absolutely needed, but their use adds additional stands and cords and the need for more electronics).

The other needed audio recording system components are a microphone preamplifier-mixer with integral 48VDC phantom power, a DAT recorder or other preferred archiving device such as a CD recorder or hard-drive, monitor earphones, and step-down power transformers (240VAC – to – 120VAC). A similar audio recording system utilized by the Solana Beach choir for their European tours rendered excellent site recordings which were later copied to CDs. These were then given free of charge to everyone in Europe who attended the choir concerts, and some of the CDs were sold to people in the U. S. to help meet the expenses of the tour.

PACKAGING:

Pack all audio equipment into lockable pro audio rack cases suitable for shipment via air and rough handling, since that's the only type of handling they will receive.

AUDIO EQUIPMENT UTILIZED FOR SOLANA BEACH CHOIR TOURS:

- (2) Neumann KM 184 small-diaphragm cardioid pattern condenser microphones for use as primary (preferred pattern) microphones

- (2) Neumann KM 184 small-diaphragm omni pattern condenser microphones for use as standby microphones
- (2) Shure 15-ft telescoping tripod microphone stands
- (2) dual microphone bars
- (1) 4-channel custom microphone preamplifier/mixer designed and built by Glass Amplifier Company
- Sony PCM-R700 Professional DAT Recorder
- (2) monitor headphones
- 240V – 120V step-down transformer (300 - 500Watt capacity, as needed).

NOTE: Use a transformer for stepping down voltage instead of a Franzus or similar solid-state device because of audio spectrum noise caused by the solid-state devices, which will ruin your recordings.

- (4) 100-ft. microphone cables
- microphone cable tester
- (4) power cords (120V, US type)
- (1) multi-power outlet (120V, US type)
- 120 minute DAT recording tape – as many as needed X 2
- (2) small flashlight + extra batteries
- (2) single microphone stand clamps
- (2) rolls of gaffer tape
- miscellaneous extra bits and pieces to bring comfort when far from home
- lockable rack mount audio equipment shipping cases, as needed
- (1) collapsible hand dolly

REMEMBER: Simple is always better than sophisticated when recording in good sound venues.

CONTINUING THE MINISTRY

The production of CDs and videos is not the only way to maintain an "Out of the Loft" ministry." Developing close relationships with those to whom you minister is an essential element of the ministry. These relationships not only involve formal contacts vis-à-vis the church and choir, but also informal contacts by tour participants via email, letter, or phone—often over a period of years. A number of choir members have maintained close relationships with people in Pohlheim, Germany. June and I, for example, continue to communicate with our friends, the Wehrenfennigs and the Jungs, and through them, with the people at the Christus Kirche. We have also kept in touch with Dieter and Brigitte Wunderlich in Berlin and Joe Leonards in Munich. June and I highly value these ongoing relationships.

Similarly, we have ongoing contact with Music Mission Kiev and the McMurrins. In the fall of 2012 our church again hosted the Kyiv Symphony Orchestra and Chorus. At that time, we gave the McMurrins 300 warm scarves made by Paula Henderson, wife of choir member Dr. Richard Henderson. The scarves were a special gift of love that Paula wanted to send to the Ukrainian widows in Kiev. Several members of our choir continue to support the MMK widows ministry through monthly financial gifts. Thus, "the song goes on" in Kiev, Ukraine.

In addition, we have developed "Out of the Loft" ministries closer to home in our local area, our state, and our region. We are also ministering in our "Jerusalem," the San Diego area. Since our return from Music With a Mission, the choir has begun a music outreach to several retirement homes; the choir even presented a program at the Meadowbrook Village Christian Retirement Community where June and I now live. Also, for the past three years we have shared our music at the Fiesta Del Sol, a street music festival held every year in Solana Beach on the first weekend of June. Participating in this festival has given the church and the choir visibility and presence in our "Jerusalem." The end of a choir's ministry tour is not the end of their ministry.

FINAL THOUGHTS

When planning your own mission and ministry, don't feel compelled to repeat or copy what we have done these past thirty years. Each time we began to explore the possibility of a new "Out of the Loft" experience, we not only tried to build on what we had found successful, but also to see how we could do it better. That was true for developing the mission thrust of the venture, as well as the logistical planning and overall preparation of the ministry. Think outside the box; be creative in all of your planning. If you can do this, you will be embarking on one of the most exciting and fulfilling times of your lives.

Made in the USA
San Bernardino, CA
05 November 2015